DESIGNING PUBLIC POLICY FOR CO-PRODUCTION

Theory, practice and change

Catherine Durose and Liz Richardson

D1613194

First published in Great Britain in 2016 by

Policy Press
University of Bristol
1-9 Old Park Hill
Bristol
BS2 8BB
UK
t: +44 (0)117 954 5940
pp-info@bristol.ac.uk
www.policypress.co.uk

North America office:
Policy Press
c/o The University of Chicago Press
1427 East 60th Street
Chicago, IL 60637, USA
t: +1 773 702 7700
f: +1 773-702-9756
sales@press.uchicago.edu
www.press.uchicago.edu

© Policy Press 2016

British Library Cataloguing in Publication Data
A catalogue record for this book is available from the British Library

Library of Congress Cataloging-in-Publication Data
A catalog record for this book has been requested

ISBN 978 1 44731 695 4 paperback
ISBN 978 1 44731 669 5 hardcover

The right of Catherine Durose and Liz Richardson to be identified as authors of this work
has been asserted by them in accordance with the Copyright, Designs and Patents Act 1988.

The statements and opinions contained within this publication are solely those of the authors
and contributors and not of the University of Bristol or Policy Press. The University of
Bristol and Policy Press disclaim responsibility for any injury to persons or property resulting
from any material published in this publication.

Policy Press works to counter discrimination on grounds of gender, race, disability, age and
sexuality.

Cover design by Hayes Design
Printed and bound in Great Britain by CMP, Poole
Policy Press uses environmentally responsible print partners

To those who have inspired, challenged
and supported us

Contents

List of figures and tables

Figures

Tables

Notes on the authors and contributors

Authors

Catherine Durose is senior lecturer in the Institute of Local Government Studies and director of Research and Knowledge Transfer at the School of Government and Society, University of Birmingham, UK. Catherine's research explores the intermediation of relationships between the state, communities and citizens, recently focusing on the politics and practice of community work participation and co-production. She has a passionate interest in how research can support progressive social change.

Liz Richardson is senior lecturer in politics and director of Undergraduate Studies for Politics at the University of Manchester, UK. She is a visiting fellow in the Centre for Analysis of Social Exclusion at the London School of Economics and Political Science, and a board member for national charities, the National Association of Neighbourhood Management and the National Communities Resource Centre. Her work is dedicated to trying out ways in which academics, practitioners and citizens can develop more democratic and participatory ways of doing politics.

Contributors

Paul Bartley is senior case manager and certified recovery coach trainer of trainers at the Acacia Network, New York, USA. He has worked with the mentally ill, homeless and substance abuse populations for nearly 17 years. He is a CRC-TOT (certified trainer of trainers for recovery coach), CASAC (credentialed alcohol and substance abuse counsellor), ICADC (international certified alcohol and drug counsellor) and a CCM (certified case manager). Paul has lived, worked and raised his three children in the Bronx for five years.

Fawn Bracy is a mother and proud recent grandmother who raised her two daughters, son and nephew in the South Bronx, where she has lived and built community for over 40 years. Winner of the Linda Powell Pruitt Women who Refuse to Surrender Award, she is a founding member of the Morris Justice Project and has worked with the New York Civil Liberties Union to reform the New York City

Police Department and bring policing with dignity and respect to the South Bronx.

Toby Blume has 20 years' experience of working in the not-for-profit sector, leading national charities for 15 years in the UK. His career has focused on supporting marginalised communities to develop innovative solutions to social challenges and influencing public policy to deliver enhanced outcomes for local people. He now divides his time between working for Lambeth Council, helping to implement its Cooperative Council vision, running Social Engine, an agency supporting public and not-for-profit organisations to find new ways of working that increase their impact and effectiveness.

Simon Burall is the director of Involve. He has long and extensive experience in the fields of democratic reform, governance, public participation, stakeholder engagement and accountability, and transparency. He has worked at the national level in Africa, Asia and Europe as well as on related issues of global governance and democracy.

Hillary Caldwell is a PhD student in environmental psychology and the Women's Studies Certificate Program at the City University of New York. Her research focuses on collective struggles over social reproduction in the context of global capitalist development. She is studying the development of knowledge and relationships through participatory action research, community-driven planning and critical pedagogy in her work with Picture the Homeless, the New York City Community Land Initiative and the Morris Justice Project.

Teresa L. Córdova is professor of urban planning and policy and director of the Great Cities Institute, University of Illinois at Chicago. Professor Córdova is an applied theorist and political economist whose focus is community development and Latino studies. Through her scholarship of engagement, she is an expert in community/university partnerships. She studies the impacts of globalisation with particular interest in global/local dynamics.

Anthony Downs joined the Morris Justice Project (MJP) after taking part in an early survey. A Bronx native of 34 years, MJP has given him a renewed energy to help end aggressive policing practices such as stop and frisk, and to educate people about abusive policing. In the summer of 2014, he participated in numerous professional conferences to speak out about police reform in New York City.

Moises Gonzales is assistant professor of community and regional planning and the director of the Resource Center for Raza Planning at the School of Architecture and Planning, University of New Mexico. He is a specialist in urban design, cultural resources inventory, landscape design, GIS mapping and analysis, and three-dimensional digital modelling. His research focus is on southwest urbanism, urban form morphology and informal settlement conditions in arid climates.

Cory Greene is a doctoral student in the critical social personality psychology programme at the Graduate Center of the City University of New York. Born and raised in the inner city of New York and committed to social justice research, Cory is one of the co-founders and co-director of HOLLA! (How Our Lives Link Altogether), a community-based organisation that is focused on facilitating the sociopolitical development of young people occupying urban spaces. He has recently won pre-doctoral fellowships from the Ford Foundation and National Science Foundation.

Jan Haldipur is an aspiring researcher and activist. As a PhD candidate in sociology at the City University of New York Graduate Center, his research interests are in urban sociology, race/ethnicity and crime, law and deviance. Prior to graduate school, he worked at a prisoner re-entry organisation where he studied barriers to employment among formerly incarcerated men and women.

Prakriti Hassan, a Bronx resident for over 12 years, has been a member of the Morris Justice Project (MJP) since 2011. She is a research assistant with the Public Science Project at the Graduate Center of the City University of New York (CUNY). She earned her bachelor's degree in forensic psychology from John Jay College of Criminal Justice, CUNY. Through MJP, Prakriti discovered her passion for research and her strong interest in statistics and police reform. She is dedicated to continuing the struggle for equality and committed to engaging education, research and action in the name of justice.

Michaela Howell is a service development manager at Bradford Trident, UK. With 17 years' experience in the voluntary and community sectors and seven in the public sector, Michaela has worked with a wide range of communities in the South Wales valleys as well as West Yorkshire. She has specialisms in community learning, community development and engagement and volunteers locally with her community association, Gala committee and Brownies group. Michaela's aspirations are about finding new ways of ensuring that local people can really influence the things they want to influence and supporting a vibrant community life in the area.

Tim Hughes is Open Government programme manager at Involve, with expertise in public participation and open government. He currently coordinates the UK Open Government Partnership civil society network and is an active member of the international Open Government Partnership community. Tim has written extensively on topics covering public participation, open government and active citizenship. He recently authored the citizen engagement topic and co-authored the public services topic of the Transparency and Accountability Initiative's Open Government Guide.

Phil Jones is senior lecturer in cultural geography at the University of Birmingham, UK. His research focuses on urban transformations and creative methods, with particular interests in technology and mapping practices. In addition to the MapLocal smartphone app, Phil has worked on projects involving video, sonification, walking interviews and the cycling body. He is currently running a large project looking at the creative economy in Birmingham and Greater Manchester.

Amina Lone has spent over 20 years working with under-served communities throughout England and is committed to empowering people to realise their full potential. Amina volunteers with marginalised groups, women's groups, young people's organisations and within working-class communities. In her day job, Amina is the founder and co-director of a community interest company, the Social Action and Research Foundation. Amina is a single mother of four, and a Manchester city councillor for Hulme ward.

Colin Lorne is an urban and cultural geographer at the University of Birmingham, UK, whose chief interests are architecture, the built environment, changing working practices and contemporary urban society. His doctoral research brings a critical geographic perspective to the entrepreneurial spaces and practices of 'co-working'. He also examines the implementation and impact of the Localism Act 2011, with particular focus on how communities are engaging in neighbourhood planning.

Einat Manoff is an urban designer and currently a doctoral student in the environmental psychology PhD programme at the City University of New York Graduate Center. Her research focuses on issues of internal displacement, land struggles and decolonisation in Israel/Palestine and in New York City through the perspectives offered by psychology, geography, urban planning and visual culture. Einat teaches urban studies at the City College of New York. She is a scholar-activist with the Public Science Project and serves as the 2014–15 Presidential Fellow with the Center for the Humanities.

Paul McCabe was born in York (UK) and began his working life as an apprentice in the city's rail industry. Sensing a richer world beyond the factory gates he set off to study philosophy and politics at the University of Bristol and, later, housing at the London School of Economics and Political Science. Craving adventure, Paul then embarked on a slow drive to India, returning with his first daughter, Lotte, who was born on the trip. He started his local government career by regenerating the then abandoned York factory from which he had once escaped.

Maura Rose is director of Balance Mediation (UK), delivering training and consultancy on mediation and restorative justice interventions. Prior to this she managed Bolton Mediation, a not-for-profit organisation which focused on restorative justice in schools, victim–offender mediation and community mediation. Throughout these years, she developed a strong interest in mediation, conflict resolution and restorative justice, seeing for herself the benefits this brought to all involved. She has a degree in psychology and a postgraduate certificate in human resource management as well as an MSc in conflict resolution and mediation studies from Birkbeck College, London. She is an accredited member of the College of Mediators.

Robert Rutherfoord is a social researcher in the Department for Communities and Local Government, UK. He is responsible for analysis on neighbourhood decentralisation and neighbourhood planning, and has a particular interest in linking up the civil service with academic research, to share insights and solve problems. Previous roles included regeneration, spatial analysis and small business research.

Nadine Sheppard is a mother of three sons and has lived in the South Bronx for over 20 years. Winner of the Linda Powell Pruitt Women who Refuse to Surrender Award, she is a founding member of the Morris Justice Project and deeply committed to ending aggressive and discriminatory policing in her community.

Dan Silver is founder and co-director of the Social Action & Research Foundation (SARF), an anti-poverty action-research think tank that aims to co-produce policy with communities. Dan has worked for several voluntary and community sector organisations as well with a local authority, with the aim of promoting equality and participation in policy development at local, regional and national levels. Dan is also doing a PhD based at the ESRC-recognised Cathie Marsh Institute for Social Research in the Department of Politics at the University of Manchester on the politics of poverty and policy evaluation.

Chris Speed is chair of Design Informatics at the University of Edinburgh, UK, where his research focuses on the network society, digital art and technology, and the internet of things. Chris has sustained a critical enquiry into how network technology can engage with the fields of art, design and social experience. At present, Chris is working on funded projects that engage with the flow of food across cities, an internet of cars, turning printers into clocks and a persistent argument that chickens are actually robots. Chris is co-editor of the journal *Ubiquity* and leads the Design Informatics Research Centre.

Lucy Spurling is a researcher in the Department of Communities and Local Government's Integration and Community Rights analytical division (UK). As an analyst at DCLG she has worked on a number of different agendas, including regeneration, worklessness, decentralisation and community rights. Prior to joining the civil service, Lucy undertook research on homelessness, drug misuse, early learning, play and childcare in both the academic and community/voluntary sectors. Lucy combines her analytical work with bringing up four boys

Jess Steele is a community entrepreneur who has been involved in local regeneration in the UK for 25 years, first in Deptford and since 2006 in Hastings, where she played a leading role in the successful battle to save Hastings Pier. She has also held national posts at the British Urban Regeneration Association, the Development Trusts Association and Locality, including developing the Community Organisers programme. She now runs Jericho Road Solutions which helps ambitious neighbourhood groups to take on challenging buildings, while working on policy and programmes at national level to make local change easier.

Brett Stoudt is an assistant professor in the Psychology Department with a joint appointment in the Gender Studies programme at John Jay College of Criminal Justice as well as the Environmental Psychology doctoral programme at the Graduate Center. His work has been published in volumes such as *Geographies of Privilege*, as well as journals such as the *Journal of Social Issues*. He is the 2012 recipient of the Michele Alexander Early Career Award for Scholarship and Service from the Society for the Psychology Study of Social Issues.

María Elena Torre is the founding director of the Public Science Project and on the faculty of the Critical Social Psychology programme at the Graduate Center of the City University of New York. She is a co-author of 'Changing minds: the impact of college on a maximum security prison'. Her writing is found in volumes such as the *Handbook of Qualitative Research in Psychology* and journals such as *Feminism and Psychology*. She is the 2013 recipient of the Michele Alexander Early Career Award for Scholarship and Service from the Society for the Psychology Study of Social Issues.

Katy Wilkinson completed an interdisciplinary PhD on evidence-based policy making in the UK government's Department for Food, Environment & Rural Affairs, before returning to the department to work as a social science adviser to the animal health and welfare team. Her research interests include the politics of crisis management and the role of interest groups in policy making. She now works in education policy support at the University of Oxford.

Margaret Wilkinson, MBE, is head of the planning for Real®Unit, part of the Accord Housing Association. Planning for Real® is a nationally – and internationally – renowned planning process that offers a range of visual, tactile, participatory and community-led techniques to give local people a real say about what happens in their neighbourhoods. Margaret has over 25 years' experience of working with local people and key stakeholders throughout the UK, and is supporting the use of Planning for Real® in different countries elsewhere in Europe.

Jacqueline Yates is a mother of two sons, a wife, and has lived in the South Bronx for more than 30 years. Winner of the Linda Powell Pruitt Women who Refuse to Surrender Award, she is a founding member of the Morris Justice Project and has been actively involved with the New York Civil Liberties Union to reform the New York City Police Department and end aggressive and discriminatory policing practices like stop and frisk.

Acknowledgements

The authors would like to give sincere thanks to our contributors – academic researchers, policy makers, practitioners and activists – who have informed our practice and thinking over a number of years and inspired this project. The authors appreciate our publisher, Policy Press, for their ongoing commitment to this unusual and innovative project. In particularly, we would like to thank Emily Watt, senior commissioning editor at Policy Press, for her encouragement and enthusiasm, and Laura Vickers, assistant editor, for her professional guidance and advice. We further acknowledge the valuable insight and positive and constructive reflection provided by our anonymous referees. We would like to acknowledge funding from the University of Birmingham's School of Government and Society, and the Institute for Local Government Studies and Politics at the University of Manchester, for their support of our writing symposium and for research assistance. Earlier versions of this work were presented at the University of Sheffield, UK and the Institute for Culture and Society at the University of Western Sydney (UWS), Australia, where we benefited from the engagement of the seminar and workshop participants, and their thoughtful questions and comments.

We give particular thanks to Tom Richardson for his challenging, considered and insightful contributions, a perspective based on a lifetime's reading, good humour, and warm encouragement and support throughout the long months of drafting and redrafting. Emily Silverman (Hebrew University of Jerusalem) helped to provoke and crystallise our thinking at an early stage. Paul James (UWS) offered comments that pushed our thinking on the heuristic. Others who have encouraged and stimulated our thinking along the way include Yasminah Beebeejaun (University College London); Catherine Mangan, Catherine Needham and James Rees (University of Birmingham) and Jo Richardson (De Montfort University).

Preface

Over the past decade or more, we have constructed our individual and joint research projects to create spaces for deep engagement with policy actors who want to do things differently. We work closely and sympathetically with policy makers, politicians and citizens, who are willing to work with us. Unsurprisingly, nearly all of these turn out to be sensitive, thoughtful human beings who are committed to behaving as ethically as possible in the service of good policy. Dark things do happen, established interests can drive decisions, but mostly there are just people muddling through trying to do the best for citizens, customers, users and colleagues. If at any point in this book, we have fallen prey to easy caricatures then this is not our intention or true perspective.

Our preferred mode is to work collaboratively and hands-on where we can. This book comes out of our respect for colleagues in central and local government, local public services, and in third sector organisations. Managing complex sets of issues, people and practices is tough, and anyone who suggests they could do better is at risk of foolishness without very careful thought about how the whole thing might actually work. Carping from the sidelines is not helpful; our efforts aim to be constructive even when being critical. While some of our schemes and suggestions may look unwarrantedly foolhardy at first glance, innovation requires some degree of targeted and strategic risk-taking. Our admiration goes to all those represented in this book and others not here engaged in co-production who have had the nerve to lead and experiment.

In our own organisations in higher education, we are exposed to similar pressures and tensions, organisational stubbornness and resistance to change, politicking, and the responsibilities of leadership. While we attempt in this book to apply co-productive approaches to our research practice, we are at a much earlier stage in attempts to apply similar principles and methods more broadly within universities. So far, our efforts have been focused outwards, showing us the gritty realities of public policy work – albeit for intense bursts. Change is a mammoth task and we are under no illusions about the dangers, and potential for serious mishaps. Still, we see efforts made and redoubled across our primary fields of practice in local areas around the UK, and in visits to other parts of the world. These concrete examples have girded our loins in writing this piece.

We have also been energised by colleagues across academia who are dealing with crises of relevance of the profession by launching themselves into policy-relevant and engaged scholarship. While we might butt heads against those who fear for our compromised souls, we welcome debate with any academic who takes time to consider their own responsibilities for social change.

Catherine Durose and Liz Richardson
May 2015

Why is redesign of public policy needed?

This book is a response to the crisis of design in public policy. It comes from the authors' and contributors' outrage at injustice, incompetence and the imposition of policy solutions, but also recognition of the inability of current policy design to deal with many of the complex problems that face modern societies. The writers involved in this book feel compelled to make this timely intervention, to reconsider how policy is conventionally made but also to draw attention to the work of policy makers, researchers, practitioners and activists who are actively engaged in doing policy making differently. An argument is made for a radically democratic alternative form of policy design: co-production.

Commentators have noted that the remarkable thing about public policy failures is how unremarkable they are. 'Policy scientists have documented time and again' (Bovens, t'Hart and Peters, 2001, p. 7) how prone the policy process is to making, 'large-scale, avoidable policy mistakes' (Dunleavy, 1995, p. 52). This book is written in the footsteps of analyses of policy failures, fiascos (Bovens and t'Hart, 1996) and other failures of great expectations of policy (Pressman and Wildavsky, 1979).

It is easy to name some of the numerous and high profile policy disasters in recent memory in most advanced democracies. For example, in the UK, the start of a list might include the 'poll tax' (Butler, Adonis and Travers, 1994); the ongoing chaos of reform of the health service (Dunleavy, 1995); poorly managed and handled public health disasters such as 'mad cow disease' or BSE (Grant, 1997). Other examples spring to mind, such as the debacle of the Child Support Agency, an organisation designed to collect child maintenance money from absent parents, as well as the spiralling costs of the private finance initiative (PFI) for the London Underground (King and Crewe, 2013). Some of these policy disasters were not disastrous for all of the parties involved; policy is not failing everyone equally. Recurring public policy 'scandals', such as tax avoidance by large corporations, or accusations of public sector contracts awarded to unfit or suspect organisations, all contribute to a sense that the odds are stacked against those with least formal power. Other tragic and seemingly sinister episodes of major abuses of power unfold in public view, such as cover-ups by senior decision makers of allegations of large-scale abuse and exploitation of children. Perhaps as insidious as identifiable large-scale events are the prosaic but equally damaging gaps between the espoused objectives of policies and the interests served by such failings, providing further grist to the mill that policy design disenfranchises citizens (Wagenaar and Cook, 2003).

These failings are coupled with a growing recognition of the limitations of policy design in the face of challenges of ever-increasing complexity. These challenges have been described as 'wicked' – cutting across many different issues (Rittel and Webber, 1973) – and 'squishy' – involving politics and human behaviour (Strauch, 1975). The alarms that these challenges sound are growing louder. The global economic crisis of 2008 suggests a future of fiscal uncertainty in the ongoing cycle of 'boom' and 'bust'. Inequities in wealth and opportunity widen as social mobility slows and precarious labour becomes the norm. Demands on welfare grow, emanating from a 'super' diverse population and the increased numbers and proportion of older people and of people a long-term health conditions. Demand cannot be met from a public purse diminished by fiscal restraint. Traditional ways of delivering public services seem impotent to meet diverse needs and tackle entrenched social problems and dependencies. Increasing the sense of the inadequacy of conventional policy making, some of this demand is arguably generated by prior and ongoing public policy failures. Major crises of urban and environmental sustainability are manifest across the globe, from climate change to depopulation to the growth of global mega cities in emerging economies. Society faces challenges in managing the sustainability and affordability of scarce resources to ensure food production and water supply. Multiple new uncertainties in developed democracies, including low or declining levels of trust in democratic institutions and leaders, political disengagement and de-alignment, make many ordinary observers wonder how and by whom these issues will be addressed. The pluralisation of spaces for political debate and protest, particularly using social media, cannot be ignored.

The litany of policy failings produced by the conventional model of policy design is long. Failures are extreme cases, but there is also a growing sense, shared by some policy makers and other policy actors, that current models are simply insufficient to generate the level of creativity and innovation needed. The wicked and squishy challenges can feel intractable and overwhelming. A fundamental rethink about how policy is done is needed. The authors share the outrage and frustrations, but also the hope expressed by earlier scholars of public policy, in continuing to work towards better policy design that produces better outcomes. They are committed to the idea that this book, in some small way, may help to construct a perception of the possibility that those inside and outside the elites of politics and technocracy can work together more co-productively to shape society for the better. The book asserts that concern with genuine democratic involvement in the policy process will be part of moving towards 'the ultimate goal [of] the realization of human dignity in theory and fact' (Lasswell and Kaplan, 1950, p. 15).Doing so presents a major challenge to conventional elite-dominated policy design, including professional cadres of policy makers, national and local elected politicians, as well as scientific or technical specialists, but also to citizens. Battle must be done with many policy shibboleths or '"Zombies" – ideas and arguments that are intellectually dead but will not stay buried ... and are repeatedly disinterred to advance interests that are very much alive' (Evans with Vujicic, 2005, p. 134). A critique of conventional policy design is set alongside a proposed alternative approach. Unlike much traditional academic work, there is a clear commitment to answering a 'so what' question, by setting out how it is considered that better policy design could be achieved. It does not eschew the strengths of conventional models, such as their focus on effectiveness, technical expertise and clear process, in favour of some romantic ill-defined other-worldly or agonistic notion. Nor is the aspiration of co-productive designs a naïve belief, as is illustrated by the rich set of practice-focused contributions. The authors and contributors do not believe in co-production as a 'policy unicorn' (Cimasi, 2013, p. xxviii), a mythical policy of beauty, which has never been seen in a practicable and replicable form. Several key areas for debate over the realisation of co-production do, however, present dilemmas and challenges, which are presented and reflected on through the literature and empirical vignettes.

Design is fundamental to the hope and optimism of these propositions (Rittel, 1988). It expresses a belief that human beings can first generate some level of shared understanding of what they would like to be different, based on which values, and then consciously remake situations into a more desired state. Design is a term that is associated with many fields of activity – manufacturing, architecture, IT, engineering, medicine and public policy – and can be used as a verb to refer to the act of designing itself, as a noun for a general framework for a complex set of strategic activities, or more specifically for the finished product (Heskett, 2001, p. 18; DesignGov, 2013, pp. 3–4).

Design thinking informs the specific ideas presented here for public policy design – including the idea that designers are not 'form givers' who dictate forms with little variation possible, but instead are 'enablers' who construct systems that allow user adaptations to deal with complexity and spectrums of needs (Heskett, 2005, p. 131). One credo is that design is about experimenting, rapid prototyping and learning-by-doing. There is a fundamental focus on how things are used, and how objects, products or services might be differentiated for different groups of users. The user is at the forefront of the designers' mind during the process, and usability suggests user-orientated testing and retesting as a minimum. Design thinking is closely linked to ideas of co-creation and co-production, as the user is at the centre of any design. Good design is unobtrusive so that users' own creativity has space to be expressed and has honesty so that designs do not make promises on which they cannot deliver (Rams, 1995). Design thinking has some of its origins in design aesthetics and it retains and harnesses a deep creative streak and sense of inventiveness. It is deeply human and touches the senses, as the consequences of policy affect people's everyday experiences. Design for democratic governance and social inclusion 'makes government policy tangible to people through objects, communications, environments, and experiences' (US National Design Policy Initiative, 2009, p. 12). The inclusion of the contributions in this book reflect a core principle of design thinking, that design is made concrete (DesignGov, 2013, p. 5)

There has been a welcome resurgence of interest in thinking about policy design internationally (Bason, 2014), for example in the United Nations Development Programme. It is exemplified in the UK by the Royal Society of Arts (RSA), the National Endowment for Science, Technology and the Arts (NESTA), the Design Council and Policy Design Lab. Across the European Union, policy design thinking has been sponsored by the European Commission. Also in Europe, leading organisations include MindLab in Denmark and Helsinki Design Lab in Finland. Australia has DesignGov and New Zealand has Better by Design. In North America, the Massachusetts Institute for Technology (MIT) hosts the Civic Data Design Lab and there have been attempts to promote design thinking for policy through the US National Design Policy Initiative. Open Government Partnerships are natural bedfellows with policy design ideas, such as in British Columbia's Government in Canada.

Contribution of the book

The book contributes to this rich body of work and practice on design thinking by situating practitioner-orientated 'grey' literature in the context of mainstream academic public policy and policy sciences literature, and vice versa, grounding public policy scholarship in practice-orientated material and original empirical contributions. It attempts to go beyond traditional scholarship and offer not solely a critique of what exists, but sets out proposals for alternatives, moving from policy description to prescription (Bason, 2014, p. 2).

The book sets out some of the frustrations with existing conventional approaches to policy design and considers alternative co-productive approaches. To facilitate this, heuristics are developed in a series of figures set out over the opening chapters of the book. The heuristics complement other work which has contrasted intuitive, emotionally literature, inductive design-based approaches with more conventional deductive, logical, rational policy mindsets (Bason, 2014, p. 6). They set out the interrelation between different elements of policy design – power, vision and grammar – and contrast between conventional and co-productive approaches to policy design. Mathematician George Polya suggested in his influential work, *How to Solve It* (1945), that heuristics offer different ways of making a problem more accessible, generating creative thinking and building theory to encourage problem solving, learning and discovery. The use of a heuristic here reflects the focus of the book on policy design and as a dialogue between theory and practice.

This approach is specifically grounded in the work on 'satisficing' by winner of the Nobel Prize for Economics Herbert Simon. 'Satisficing' – a splicing of the words satisfying and sufficing – is a practical approach resulting from Simon's recognition that life does not usually deliver optional solutions. Instead, people can look for answers that are 'good enough' (Simon, 1996, p. 27) for a particular purpose and when the costs of working out how to best optimise solutions outweighs the policy benefits, or is simply too big or uncertain a task. A heuristic is not intended to be a perfect reflection of current policy design or suggest an optimal alternative policy design, but to enable understanding of policy design. To offer such optimal or perfect solutions would 'defeat the very premise of our argument'; rather, the value of theorising – through the use of dialogue and heuristic – 'lies in the options that are generated rather than the uncertainties that are resolved' (Garud et al, 2008, p. 356). In these ways, the book is original in its form and its contribution to the field.

The book is collaborative in two senses: its engagement with existing work within the academy but also in drawing in analysis and expertise from beyond the academy. Its intention is not merely to deconstruct but to offer theorisations of and suggestions for alternative normatively grounded constructions of policy design. Its rigour lies in the scholarship that created the heuristic and the interaction with reflections from practice, which generate an explicit discussion of tensions between concepts, how to manage these tensions. Sections One, Two and Three contain 12 reflective contributions, which form vignettes in the method underpinning the book. Vignettes are stories about individuals, situations and structures, which can make reference to important points in the study of perceptions, beliefs and attitudes (Hughes, 1998, p. 381). The 'focused descriptions' were selected by the authors and curated for this book based on their status as 'emblematic' (Miles and Huberman, 1994, p. 81) or typifying in some way the phenomena under investigation. 'Zooming in' on specific practices complements, develops and balances the 'zooming out' of theorising (Nicolini, 2013). Vignettes are aim to 'expand and generalize theory' (Yin, 2009, p. 15), providing analytical robustness, rather than empirical generalisability of cases. These vignette examples variously provide a narrative about a particular instance of 'doing' policy making or a reflection over time of the values, dynamics and opportunities that may underpin taking a more co-productive approach to policy making and analysis. In conventional research, they can be constructed by the researchers as composites, but are constructed here by the participants in dialogue with the authors.

Development of the book

This book is conceived as a conversation between theory and practice. It models some of the substantive ideas that we seek to convey: valuing and respecting different types of knowledge and expertise as part of a more dialogic form of knowledge production. In this sense, we regard the book as a co-production between us – as academic researchers – and other researchers, policy makers, practitioners and activists. However, co-production does not mean abandoning our role or expertise as researchers. Nor does it mean that everyone involved should or has played the same role in the development of the book. As such, Catherine Durose and Liz Richardson have been identified as 'authors', providing the initial theoretical grounding in Chapters One to Three, framings of each contribution, discussion in Chapter Four, and governance implications in Chapter Five and Epilogue. Others involved have authored their own contributions, sharing their insights and reflexive analysis related to their own practice.

Durose and Richardson developed the proposal for the book in consultation with the contributors. A writing symposium provided a forum early in the development of the book to share and exchange ideas and clarify the core thesis of the book. The authors suggested a focus for each contribution based on their understanding of the contributors' practice. Contributors shared their drafts for discussion with the authors, who then provided a framing for each, which was again clarified through exchange and discussion. The authors used the agreed framings of how the contributions were situated in the literature to inform the theory-building work of the opening chapters. Theoretical tensions set out in the opening chapters are revisited in the discussion in Chapter Four, where the argumentation is supported by the analysis provided by the contributions.

In this work, we have sought to surface, if unable to fully mitigate, the power dynamics at play within mainstream academia. Seeking to integrate different forms of expertise recognises the usual exclusion of subjects of research from processes of knowledge production and attempts to rectify this. The book values complementary contributions from academic literature and practice, in generating and grounding critiques and constructing alternatives for the policy process. Providing a platform for these voices offers 'a pungency and vitality' often 'absent from mainstream social science' (Maynard-Moody and Musheno, 2003, p. 30), which often militates against transdisciplinary, problem-centred and applied work. However, the tropes of academic work are powerful, and these are complex issues, which the authors return to in the Epilogue.

Structure of the book

There is an acknowledgement, agreed by the contributors at the outset, that artificial resolutions of differences, or avoidance of difficult questions, are inimical to this shared endeavour. The chapters attempt to share discussions that do not avoid some of the tough issues raised by the interactions between theory and practice. In the opening chapters of the book, the authors critically reflect on the conventional policy process and contrast this with a co-productive alternative.

Chapter One introduces the concept of policy design and begins to build a heuristic to understand the interrelationship of different elements in policy design: power, vision and grammar. Chapter One focuses on contrasting understandings of power – constituted and constitutive - which underpin and inform policy design. Chapter One continues advancing a critique of constituted power. Chapter Two develops the argument setting out the vision and grammar that characterise conventional constituted policy design. Chapter Three poses the contrast, exploring the policy design that may characterise constitutive co-productive approaches. The book then presents a series of empirically grounded contributions from researchers, activists, policy makers and practitioners who are interested and actively involved in doing policy differently. The authors frame and reflect on each of these contributions. The contributions are divided into three sections: challenge and change within conventional policy design, vision in co-productive policy design and grammar in co-productive policy design.

The contributions in the first of these three sections take us inside central and local government, exploring the vision and grammar of conventional policy design. In this section, Katy Wilkinson reflects on the impact and handling of crisis at the national level, using the vivid example of emerging animal disease threats in the wake of the 2007 foot and mouth crisis. Paul McCabe reflects on the dynamics at a local government level of engaging communities in a hotly contested area of policy, housing development. Simon Burall and Tim Hughes contemplate an attempt to develop collaborative policy making at a national level on open government, revealing the transparent values and hidden politics that shape the collaboration. Robert Rutherfoord and Lucy Spurling document an attempt at the centre to move towards more participatory and open forms of policy. Toby Blume reflects on how a local authority can instigate and manage policy design differently, using creative disruption to deliver cultural change.

Following these insights into the appetite and potential for change from within, the contributions then turn to look at the policy design of co-productive alternatives. Section Two, vision in co-productive policy design, focuses on the vision-led work of different coalitions with the stated intention to effect policy change. Teresa Cordova and Moises Gonzales share their reflections of being part of the Resource Center for Raza Planning. These planners worked with traditional communities, drawing together different forms of expertise in order to intervene and influence policy decisions on infrastructure and development. Jess Steele then shares her story of working to challenge the policy process on a series of planning and regeneration decisions. She relates how she used the tactics of community organising to build community power and challenge decision making. The section concludes with the Morris Justice project detailing how they used participatory action research to challenge the 'stop and frisk' policy of the New York Police Department.

The third section focuses on the grammars of policy design, and its co-productive alternatives, focusing on different forms of facilitation to bring together experts within the policy process with communities and citizens. Phil Jones, Colin Lorne and Chris Speed reflect on the development of a smartphone app to allow communities to contribute more meaningfully to neighbourhood planning. Amina Lone and Dan Silver illustrate how social researchers and activists were able to generate community conversations in the wake of the summer 2011 riots in Northern British cities. Michaela Howell and Margaret Wilkinson show how co-design was used to reshape a national policy initiative to meet local needs around employment training and support. Maura Rose details a series of principles that can be used to mediate and resolve conflicts.

The book then moves to a discussion chapter by the authors, Chapter Four, which reflects on how the analyses generated through the contributions challenge, deepen and advance the theorising of the earlier chapters. The contributions generate complex issues, which cannot be ignored if co-production is to become a serious contender. These include the feasibility and possible methods of change, the degree to which this is idealistic, how co-producers might protect themselves from being co-opted, how to take account of deep value conflicts, and how to reconcile strong leadership with less hierarchical structures, and retain leadership while valuing a range of different forms of expertise, including experiential expertise. So as to exemplify the ideas advocated as possible, the book is structured so that the discussion chapter critically reappraises the ideas set out in the opening chapters. This is a relatively unusual approach to the structure of a book, and one which reflects a more dialogic approach to generating knowledge. Finally, Chapter Five looks at the governance implications for the further development of design for co-productive policy making. An epilogue reflects on the implications of the book for the authors' research practice.

CHAPTER ONE

Possibilities for policy design

Taking a design approach to addressing policy failings is about having a strong sense of what the alternatives could be; it is an inherently optimistic approach. Design principles have clear appeal in the current policy context. Design presents an alternative to mass-processing, allowing user adaptations to facilitate differentiation and deal with complexity. Rather than being wedded to a 'policy presumption', design opens up the possibility to experiment and learn through doing and possibly failing. Moreover, design places the citizen or user at its core. These principles have a broad appeal to those seeking greater democratic legitimacy for policy. But this normative thrust is not naive. A design approach is fundamentally about the substantive and instrumental ambitions to achieve better policy outcomes. Grounding this approach in the work of Herbert Simon means that design is not about generating an optimal prescription of policy in a perfect world, but about questioning that 'policy presumption'. If we understand policy design as 'the pursuit of valued outcomes through activities sensitive to the context of time and place' (Bobrow and Dryzek, 1987, p. 19), it both opens up the inner workings of policy making, allowing us to understand the interrelations and interreliance of different elements of current policy, but also provides a means of generating alternatives.

This chapter considers the parameters of debate on policy design before setting out its key elements of power, vision and grammar. These elements are common to different policy designs, but are manifested differently. The chapter begins to build a heuristic as a means of understanding policy design. The heuristic sets out contrasting policy designs – conventional and co-productive – based on the notions of power that underpin them. This contrast encourages lateral thinking about how policy design works and the potential for redesign. Power is often a hidden struggle in policy design, but it fundamentally informs and shapes the vision – the valued outcomes pursued – and the grammar – the activities used in this pursuit. To bring this hidden element out into the debate, we develop our heuristic further by setting out the contrasting ways in which power is interpreted in conventional and co-productive policy designs. These different interpretations are then used to inform a discussion on the feasibility and desirability of policy redesign.

What is policy design?

Policy design, in the field of the policy sciences, is an idea associated with Herbert Simon's *The Sciences of the Artificial* (1996), originally published in 1969, as well as other design theorists like Horst Rittel (1988). The recognition of contemporary, complex policy challenges has led to a resurgence of interest in using design in an applied way to public policy (Burns et al, 2006; Boyer, Cook and Steinberg, 2011; Design Council 2013; DesignGov, 2013; Allio, 2014; Bason, 2014). At its core, policy design is the idea that human beings can have some degree of control over outcomes through policy, by setting socially desired and democratically agreed goals, and then attempting to fulfil those goals through their individual and collective actions and institutions. Simon (1996, p. 111) said, 'Everyone designs who devises courses of action aimed at changing existing situations into preferred ones.' Pioneering design thinker John Heskett (2001, p. 5) described design as 'the human capacity to shape and make our environments in ways ... to serve our needs and give meaning to our lives'. Policy design is inherently optimistic and normative, engaging in innovative problem solving aimed at producing outcomes 'concerned with how things ought to be ... in order to attain goals and to function' (Simon, 1996, pp. 4–5). 'Little-d design is what translates abstract policy Design into experiences everyday people can see, hear, touch, smell, and taste' (US National Design Policy Initiative, 2009, p. 8).

Given the many examples of ineffective policy (Horst Rittel's (1988, p. 2) 'Type 1 failure'), policies that resulted in perverse or unintended consequences (Rittel's (1988, p. 2) 'Type 2 failure'), or policies with inequitable outcomes, it seems like a bold claim to argue that policy can be consciously made, or dictated by a set of designers. In Herbert Simon's original work, critics felt he had overemphasised the capacity or desirability for policy to be designed for optimal solutions, and underestimated how policies evolve as an accidental by-product of the accretion of many byzantine incidents over many years by many different actors. However, these associations with the idea of policy design are misplaced. Some misconceptions or concerns about design thinking have been caused by the use of engineering or computing analogies to address human problems, as public policy is not amenable to this type of ultra-rational approach. Policy design accepts that policy actors are boundedly rational, and recognises the limits to pure technical-rational thought, to include answers that are feasible, and able to be practically used, or are 'good enough' (Simon, 1996, p. 27).

Policy design offers an antidote to what Charles Lindblom (1959) called 'disjointed incrementalism' rather than being the outcome of conscious deliberation. Policy design is based on the premise that policy making has the potential to be more than a 'fuzzy gamble' (Dror, 1986, p. 168). Policy design integrates the benefits of structured planning with the caution and nuance of intuition (Boyer, Cook and Steinberg, 2011, p. 36), experience, practitioners' creativity and their 'reflection-in-action' (Schön, 1983). It is what Wildavsky (1979) called a 'sixth sense' policy making, which is about advanced skill in judging or sensing a very specific set of circumstances. A designer's toolbox should contain not a grand theory or single big idea, but 'an expandable set of little methods', each grounded in empirical and detailed understandings of the context: 'The philosopher Isaiah Berlin … famously divided people into hedgehogs and foxes. The former know one big thing, or think they do. The latter know lots of little things. Design is a methodology for foxes' (Design Council, 2013, p. 24). Redesign is inherently ambitious, given that 'institutional layering' means that the new lies on top of and coexists with the old (Thelen, 2004, cited in Lowndes and Roberts, 2013, p. 184). However, 'attempts at reform remain enormously important, because they express social values (and reveal struggles over those values) that are generally hidden

Figure 1: Elements of policy design

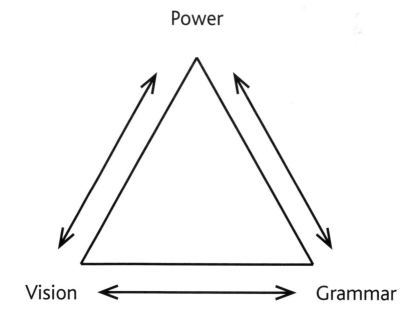

Power

Vision ⟷ Grammar

below the surface of political institutions' (Lowndes and Roberts, 2013, p. 186). Policy activities need to be 'sensitive to the context of time and place' and understand the detail and nuances of the policy context (DesignGov, 2013, p. 5), including the complexity of the policy issue and the 'degree of control ... over execution of actors in the process' (Bobrow and Dryzek, 1987, p. 19). Within these contexts, policy design, as understood here, is made up of three elements: vision, grammar and power, as shown in Figure 1.

Vision is about the clarification of values in order that these can be used to assess policy options and make choices about policy goals. Vision for policy making is critical to policy design because it acknowledges that policy is political in both a 'big-P' and 'small-p' sense. Policy is ideological, sometimes more explicitly than others, but is nevertheless a value-driven process. Vision provides a basis to inform, mobilise and channel action. Action takes place around 'grammar' (Fung, 2001, p. 101), or institutional arrangements – that is, 'how things are done round here' or the 'standard operating procedures' (Hall, 1986, cited in Lowndes and Roberts, 2013, p. 47). To achieve policy goals and actualise the vision, policy design also needs to have supportive rules and practices, embedded in structures of resources, and structures of meaning (March and Olsen, 1989). As Schneider and Ingram (1997, p. 2) remind us: 'Policies are revealed through texts, practices, and symbols ... that define and deliver values'. Grammar requires an identification of the audience and their mutable 'proclivities' as part of 'the creation of form (which can apply to both the content and process of policy)' (Bobrow and Dryzek, 1987, pp. 19–20). This element recognises that it is

> actors who make and remake institutions on a daily basis ... political institutions may change gradually through individuals' efforts to match institutions to changing situations, which includes adapting rules, practices and narratives over time. (Lowndes and Roberts, 2013, p. 180)

Vision alone is hard to act on, and needs translating into action via 'strategic intent' (Boyer, Cook and Steinberg, 2011, p. 23). The elements of the vision and grammar are interreliant: 'ethos may amount to nothing more than good intentions ... [but] tools or processes in themselves can be disempowering if used without an underpinning ethos'. Thus, 'methods need to be applied within a wider set of values', but further to that, there is a dynamic relationship between method, or what is termed here grammar, and ethos or vision (Beebeejaun et al,

2013, p. 17i). Underpinning them are some very different competing understandings of power, shaping them into more or less co-productive approaches.

Power in policy design

One of the significant hidden struggles in policy design is the deep notions of power that underlie competing visions and grammars. Figure 2 shows the start of the heuristic of policy design, setting out two contrasting approaches to policy design: conventional and co-productive.

In this chapter, an argument is made that a key dividing line between conventional and co-productive designs is their understanding of power. Conventional policy designs see power as a zero-sum resource held by one body over another in a hierarchical relationship, sometimes referred to as constituted notions of power. More co-productive designs have a view of power as a positive-sum resource that can be used in a non-coercive way for mutual benefit, sometimes known as constitutive ideas of power. More importantly, co-production is based on the idea that it is possible to bring constitutive power into formal 'constituted' policy institutions. This idea has been controversial and some of the major points of debate are discussed here.

Figure 2 illustrates the contrast between constituted and constitutive notions of power. Constituted power is a zero-sum game, an either/or: you either have power, or someone else has. Power exists for the taking, and is not shared or jointly created (Lukes, 2005). Pioneering twentieth century thinker, Mary Parker Follett (1924, p. x), described constituted power as 'power over', dominating or coercive power. In contrast to constituted hierarchical power, constitutive power is a 'non-dominating' form of power (Pearce, 2011). Constitutive power conceives of power as a 'positive-sum' game (Clegg, 1989). Power is not indivisible – something to be given or taken – but instead is the property of relationships between people, what Lasswell and Kaplan (1950, pp. 75–76) describe as an 'inter-personal process'. It can be generated, shared and is not diminished by being distributed. This perspective is what Parker Follett (1924, p. x) calls 'power with' or co-active power.

More co-productive approaches to policy design argue that constitutive power could be used to develop co-productive policy making. For example, there are many initiatives across the world to decentralise decision making down to a local level, and to include citizens in making tough policy choices or in controlling resources.

Figure 2: Power in conventional and co-productive policy design

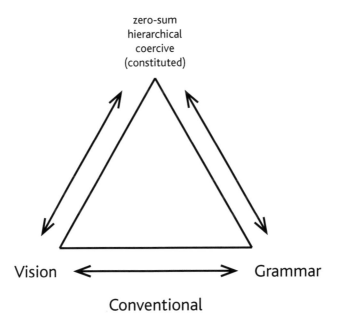

Conventional

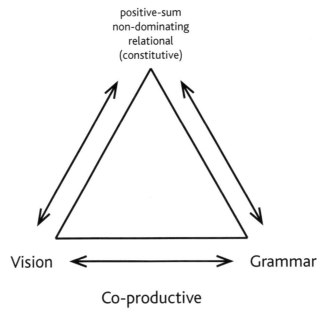

Co-productive

These moves often require elected politicians to share power and control, and can be challenging to achieve for that reason. But there is a conviction that such change is possible. This is because neither constituted nor constitutive notions of power are seen as inherent in a specific site or group of people. Constituted power is not conflated with formal institutions, in this case government. Constitutive power is not seen as the sole province of citizens. Considering constituted and constitutive power in these ways opens up space to apply different concepts of power in different ways to policy design, and allow for change towards co-production.

Why some believe co-productive policy design is not feasible

A zero-sum notion of power leads to the conclusion that it is not possible to have constitutive forms of formal governmental institutions. If power is indivisible, it can only be held by one side or the other, by one body against another. It is this core idea that leads to the questioning or rejection of the possibilities of more constitutive approaches to policy. The case that change is not possible, or even undesirable, is often based on the premise that constituted power is situated in governments, constitutive power situated with citizens, and the two are mutually exclusive. Constituted power, formal political institutions and sites of policy making are seen as irrevocably bound together. This premise has its origins in the eighteenth century at the time of the French Revolution (Sieyès, 1789), with the promotion of the radical idea that ordinary people – constituents – should be the democratic basis for the authority of the *constituted power* of formal political institutions. More modern debates have mutated the idea of constituent power – as something possessed by citizens – into the more dynamic idea of *constitutive power* as something actively created by citizens (Benjamin, 1921; Arendt, 1963; Hardt and Negri, 2002; Agamben, 2005; Lindahl, 2007).

The modern democratic state relies on the delegated authority it has from constituents, via representative elections: citizens 'hand over' power to elected representatives and delegate authority to a small set of decision makers. It can be seen that the notion of power here is indivisible, and therefore giving it up through the ballot box means citizens no longer have it. As constituted power is hierarchical and dominating, elected representatives make decisions on behalf of citizens, sometimes in opposition to citizens' expressed wants if politicians consider that such decisions are in citizens' best interests. What results from this line of thinking is one of the paradoxes of constituent power. That is, if citizens have the power, but then give it up to others, how can they then exercise that power? What control do citizens have over constituted institutions in a representative democracy, other than through the ballot box?

So, one of the reasons that some people believe co-productive policy designs are not feasible is that formal institutions of policy are based solely on constituted power. In this argument, there are ways that citizens can try to exert some influence over formal institutions and elected decision makers. These include bringing fresh faces into politics; new systems for electing political leaders; encouraging policy makers to explain if citizens disagree with their decisions; citizens demanding to know why decisions have been made by politicians; gathering public opinion between elections and getting involved in consultation (Esaiasson and Narud, 2013; Richardson and Durose, 2013). If citizens want to try and influence policy making, then they can attend public meetings, hope their preferred candidate gets voted in at election time, stand for election themselves and campaign and protest while trying not to be co-opted by the (constituted) powers that be. Mechanisms for holding those in power to account or challenging decisions may also be used, such as lobbying, direct action, protest and demonstrations. One idea proposed by Hannah Arendt (1963) was town hall meetings, which she saw as 'spaces of freedom' that would support deliberation and debate among citizens. This account is perhaps something that people who have been to a town hall meeting might contest. However, citizens themselves have created alternative institutional 'spaces of freedom' to hold authorities to account, such as in the Occupy movements seen across the world in 2010 and 2011. The broader idea of citizen engagement through public meetings and other forms of democratic innovation remain extremely popular (Smith, 2005).

Why some believe that co-productive policy design is not desirable

If, and when, formal institutions are at odds with citizens, all of the options listed above are vital potential correctives. These are all attempts to resolve the paradox of constituted power of how citizens can exercise their power after having given it away. But they are ultimately unsatisfying, as they remain in a broader framework which offers citizens a largely passive role and little genuine power or control. Therefore, the next step is for citizens to not give so much power away, and have greater control over decisions. In a positive-sum notion of power, this is a logical and feasible next step. In a zero-sum notion of power, this attempt to cure the paradox only leads to another one. The mere process of constituting something may mean the loss of constitutive power. By this reasoning, bringing constitutive power into constituted arenas would co-opt it to become part of the 'machine' and therefore tainted with the same inherent problems of formalised power. In this zero-sum based argument, these two types of power are interdependent, but they are also seen as mutually exclusive and excluding.

Notions of mutual exclusivity between constituted and constitutive power are popularly translated into debates between 'top down' versus 'bottom up' policy making. What happens if the 'bottom' becomes the 'top' – for example, when control over policy decisions is transferred to citizens and communities? Does the bottom simply end up replicating the things it fought to reject and replace? Influential 1960s radical writer and community organiser Saul Alinsky (1946, 1971) fought for citizens to realise their power in numbers, organise for change and get a seat at the (decision-making) table, but he was later accused of becoming part of the system that he and others had opposed. Critics said they had replicated 'machine politics' (Weil, 1986; Sen, 2003; Mills and Robson, 2010; Beck and Purcell, 2013).

This zero-sum logic explains why some argue for a position of perpetual resistance and opposition and standing 'outside the system' in order to guarantee that there is always a check and challenge to power (Mouffe, 2000, 2013). By never tying this power down, the risk of it solidifying into the very thing it is opposing is avoided. For some thinkers and activists, it is necessary and desirable to keep constitutive power separate from formal power or decision making, which are seen as not amendable or capable of significant reform. Recent challenges to global corporate power and social injustices by anti-globalisation and other social movements, have seen some urge caution that social movements must not be co-opted by the constituted powers of a globalised security state. Roberto Unger (2004) advocates resistance or 'denial' where there are fixed social hierarchies and institutional contexts that create oppression or injustice.

Where there are stubborn notions of constituted power held by those who have the ability to act in ways that are dangerous, damaging or corrupt, then it makes sense for others to provide resistance, protest and to hold those in power to account. Effective co-production is facilitated by supportive conditions; it is not appropriate in all cases. Chapter Four returns to some of these debates. But the aspiration advocated in this book is based on a positive-sum notion of power which underpins co-productive approaches. It rejects the case that .co-productive policy design is either unfeasible or undesirable.

Conclusion

This chapter begins to develop heuristics which help us to think laterally about policy design. By linking contemporary practice using ideas of design in policy with political science and public administration thinking, we are able to challenge the 'policy presumption'. By using heuristics as design tools, we are able to understand more clearly the 'black box' of policy, but also generate alternative designs.

Using heuristics to generate contrasting policy designs, this chapter was able to reflect on the theoretical tensions between policy designs premised on constituted and constitutive understandings of power. Power is often the elephant in the room in debates on policy design. Drawing out some of the paradoxes of constituted and constitutive power opens up spaces to consider how these different views of power can apply in different ways to policy design. Viewing power as a zero-sum resource held by one body over another or as a positive-sum resource generated in relationships between people, which can be used in a non-coercive way for mutual benefit, lets us consider the implications which differing interpretations of power have for policy design.

Positive-sum notions of power unshackle formal policy institutions from negative forms of hierarchical power, and allow us to consider how constitutive power can be brought more into constituted policy design without co-option. They also challenge some of the underlying presumptions made in the paradoxes of constituted power, primarily the conflation of constituted forms of power with formal policy institutions, and constitutive power with citizens. The next two chapters consider the other core elements of policy design. Chapter Two focuses on vision and grammar in conventional policy design, Chapter Three on vision and grammar in co-productive policy design.

CHAPTER TWO

Conventional policy design

Chapter One set out heuristics that illuminated the underpinning and interlocking elements of policy design – power, vision and grammar – and contrasting policy designs, conventional and co-productive. It focused on the first of these elements – power – and how differing interpretations of power informs contrasting notions of policy design. This chapter builds on these heuristics to consider the vision and grammar of conventional policy designs. Vision reflects the recognition that policy design is political and value-based and provides a basis to inform, mobilise and channel action towards desired policy outcomes. If vision is the politics and values that inform the desired policy outcomes to be pursued, then grammar is the institutional practices employed in the pursuit of those goals.

The Introduction outlined some of the failings and consequences of conventional constituted policy design. In this chapter we develop the heuristic to try and explain the causes of these failings and consequences. Decisions are made about where to build new houses, waste incinerators, wind farms and roads which make citizens angry or suspicious of policy makers' intentions. Public services seem to be stretched to capacity and fail to offer quality tailored care. Or there might be disparities in life chances and quality of life between those at the top and those at the bottom which make us worry that some are left behind. What is going wrong in cases like these? Is it that decision makers do not understand the situation well enough? Is it that decisions are made based on party politics? Is it that the loudest voices have dominated? How can we get a deeper understanding of these issues? Just as the specifics of good policy design vary depending on context, so do suboptimal policy designs – each problem has its own unique features. While this is true, it is also possible to identify some common aspects of conventional approaches to policy that hamper their problem-solving capacities. Figure 3 shows the most salient and problematic negative features of vision and grammar that characterise the limitations of conventional policy design. This chapter will look first at these specifics of vision in conventional policy design, then of grammar, in order to understand the characteristics which generate some of the limitations of conventional policy design.

Figure 3: Conventional policy design

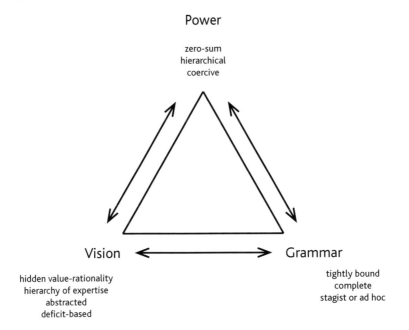

Vision

Vision reflects the recognition that policy design is political and value based and provides a basis to inform, mobilise and channel action towards desired policy outcomes. What is the vision that underpins conventional policy making? Following Figure 3, the next section looks at three aspects of the vision: hidden value rationalities; a hierarchical ordering of expertise, where technocratic elites dominate; and a deficit based model of citizens abstracted from engagement and dialogue with people's complex views.

Hidden value rationality

One element of the vision of policy design concerns the interplay and balance between value rationality – an assessment of whether the goal is worth it – and instrumental rationality – an assessment of how to reach a particular goal. An issue with conventional policy design is where value rationalities are occluded, although they are not displaced, so politics becomes something which is hidden, and even more easily manipulated. The issue is when instrumental rationality is seen in isolation from debates about the values of policy, as was set out in 1954 by British polymath Bertrand Russell (1954, p. 8):

Historically, the most influential conception of rationality in policy analysis has been the instrumental (or means–end) conception of rationality, in which determining whether a policy is rational is a matter of determining whether it efficiently and effectively accomplishes given goals; the goals themselves cannot be either rational or irrational.

While instrumental rationalities – outcomes – are crucial in policy design, the lack of transparency of the value rationalities underpinning desired outcomes leads to a shallow vision of policy design.

To cite Harold Lasswell (1936), one of the founding 'fathers' of the study of public administration, policy design is about who gets what, when and how. Policy design is, in this sense, deeply political and importantly shaped by ideology and values (Mrydal, 1972; Etzioni, 1988; Weiss, 1993; Walt, 1994; Davies, Nutley and Smith, 2000; Duncan, 2005; Mulgan, 2005). Yet in a Laswellian sense politics is often obscured in debates on policy making. For example, a UK think tank's proposal for how to change policy making describes how 'very little attention' is paid to the role of politics. It points to an official government guide to *Professional Policy Making* (Cabinet Office, 2001) which 'treats politics briskly ... as something external to the policy process, as a "context" that must be "understood" or "managed"' (Hallsworth, Parker and Rutter, 2011, p. 35). If and when politics is hidden in policy, then some ideological biases and interests are not fully transparent. In instances where major vested corporate and financial interests are involved this can be dangerous, for example if attempts are made to sway policies in their own favour through underhand means (Hatchard et al, 2014), for example through what is known as 'astroturfing' where apparently grassroots lobbying movements are actually sponsored or directed by commercial firms. When politics is present not as a set of transparent interests, it can reappear in less seemly guises, such as politicking and power games, referred to as 'palace politics' (Allison, 1971). Whether party political, or concerning the vested interests of particular groups, 'palace politics' invades conventional policy design in many iniquitous and insidious ways. This lack of transparency around the Lasswellian politics of policy making is the source of much cynicism about the conventional policy process.

However, attempts to manage politics out of policy are no better. As policy is seen as being 'shot through with value conflicts, political decisions and priorities', some argue that it would be bettered not by a more transparent articulation of the values at play but by the application of 'relatively neutral' research (Geva-May and Pal, 1999,

p. 259). A lack of transparency about values has been converted into an argument that policy making should be value neutral, driven instead by 'what works'. In the modern policy context, this view is sometimes articulated through calls for 'evidence-based policy making' (EBPM). Of course, policies should be designed based on whether they are likely to accomplish specified goals; this is merely common sense. What is problematic is where a combination of instrumental rationality, isolated from a debate on values, coupled with supposedly value-neutral evidence-based policy making, results in a hollowing out in debates over policy goals. As Wayne Parsons (2002, p. 56) argues, the particular conventional rendering of evidence-based policy making depoliticises knowledge production and utilisation, and is therefore working against a 'Lasswellian approach [which] is about ensuring that knowledge is politicised'. A more co-productive interpretation of the use of useful evidence in policy making would strike a different balance between value and instrumental rationalities in policy design (Rittel, 1966). For example as Carol Weiss (1993, p. 94) argues, the idea of an objective 'evidence base' needs also to recognise the values and assumptions underlying 'neutral' facts and the value-laden process of selecting and weighting that evidence.

Hierarchical ordering of expertise

The particular balance between value and instrumental rationalities in the vision of conventional policy design is reflected in a hierarchical ordering of expertise within the policy process. That is, particular forms of expertise are given greater legitimacy than others within the policy process. On the one hand, debates about hierarchies of expertise reflect widely shared critiques that policy making is dominated by elites. The expression of concern about 'policies without publics' (May, 1991, p. 190) is often readily dismissed with hand wringing and recourse to arguments about a lack of appetite or incentives for public participation. What such a dismissal reinforces is a sense that expertise is useful for policy making primarily when it meets either instrumental rationalities or the demand for supposedly neutral evidence. Expertise is 'restricted to technical and scientific communities' (May, 1991 p. 190), where 'science' is 'the model for political thinking' and 'technocrats' are the 'model actors' (Boyte, 2005, p. 521).

Yet even within these elites, a hierarchical ordering of expertise can be detected (Porter, 2010; Newman, 2012). While elected representatives are in theory the decision makers, technocrats are recognised to have 'gr[o]w[n] increasingly powerful throughout the twentieth century' (Boyte, 2005, p. 522). 'Technocrats' is a term used to describe a professional cadre of policy analysts and advisers who are often generalists rather than specialists in any one policy field. Their role is not to generate research or science but to marshal it for use in policy. They are the courtiers in the 'palace politics'. Boyte (2005, p. 522) attributes the growth in their importance to a policy design that 'hide[s] values, interests, power and authority relations under a scientific and neutral pose and undermine[s] the authority of those without credentials'.

This perspective is not to debase the value of scientific knowledge in policy design. Indeed, one widely bemoaned flaw of conventional policy designs is that potentially useful or life-changing scientific advice and evidence is frequently ignored. Academics and professionals, who offer these forms of scientific and specialist expertise, often complain of neglect and mistreatment by their target policy audiences (Richardson, 2013; Stoker, 2013). Many such commentators now see the enactment of 'evidence-based policy making' as serving to exacerbate technocratic privilege (Fischer, 2000; Collins and Evans, 2002), where evidence is used to close down challenge or is drawn on after the fact to legitimate a decision – what some have described as 'policy-based evidence making' (House of Commons Science and Technology Committee, 2006). Policy is instead often determined by the 'seat-of-the-pants intuitions' (Green and Gerber, 2003, p. 105) of technocrats and politicians about what might work.

This technocratic privileging also serves to devalue experiential expertise. While politicians' accumulated experiences inevitably shape their underpinning belief systems and frames for understanding, their legitimacy derives from election not experience. Experiential expertise or lived experience features in occasional explicit references to politicians' personal experiences and more commonly their translation of the direct experiences of constituents and voters, for example a piece of casework in their constituency surgeries or an inspirational visit to a project. This 'policy by anecdote', where the fad of the day is promoted with a single heart-warming example, is often viewed by scientists and researchers as an attempt to displace other more robust, reliable and relevant forms of expertise. Citizens' own presentations of their lived experience rest further down the hierarchy of expertise. As others have reflected, for many citizens policy making and analysis feels, at best, an abstraction or irrelevance, and at worst, a deliberate attempt to perpetuate a technocratic, high-handed elitism (Wagenaar and Cook, 2003).

Abstracted and deficit based

Non-elite or mass participation in policy is now rhetorically de rigueur, but direct forms of participation remain heavily managed and partial in many places. Democratic innovations that give citizens the opportunity to participate in policy design in practice often run the risk of perpetuating, reproducing and institutionalising power inequities (Freire, 1996; Gaventa, 2005; Skelcher, Mathur and Smith, 2005; Porter, 2010). Such forms of 'co-'decision making, for example in collaboration or partnership, often give responsibility without control and fail to share power (Arnstein, 1969; Cooke and Kothari, 2001). As such, they can also misinterpret and misrepresent the identities and aspirations of communities (Denis and Lomas, 2003; Durose, Greasley and Richardson, 2009).

Misinterpretation of citizen knowledge, experience and expertise also often occurs through abstraction by aggregation in public opinion surveys and official statistics, which further reinforce the position of technocratic elites in policy design. Although 'reliable official statistics are a cornerstone of democracy' (HM Treasury, 1998, p. 5), the process of aggregation necessary to provide this statistical data has a necessarily homogenising effect, neglecting minority views. Surveys often show that people's views are complex and sometimes appear to be contradictory. While it is possible for sophisticated data to be able to show people's preferences in all of their conditional and nuanced glory, there is a risk that by itself it offers only an abstracted take on the views of citizens, which makes those views easier to devalue. Looking at survey data for any length of time, it is easy to develop a jaundiced view that citizens are victims of Orwellian 'double-think' or cognitive polyphasia, which is the ability to seem to simultaneously hold contradictory views without cognitive dissonance.

If policy is designed without a dynamic two-way process of direct citizen engagement, people have too few opportunities to discuss, explain, justify or defend the meaning, intention or contradictions of their quantified behaviours, preferences and opinions. Nor are there ways for respondents to amend their policy preferences in light of new information or arguments in conventional survey data. Longitudinal data and repeated cross-sectional data both show changes in citizens' views and behaviours, but even with in-depth statistical analysis, sometimes it is not clear whether these changes are the result of reasoned deliberation, stupidity, confusion or being too easily influenced by external forces like the media. No wonder then that policy makers might see citizens' preferences as simultaneously both stubbornly fixed as well as frustratingly inconsistent and fluid.

This abstraction, misinterpretation and marginalisation all work to pathologise citizens in the policy process. Citizens become the objects of policy – the units to which policies happen rather than active subjects who are constitutive of their own action and power. From this perspective, citizens become 'clients and consumers who are serviced by experts' (Boyte, 2005, p. 522). Some people have begun to think about this as 'deficit model' policy design (Kretzmann and McKnight, 1993). Deficit-based positions often – however inadvertently – focus on and direct resources towards a 'community's needs, deficiencies and problems' and encourage them to see themselves as reliant on outside expertise in order to solve problems (Kretzmann and McKnight, 1993, p. 2). Ultimately, if the underlying model of citizens is deficit based, then where citizens' views are inconsistent, contradictory or conflicting it makes sense that citizens need protecting from themselves. Different mechanisms for democratic innovation (Smith, 2005), for example deliberative polling (Fishkin, 1997; Fishkin and Luskin, 2000), and models of representative yet responsive governance (Richardson and Durose, 2013) may offer ways to elucidate, debate, evolve and even amend citizens' views in the policy process. However, the deficit model is persistent, with lingering questions over the capacity of citizens to engage in meaningful policy debates (Richardson and Le Grand, 2002).

Grammar

The chapter will now turn to consider the grammar of conventional policy design. If vision is the politics and values that inform the desired policy outcomes to be pursued, then grammar is the institutional practices employed in the pursuit of those goals. The chapter will focus on three types of grammar: the tightly bounded and demarcated nature of different groups; the approach completed and planned in advance; and an understanding of policy making either as a linear process composed of a set of stages that follow each other or as ad hoc, complex and chaotic.

Tightly bounded

One set of grammatical rules in constituted approaches is that the various actors in the policy process are delineated into a set of tightly bounded groups that each play a defined set of roles or functions (Agranoff, 2007). Generally, this approach exhibits low levels of permeability and porosity, for example in the boundaries between the 'two communities' (Caplan, 1979) of academics and policy makers. Occasionally, some determined individuals break through the boundaries, in the form of academic 'policy entrepreneurs' for example (Kingdon, 1995). A few people are members of multiple groups, such as activists who are also academics and vice versa (Wright Mills, 1959). However, generally each policy 'community' has a defined set of cultural norms. The high strength of in-group affiliations and loyalties means some feel they might be better described in a more rugged and primal sense as 'tribes' (Orr and Bennett, 2010, p. 199).

Not only are the groups tightly bounded, but distinct functions are attached to them. The different functions in the policy-making process, such as assembling the evidence, or projecting estimated outcomes, or estimating risk, which are usually performed by specific groups. In public policy contexts, the ultimate decision makers are (in theory) the elected politicians. Policy analysis is often seen as a role for professional civil servants, or a function that might be performed by policy advisers outside the administration. Analysts bring together the resources, information, intelligence and skill needed to go through the various stages. These analysts may not be themselves political, but are aware of the political context of decision making. Policy analysts advise policy makers. Policy evaluation, as sometimes portrayed, is a more specific function of looking at objective evidence and is a role usually occupied by academics or scientists. It is not entirely clear where citizens fit into the process, other than as opinions represented by data in the analysis, or perhaps as constituents represented by the elected politicians. Where this leaves policy making is a highly prescribed set of roles, behaviours and bases of understanding for each group. Poor communication, misunderstandings, disjointed processes, the actors lacking a holistic grasp of an issue and lack of respect between the groups is almost 'programmed-in' from the start.

Complete

A further aspect of conventional grammars being scrutinised here is the notion that a good policy design is one in which everything can be known and planned for in advance. It rules out uncertainty, flexibility and developmental change. It is a fiction of constituted grammars that plans can take into account all eventualities and circumstances. Understandably, when serious consequences for people's lives and public resources are at stake, there is a necessary demand for certainty about the possible results of choices, and careful forethought about how to realise choices in practice: 'Large public-works [and public-service programmes] are effectively irreversible, and the consequences they generate have long half-lives. Many people's lives will have been irreversibly influenced, and large amounts of money will have been spent – another irreversible act' (Rittel and Webber, 1973, p. 163). However, a lack of pause for reflection, or the capacity to amend and adapt plans, can lead to the continued implementation of unsuitable policies long after their unsuitability has been recognised.

This prescriptive approach is underpinned by an expectation of completeness – that the institutional arrangements for how citizens contribute have to be worked out fully in advance. Much of the discourse on policy design has 'extolled the virtues of completeness' as it is perceived to allow 'for the pre-specification of a problem, the identification of pre-existing alternatives and the choice of the most optimal solution' (Garud, Jain and Tuertscher, 2008, p. 351). Incompleteness in conventional design is seen as a hindrance to proper policy making. However, the expectation of completeness can close down the scope for citizens to make meaningful contributions, for example when the 'most optimal solution' or other fundamental choices such as desired policy formats have already been decided before citizen engagement takes place. Small wonder then that one of the gripes about participation in policy is that it is at times overly constrained or tokenistic. This sense of completeness informs participation, being seen by many as an 'empty ritual' (Arnstein, 1969).

Stagist or ad hoc

The third key aspect of the grammar of conventional policy design is its depiction as a linear series of logical, orderly and neat stages. One author has called this stagist portrayal of policy design the first 'grand age' of public policy scholarship (John, 2015). These stagist models typically set out how the process of policy making falls into a number of stages or broad phases: for example, problem identification and definition, sometimes called agenda setting, followed by policy formulation, involving the assessment of options and trade-offs, decisions about choices and adoption. Adoption is followed by the policy being implemented and delivered, monitored and evaluated, and subsequently maintained, or terminated, or renewed and/or amended (Brewer, 1974; Hogwood and Gunn, 1984; HM Treasury, 2003; Bardach, 2011). At their core, these models extol the idea that policy making proceeds at a steady pace, in a logical orderly fashion, informed by rational thought and reflection, and grounded in high-quality evidence and analysis.

Were the stages model of policy to be empirically accurate, it already suggests some of the suggested problems with conventional policy making: that only certain sorts of groups of experts and professionals take part in policy making and that once a stage is completed, the process inevitably moves forward. Going backwards would be just that, a backwards move and a negative development. Failure to conform to these stages is described in pejorative terms, with the only alternatives being messy and irrational. When much of 'real world' policy making does not conform to this ideal type, it is seen as a demonstration of irrationality, a distortion of what should otherwise be poor practice. The flexibility and iteration implied by a non-linear process are not acknowledged or accepted as positive in conventional design.

Not only are the features of the stagist model problematic in theory, they are also problematic in reality. Much has been written about how the stagist model is empirically unsupported – it simply is not how real policy is made or works (Hallsworth, Parker and Rutter, 2011). Academic and policy writers have pointed out that real policy is a world away from a neat linear process of stages that happen in the desired order, with decisions being made in a thoughtful, rational way, informed by evidence and quality analysis. For example, over 50 years ago, Charles Lindblom (1959) described the 'science of muddling through' and argued that policy somehow emerges from a complex set of forces. Another major writer relied on an organic metaphor to express the chance nature of how and why some policy ideas 'catch hold': 'people plant seeds every day … When you plant a seed you need rain, soil and luck' (Kingdon, 1995, p. 81). Others have argued that what replaces the linear process is 'ad-hocery' (Hallsworth, Parker and Rutter, 2011).

Following these ideas, better, more complex, empirically accurate and thoroughly tested descriptions of the process have been put forward in what John (2012, 2015) calls the second 'synthetic' age of public policy studies. This second period saw new ways to understand and explain some of these odd features of policy, such as the combination of policy flux and policy stasis (Baumgartner and Jones, 1993; Sabatier and Jenkins-Smith, 1993). Empirically grounded descriptions of policy making revealed 'tooth and claw' portrayals of a competitive melee of messy real-world processes. One highly influential piece of academic writing drew the analogy of a 'garbage can' (Cohen, March and Olsen, 1972), which was later adapted by Kingdon (1995) into the policy window model. Within the garbage can, policy is not just a free-for-all of half-digested and out-of-date ideas decomposing together into a mush. Ideas, their proponents and the environments they operate in all interact, out of which policies emerge, bruised but ripe for serving up on the implementation table. Particular confluences of factors coincide to make it more likely that one group or set of ideas or interests will win over the others. An idea suddenly catches hold of political imagination or popular debate – what is going on? Some perfect policy storm – a public crisis, a new Minister, a canny policy wonk – creates a window for policy change as problems, policies and politics interact. Political receptiveness and congruence with dominant values are some of the selection mechanisms in the survival of the fittest in the primeval policy soup (Kingdon, 1995).

Conclusion

Conventional policy design is based on an assumption of a zero-sum notion of power. A sense that power is held in hierarchical relationship: it may be given and taken, but it cannot be shared. This underpinning premise colours the vision and grammar of this policy design and their enactment in policy making. This zero-sum perspective has prompted a masking of the value rationalities at play within policy design, privileging instrumental rationality within conventional design, a focus on achieving goals, which leads to a lack of transparency concerning the value rationalities at play. The predominance of instrumental rationalities, in turn, supports a privileging of those able to play 'palace politics', those technocrats who are able to effectively marshal evidence and expertise to the rhythms and demands of policy making. This 'vision' of policy making marginalises and disenfranchises citizens at every turn. Beyond the ballot box, their potential contribution or expertise is dismissed, unrecognised and devalued. They are locked out of policy making, excluded from a process of policy design intended to determine the vital questions of who gets what, when and how in a democratic society.

The concordant grammars of conventional policy design, as demonstrated in the first and second grand ages of understandings of public policy draw broad and contrasting pictures. The first gives us a sense of a reassuringly logical, thoughtful and intelligent world inhabited by elites who can best look after citizens' interests. The second draws back the curtain to reveal a harsh, contingent world of hard-fought and brutish policy competition between sets of unlikely and unpredictable allies in a chance world where events align in unforeseen combinations to favour one idea over another. The former seems unrealistic; the latter seems undesirable. Choices appear to be cold rigidity or bloody chaos. Neither seems well suited to addressing complex seemingly intractable global public policy challenges.

Both sets of ideas in the first and second ages of public policy studies offer competing conceptualisations of the existing conventional process. The development of more accurate descriptions of the policy process is always useful and some branches of the third age of public policy scholarship are moving into ever more advanced understandings of the complexities of human and institutional motivations (John et al, 2013; Lowndes and Roberts, 2013). This book attempts to move into territory that is more normative. How can those interested in creating more co-productive approaches move from description of the existing, to design of alternatives? How can policy designers find ways to integrate co-productive elements into conventional spaces?

CHAPTER THREE

Co-productive policy design

Design is about 'designing schemes for designing institutions' (Goodin, 1996 p. 28 cited in Lowndes and Roberts, 2013, p. 187). But design is 'not a cookbook'; there is no simple fail-safe recipe to follow (Bobrow and Dryzek, 1987, p. 207; Boyer, Cook and Steinberg, 2011, p. 87). The stagist model of the policy process has been rejected in favour of an acknowledgement that policy is messy, political, chaotic, with many unforeseen and/or uncontrollable contingencies affecting outcomes (Bovens and t'Hart, 1996). However, a commitment to the potential for policy to be more than a 'fuzzy gamble' (Dror, 1986, p. 168) on outcomes and the lives of citizens can be retained. Building on the heuristics of policy design in the opening chapters, this chapter returns to the notion of power as positive sum, non-dominating and relational set out in Chapter One to explore the vision and grammar of co-productive policy design. Chapter Three considers the possibility of introducing co-productive elements into conventional policy design through vision and grammar.

Thinking through the vision and grammar of co-productive policy design and the possibilities for introducing such elements resonates with wider debates on co-production. In its origins, and in the sense used in this book, co-production is a term associated with the research of Elinor Ostrom. In her work on the management of common-pool resources, such as access to water, Ostrom (1996, p. 1073) used 'co-production' to describe a process through which 'inputs from individuals who are not "in" the same organisation are transformed into goods and services'. The term 'co-production' suggests a relationship between 'regular producers' (policy makers and practitioners) and 'clients' (service users) (Ostrom, 1999), specifically where the 'client' acts not as a 'consumer' of services, but as a 'co-producer' of them. The implication here is that citizens can play an active role in producing public goods and services of consequence to them (Ostrom, 1996, p. 1073). Co-production has become a ubiquitous term in contemporary policy, which builds on a rich, diverse and contested lineage of theory and experimentation. Chapter Three considers this background before looking at how ideas of co-production can help to inform the vision and grammar of more co-productive policy design.

What is co-production?

Co-production is a resonant, widely applied term in policy, arguably fuelled by but reinforcing its conceptual ambiguity (Vershuere, Brandsen and Pestoff, 2012). In this chapter, the parameters of debate on co-production are mapped and reflected on, to consider how co-production can inform the vision and grammar of co-productive policy design.

Co-production can take place at the individual, group or collective level (Brudney and England, 1983). Individual co-production describes arrangements where an individual (and their family) is the producer and beneficiary; examples include expert patient programmes and home-schooling contracts. Group co-production involves producers and beneficiaries as a specific group or category of citizens, such as users of a particular service or residents of a particular neighbourhood – e.g. pooled social care budgets and neighbourhood watch schemes. In collective co-production, a group of citizens will act as producers – for example, time-banking or school governors – but the beneficiaries are the wider community (Durose et al, 2013a). Brudney and England (1983, pp. 62–63) 'consider the collective forms of co-production more important, simply because they are likely to have greater impact on who receives the benefits derived from co-productive activities'. The premise of this argument is that these relationships are the basis for a different form of efficiency in managing resources and delivering services, one which challenges the traditional economic arguments of an 'economy of scale' to instead assert an 'economy of scope' (O'Donovan and Rubbra, 2012) based on generating creative synergies in resources and expertise (Ostrom, 1996).

In some of the literature, co-production is used simply as a new way of describing or recognising how service users, citizens and communities contribute to public services (Needham and Carr, 2009). Such contributions can include attending school, taking medicine or recycling waste. While such examples highlight the familiar and everyday nature of co-production, they perhaps offer an overly passive version of citizens' roles in co-production (Sharp, 1980). Others instead cite the caring responsibilities that many citizens take on for families, friends and neighbours. Seeing caring as co-production offers recognition of the often hidden and undervalued contributions of citizens in the provision and delivery of public service. The example of caring also reflects that co-production may be most appropriate and significant in 'relational' rather than transactional public services (Berry, 2012) or in instances 'where the social issues are chronic and complex, and the solutions are contested (Horne and Shirley, 2009, p. 25). Some of the commentary that comes closest to co-productive policy design goes further and sees co-production as a means of transforming public services, by challenging traditional relationships of power, control and expertise (Arnstein, 1969) and demanding that 'producer and product, process and outcome are changed' (Cahn and Gray, 2012, p. 131).

In this way, transformative co-production relies on an emotionally charged process of reciprocal change (Ewert and Evans, 2012, p. 76). Such reciprocity requires that citizens and professionals challenge their perceptions of themselves, their role and of each other (Bradwell and Marr, 2008, Conroy, Clarke and Wilson, 2012). Doing so demands a process of 'mutual readjustment' where 'the actions taken by both the service agent and the citizen are based on their joint consideration of a problem' where both 'share responsibility for deciding what action to take [and] each accords legitimacy to the responsibility of the other' (Whitaker, 1980, pp. 241, 244). As Bovaird (2007, p. 856) reflects, 'the service user has to trust professional advice and support, but the professional has to be prepared to trust the decisions and behaviours of service users and the communities in which they live rather than dictate them'. So that local public services are meaningfully seen as the 'joint product of the activities of both citizens and government', 'rather than an agent presenting a "finished product" to the citizen, agent and citizen together produce the desired transformation' (Sharp, 1980, p. 110).

Critiques of co-production

As with many similar terms and concepts, co-production is now pressed into service in support of many wildly different causes. In academic writing, part of the intellectual battles around the term are a product of its origins and use, emerging in a largely US-based academic literature on public service management, premised on the recognition that the involvement of citizens and communities is crucial to delivering more effective public services and better local outcomes (Sharp, 1980; Whitaker, 1980). It has a mixed lineage drawing on ideological or normative positions from across the political spectrum. For example, some work could be identified with more right-leaning orientations, and draw from advocates of 'public choice', characterised by an antipathy to 'big' government, and to its support of marketisation and privatisation (Bussu and Galanti, 2014). From a wholly other tradition, co-production is informed by the literature and practice of citizen participation and development. For some, co-production denotes a clear commitment to asset-based community development in recognising and engaging a community's capacities and assets (Kretzmann and McKnight, 1993). It also draws on theories of communitarianism (Etzioni, 1993) and social capital (Putnam, 1995), reflecting their shared emphasis on balancing rights with responsibilities and recognising the importance and value of voluntarism, association, civic duty and self-organisation. This diverse lineage has fuelled both the growing prominence of co-production in contemporary political debates and its perceived lack of conceptual clarity.

The criticisms that broader efforts and experimentation with participation in decision-making have faced, of perpetuating 'power imbalances between participants, explicit and implicit co-option, cost-shifting and continuing centralisation' (Taylor, 2007, p. 297), continue to be made in debates about co-production. Many commentators who are wary of the term take a line of critique arguing that the apparent opening up of agenda setting and decision making articulated in the discourse of co-production masks new forms of state control, as state power is reproduced at a distance from or beyond the state. This work on 'governmentality' was initiated by the French social theorist Michel Foucault (1979), and focuses on the organised practices or techniques of the state through which citizens are governed, configured, regulated and controlled (Rose, 1999). Critics of co-production argue that it is used by the state as a means of re-centralisation. By establishing the 'rules of the game', the state is able to determine the parameters of local solutions (Swyngedouw, 2005). For example, by using co-production to challenge the public sector monopoly on the provision of public services, the state is able to open up previously public space and accelerate its drive for marketisation. Thus, the new governance spaces of co-production are said to be 'inscribed' by the existing distribution of power and create privileged pathways and access for the more powerful actors while serving to co-opt and colonise the less powerful, and silence, marginalise and ignore alternatives.

Another line of attack on co-production centres on its use as a technique to make citizens responsible for aspects of welfare, which previously the state had supported, described as 'responsibilising' citizens. To responsibilise is to mobilise and harness community resources for self-management (Clarke, 2005), thus divesting the state of its responsibility for welfare and social justice. Citizens are thus activated, but also compliant. Given that interest in co-production of public services re-emerged in the wake of the financial crisis, this served to strengthen the responsibilisation critique. The case for co-production is now often made on the basis of its 'strong potential relationship' with efficiency (Ostrom, 1993, p. 231). Indeed, it is on this basis that co-production seems to have caught the imagination of those within conventional policy design. This interest, particularly in a context of austerity is often underpinned by a 'substitutive' logic of divestment from the state (Barker, 2010). Specifically, that co-production offers the opportunity for cost substitution through shifting responsibilities to citizens.

Reclaiming co-production for co-productive policy design

Depictions like those of the governmentality theorists of the ceaseless reproduction of state power neglect not only the potential for unintended consequences, but also of heterogeneous local response. As discussed in Chapter One, some writers believe that the pervasiveness of constituted logics means that radical change to conventional systems is either not possible, or has dire consequences of co-option into the system for those who dare try. In this book, these arguments are rejected; policy does not always work out the way that government intends, nor do citizens, communities and localities always behave in the ways sought by government. The interest and drive for co-production from government can help to legitimise the presence of communities in decision making and strengthen the hand of allies within the system who want change (Taylor, 2007, pp. 308–309). More significantly, it may help to mobilise communities, not just denying or constraining, but creating opportunities for social action (Taylor, 2007, p. 308). While often understated, the governmentality literature itself allows the possibility of 'active subjects' who can resist the reproduction of state power and articulate and implement alternative agendas (Atkinson, 2003, p. 117). Many communities have seized on opportunities to assert their independence, shape government interventions and ensure resources meet community need. There is also evidence of a wider latent interest from citizens and communities in becoming involved in shaping and making the decisions that affect their everyday lives (Hansard, 2013, p. 71). As Taylor (2007, p. 309) comments, 'one community's "responsibilisation" can be another's community empowerment'.

While co-production recognises the limitations of government in being able to access specific resources or expertise (Verschuere, Brandsen and Pestoff, 2012), attempts to use co-production to substitute for cuts in state support for the most vulnerable misconstrues Ostrom's 'additive' logic (Barker, 2010). An additive logic argues that efficiencies in public services can be delivered through bringing together existing

Figure 4: Power, vision and grammar in policy design

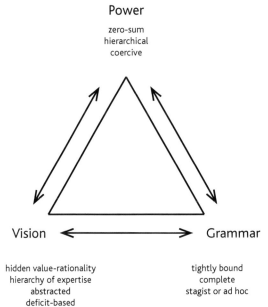

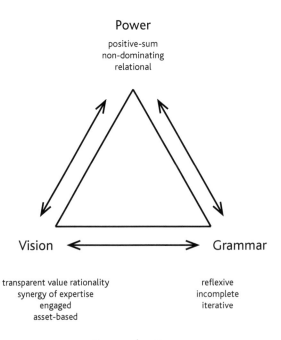

resources and assets in new and creative ways (Durose et al, 2013a). So, recognising that while community assets are 'absolutely necessary' in achieving efficiencies in public service delivery, they are usually 'not sufficient to meet the huge development challenges ahead' without the contribution of, among others, government (Kretzmann and McKnight, 1993, p. 6). From this perspective, there remains a possibility to see co-production as an empowering and socially just proposition, which facilitates citizens in acting collectively and generating additive, voluntary and transformative social action (Bussu and Galanti, 2014). It is this latter view which has generated interest beyond the design and delivery of public services and for co-production to be used to denote an approach to both research (Durose et al, 2011; Beebeejaun et al, 2013, 2014) and conflict resolution (Susskind and Elliott, 1983).

This exploration of the lineage and debates surrounding co-production shows that it is a loaded term. This book seeks to reclaim this term and draw on this intellectual lineage to inform the vision and grammar of co-productive policy design. Figure 4 builds on earlier heuristics to set out the key elements of co-productive policy design.

Vision

Vision reflects the recognition that policy design is political and value based and provides a basis to inform, mobilise and channel action towards desired policy outcomes. What sort the vision underpins co-productive policy design? Following Figure 4, the next section looks at three aspects of the vision: transparent value rationality; synergy of expertise; and an asset-based perspective of citizens, where people are engaged in two-way discussion.

Transparent value rationality

Laswell's view of policy design is inherently political; the decision of 'who gets what, when and how' is shaped by values. The isolation or masking of instrumental rationality from the necessary complement of value rationality was identified in Chapter Two as a feature of conventional policy design. Alternatives add to the evidence base about 'what works' with greater transparency about what is working, for whom and to what ends. Co-productive designs do not reject evidence about what is most likely to be an effective policy, nor do they eschew outcomes. Instead, they place debates about how to achieve much-needed outcomes in debates about what the values are underpinning the outcomes. There is an openness about debating and defending those values. Tools can be used to assess value rationalities alongside instrumental rationalities – for example, societal-level social vindication (Fischer, 1995) is where policies are designed and assessed against higher order principles or political values such as equality or justice (Stone, 1997; Rawls, 1999) and how they will affect whole systems. More transparent articulation of underlying value rationalities offers the opportunity to generate an explicit commitment to wider transformative social goals (Beebeejaun et al, 2014), aiming at 'actively alter[ing] the social conditions' (Robinson and Tansey, 2006, p. 152).

The explicit articulation of value rationalities offers a means of 'politicising government and retrieving older practices of democratic politics' (Boyte, 2005, p. 519). It means the rediscovery of democratic politics recognising that the ethical and political legitimacy of policy is strengthened by the presence of those affected in the development of that policy (Young, 1990) and that knowledge creation is part of the wider rights of citizens (Freire, 1996; Gaventa, 2005). Further, it revives a form of democratic citizenship where 'an ethos of public responsibility, accountability and authority' becomes diffused as a function of the general civic culture' (Boyte, 2005, p. 519). Such politicisation 'advanc[es] three democratic goals: participation, deliberation and empowerment' (Fung, 2001, p. 87) and in doing so has a beneficial effect, not only for citizens (Pateman, 1970). A co-productive vision intends to bring a range of benefits for the policy process (Pelletier et al, 1999). These are 'substantive', providing an informed knowledge base for policy making; 'normative', strengthening the democratic legitimacy of public policy; but also 'instrumental', with communities feeling greater ownership of policy (Verschuere, Brandsen and Pestoff, 2012) and therefore being willing and enabled to contribute to improved outcomes and achievable solutions (Ostrom, 1996).

Synergy of expertise

Conventional policy design in its worst or most extreme forms is perpetuated by an elitist technocracy, which privileges a particular – technocratic – form of expertise over other forms of expertise, including science, but also experiential, local, applied and creative knowledge (Fung, 2001; Collins and Evans, 2002; Yanow, 2004). In these cases, citizens can be left 'disconnected and dispirited' (Wildavsky, 1979; Mintzberg, 2005) and disempowered as their 'practice wisdom' is devalued (Boyte, 2005, pp. 521, 522) and they are credited with 'little or no ability to solve collective problems among themselves' (Sugden, 1986 cited in Ostrom, 1993, p. 226). The aim in co-productive policy design is not to reorder a constituted hierarchy of expertise, so simply advocating a different type of hierarchy which privileges experiential expertise over other forms. Instead, co-production suggests the value of involving different forms of knowledge and expertise in the policy process, and moves towards synthesis of different 'ingredients' of a policy puzzle (Boyer, Cook and Steinberg, 2011, p. 34), while ensuring that these different forms of knowledge are 'integrated, not annihilated, not absorbed' (Follett, 1924). Note that it is forms of knowledge that are respected, without presuming which groups hold those forms. For example, citizens do not need to be pigeon-holed as experts only based on their personal experience. As with the authors and contributors to this book, people may have multiple roles and forms of expertise to offer to policy. In his autobiography, Herbert Simon talks about the varied threads of his career and life, saying: 'Which of the wanderers through these different mazes will step forward at the call for the real Herbert Simon? All of them ... We live each hour in context, different contexts for different hours' (Simon, 1991, p. xvi).

A co-productive policy design is instead based on 'creative synergies'. This term, borrowed from Ostrom (1996, pp. 1082, 1079), reflects that 'when co-productive inputs are diverse entities and complements, synergy can occur. Each has something the other needs ... if inputs are strictly substitutable, no potential for synergy exists'. So, while co-production of policy is importantly grounded in the local knowledge (Yanow, 2004) and experiential expertise (Collins and Evans, 2002) of citizens, co-production does not seek to initiate a 'zero-sum substitution' of the different forms of expertise – a loss of scientific data or professional insights in favour of experiential understanding or local knowledge. Instead, there is a recognition that each form of expertise is 'absolutely necessary', but 'not usually sufficient' to tackle significant contemporary policy challenges (Kretzmann and McKnight, 1993, p. 6). An 'additive' approach to co-production is required (Barker, 2010), bringing together existing – but perhaps hidden and untapped – resources, assets and expertise in a beneficial mutually reinforcing configuration (Mintzberg, 2005; Durose et al, 2013b, p. 329). In this sense, co-production is about the 'dynamic interactions between participants, rejecting the notion of a 'binary relationship' (Orr and Bennett, 2009; Pohl et al, 2010), and instead positing 'the idea of mutual learning and interaction between parties with distinct roles and claims to knowledge' (Beebeejaun et al, 2014, p. 40).

Political scientist Aaron Wildavsky's classic work, *Speaking Truth to Power* (1979), helps us understand that policy design is an 'art' as well as a 'craft'. Iris Geva-May (1997, p. xxiii) refers to art 'because it demands intuition, creativity and imagination in order to identify, define and devise solutions to problems' and to craft 'because it requires mastery of methodological, technical and inter-disciplinary knowledge in fields ranging from economics and law to politics, communication, administration and management'. This perspective reinforces some of the critical aspects of policy design, and parallels the design thinking literature, in that policy design ought to blend creativity and imagination, with hard skills drawn across specialisms. And it suggests that what is also important in co-productive policy design is the involvement of different types of knowledge, not to fixate on which groups are seen as holding these types of knowledge. Using some of the same terms, organisational theorist Henry Mintzberg (2005, p. 151) argues that policy must proceed relying not only on 'science', but also drawing on 'art' – vision, leadership, imagination and intuition – and 'craft' – knowledge based on experience and applied knowledge. Policy can be 'disorganised', 'disconnected' and 'dispirited' if one form of expertise is left out, or overly dominates (Mintzberg, 2005, p. 153).

In practice, 'craft' in the form of direct experience is the form of expertise that is least likely to be in balance. Proposals for co-productive designs do not seek to redress this by simply tilting the emphasis the other way, and neglecting leadership, or evidence, but to rebalance art, craft and science. In different circumstances, there might be a greater urgency for more creative solutions which demand more 'art' – i.e. intuition, novel ideas and leadership. In other situations, the priority will be to inject more 'science' or evidence, or to use 'craft' – e.g. direct experiences of policy implementation from the perspective of users, citizens or practitioners, to assess feasibility. Each situation will make its own demands, and these will change over each iteration.

Engaged and asset based

Co-productive policy design rejects the idea that certain areas of life are necessarily elite-only activities (Dewey, 1934). Philosopher and educational reformer John Dewey challenges the assumption made in conventional policy design of a passive audience of citizens who are the recipients and subjects of decisions, services and products made by elites. He instead suggests that citizens are all potentially creative makers in their own right. For policy design, this means seeing citizens as 'co-designers'; doing so 'turn[s] people into participants ... they become innovators and investors, adding to the system's productive resources rather than draining them as passive consumers waiting at the end of the line' (Leadbeater and Cottam, 2007, p. 98).

Thus, a co-productive policy process begins 'with a clear commitment to discovering a community's capacities and assets' (Kretzmann and McKnight, 1993, p. 1). It is an asset-based approach (DesignGov, 2013, pp. 5, 20) and recognises that citizens have 'something useful and sensible to add as experts in their own right and in their own lives' (Richardson and Durose, 2013). An asset-based perspective asserts that 'problem-solving efforts would work best with deep citizen involvement' (Fung, 2001, p. 74), challenging the embedded hierarchy of the expert versus the layperson (Porter, 2010). It avoids privileging particular forms of expertise, so that different claims to knowledge are acknowledged and communication within the policy process is not seen as 'a one-way transfer from a knowing subject to a supposedly ignorant one' (Pohl et al, 2010, p. 217). This perspective maintains that the contributions of citizens serve to enhance the policy process through raising questions and offering insight that may be otherwise neglected by technocratic 'experts' (Fischer, 2000; Agger, 2012).

Grammar

While recognising the importance of articulating the vision of a co-productive policy design, it is acknowledged that realisation of this vision may seem like a 'daunting' challenge (Ostrom, 1996). Without designating institutional practices which could be employed in the pursuit of the vision, it may amount 'to nothing more than good intentions' (Beebeejaun et al, 2014, p. 48). The chapter will focus on three types of grammar: reciprocal and reflexive relationships between different actors; incomplete approach allowing policy design to be affected in use; iteration, involving experimentation and learning-by-doing.

Reciprocal and reflexive

Co-production requires that participants 'build a credible commitment to one another so that if one side increases input, the other will continue at the same or higher levels' (Ostrom, 1996, p. 1082). The tightly bounded 'tribes' of conventional policy design (Agranoff, 2007; Orr and Bennett, 2010) offer little opportunity for generating reciprocity and reflexivity (Ward, 2006; Orr and Bennett, 2009). Without the reciprocal contributions of all policy actors co-productive policy cannot happen. Reciprocity is necessary for co-creation of outcomes and synergies of expertise to be made concrete. Reflexivity – the ability of people to adapt, be self-aware and self-conscious – has been seen by those such as Dewey as one of the conditions for expanding participation in democratic governance. Policy actors who have typically been marginalised need to apply and adapt their assets and skills to the complex task of policy making. Those actors who might be unfamiliar with each other need to be brought together in co-design spaces, which facilitate reflexivity.

Reciprocity is one feature that pessimists fear will be extremely hard to achieve, because of worries about low levels of civic participation. While the decline of traditional forms of political participation is often lamented as meaning that citizens have 'opted out of politics' (Diers, 2004, p. 6). Other evidence shows that citizens have begun to adapt and forge new political identities that recognise the shift demanded in co-production from 'seeing citizens as voters, volunteers, clients or consumers to viewing citizens as problem solvers and co-creators of public goods' (Boyte, 2005, p. 519). Hendrik Bang (2005) coined the term 'expert citizens' to describe citizens who see themselves as an 'effective partner' to the state and 'feel they can do politics and make and implement policy as well as the old authorities' (Li and Marsh, 2008, p. 250). To them, 'politics is a fusion between representation and participation in a new form of political participation where you use your knowledge, skills and strategic judgement to influence others' (Li and Marsh, 2008, p. 250). Bang (2005) also identified 'everyday makers', citizens who are 'concerned to enhance their personal capacities for self-governance and co-governance' within a 'democratic political community that allows for the reciprocal acceptance and recognition of difference' (Li and Marsh, 2008, p. 251). While not underestimating the challenge, the emergence of these new democratic innovations and shifting identities should be acknowledged.

Citizens are often incentivised to get involved 'when they think that their efforts will not be wasted' (Bovaird and Loeffler, 2012, p. 1) and 'when they receive, or expect to receive, something at least as valuable in return' (Alford, 2009, p. 188). It is likely that citizens will be motivated to get involved by the 'importance or salience' of an issue and whether it makes 'a direct impact on their life and/or life chances'. Such 'enduring' issues can include planning and infrastructure developments, employment and skills, public order and criminal justice, health and social care and environmental sustainability (Pestoff, Brandsen and Verschuere, 2012, p. 24). The motives of citizens can move beyond immediate self-interest and involves intrinsic rewards, solidarity incentives or normative appeal (Alford in Pestoff, 2012).

Design thinking is said to be 'disorderly not due to intellectual sloppiness but rather to the nature of design problems' (Rittel, 1988, p. 2), which have 'no clear separation of … problem definition, synthesis and evaluation' (Rittel, 1988, p. 2). Managing deliberately 'disorderly' thinking requires reflexivity. Desire for reflexivity has led to calls for the creation of new mediating institutions or 'boundary spaces' to replace the declining spaces of political parties, trade unions and churches (Diers, 2004, p. 11). Such mediating institutions help different 'social worlds' to work together and develop a 'shared thought style' (Pohl et al, 2010, pp. 268, 271) while providing opportunities for citizens to 'learn the political skills of dealing with different sorts of people – negotiation, discussion, the messy open-ended ambiguity of public life'. The practices that inform these mediating institutions are also of importance. The term, 'boundary spanner' (Williams, 2002, 2012) has been used to describe the practice of intermediation between different organisations and with their wider environment (Thompson, 1962). The skills and positioning that boundary spanners may require and occupy are the subject of wide-ranging debate, considering whether public servants have the appropriate skills for this twenty-first century challenge (Needham and Mangan, 2014) and whether boundary spanners need to be located or employed within public institutions. Paul Williams' (2002, p. 119) influential work describes 'boundary spanners' as a 'jack of all trades', creative, innovative and entrepreneurial. His boundary spanner is excellent at listening empathically, building relationships and sustaining them, and managing conflict. These 'soft skills' are also found in John Forester's work (1999) on deliberative planners working in complex urban environments. For co-production, intermediation may help 'parties arrive at a common definition of their relationships, define their separate goals clearly and through facilitated analysis discover options which meet the needs of all' (Burton, 1986, p. 125). The boundary spanner aims 'to be innovative in guiding the translation of discovered shared political values into political structures and institutions that will promote their fulfilment' (Burton, 1986, p. 128).

Incomplete

Encouraging reflexivity or reciprocity is difficult within the expectation of 'completeness' which characterises conventional policy design. Completeness is where the options for who gets involved in policy, how this happens, what the policy options are and what the scope for dialogue is are closed off from the start of a design process.

Completeness forecloses options for how multiple forms of expertise across traditional elite and non-elite policy actors can be involved in the policy process (Garud, Jain and Tuertscher, 2008, p. 352). Instead, policy design should be more incomplete, and open to being 'palpably and directly affected' by participation (Fung, 2001, p. 79). In design thinking literature, the emphasis is on design as a user-centred activity (Burns et al, 2006, p. 18; Bason, 2014, p. 4), which includes citizens in problem identification (DesignGov, 2013, p. 10), and is also incomplete in that 'design is never done' but instead is open to continual adaption and innovation, change and reconfiguration (Burns et al, 2006, pp. 21, 26). Co-productive design challenges the tightly bounded or elite-dominated nature of policy by not just seeking to 'give people a say in the answer to pre-defined problems' but by acknowledging the control which a wide range of policy actors, including citizens, can have in 'identify[ing] the kinds of problems to which [policy] responds' (Bradwell and Marr, 2008, p. 18).

To increase the likelihood of successful co-production, 'options must be available to both parties' (Ostrom, 1996, p. 1082), which is about reciprocity and incompleteness. Ostrom argues that centralised and prescriptive approaches have the effect of removing opportunities for local discretion and specificity – i.e. they are overly complete. She offers an example from development education of being able to alter the timing of the school year to fit with the agricultural activities of the families of pupils. The implication is that providing scope for flexibility is likely to encourage and incentivise participation (Ostrom, 1996). Incentives for reciprocal contributions to co-productive designs include the expectation that policy will lead to outcomes that matter to citizens. What is incomplete is the dialogue about policy priorities and methods of achieving them. Incomplete does not mean directionless. Incompleteness rejects pre-set prescriptions on solutions, and instead posits a clear outcome specification. Scope is left within the broad specification for policy actors to agree collectively what creative solutions will best achieve goals and deliver on values.

Incompleteness rather than 'completeness' is important to reflect change in the social context and in the positioning and perspectives of different participants (Olsen, 1997; Pierson, 2002). Successful co-productive arrangements are unlikely to be 'the result of masterful design', but instead often 'ar[i]se haphazardly – themselves the result of fitful informal deliberations' (Fung, 2001, p. 76). It is not the proposition here that policy design is left to haphazard encounters, but that spaces for informal interactions are incorporated, and sufficient plasticity is programmed into the design for improvements and innovations generated in this process. Incompleteness requires designs to be carefully structured in ways that allow the space for new actors to get involved, and for lateral solutions to be added to the discussion at many different stages, rather than be closed down at too early a stage.

'Incompleteness' of design has a number of benefits for co-production. It can provide a 'trigger for action' (Garud, Jain and Tuertscher, 2008, p. 364) facilitating innovation and improvisation as 'actors mediate the relationship between extant structures and the external environment' (Durose et al, 2015, p. 11). A starting point of 'incompleteness' also has the potential to blur the distinction between 'designers' and 'users', leading to 'a community of co-designers who inscribe their own contexts into the emergent design, thereby extending it on an ongoing basis in diverse and non-obvious ways' (Garud, Jain and Tuertscher, 2008, p. 364). Incomplete design is underpinned by a belief that it can 'outperform traditional designs by being extremely adaptable to continually changing contexts' (Garud, Jain and Tuertscher, 2008, p. 360).

Iterative

Stagist models of public policy making are simultaneously discredited for their lack of empirical grip and reified for their normative reassurance and simplicity, or the seeming chaos of alternatives. A design approach would emphasise an alternative, which emphasises and encourages iteration through experimentation and learning by doing. Iteration builds on the idea of policy design for foxes, and is operationalised in design thinking through things like rapid prototyping (Boyer, Cook and Steinberg, 2011, pp. 16, 327; DesignGov, 2013, p. 6). It leads from the grammar of incompleteness, as being open to new inputs requires co-productive designs to be dynamic and amendable in response to rapid feedback. This iterative approach acknowledges the human capacity for what John Keats called 'negative capability', and cited by Dewey as an influence on his philosophy. Dewey (1934, p. 41) embraced Keats' admonishment to embrace doubt to reinforce learning that 'accept[s] life and experience in all its uncertainty, mystery, doubt, and half-knowledge and turns that experience on itself to deepen and intensify its own qualities'. Rittel (1988, p. 5) reminds us that designers have 'no algorithms [and] no limits to the conceivable', that this 'epistemic freedom' is 'not easy to live with', and testing, prototyping and iterations are one way to address this: 'Whenever actions are effectively irreversible and whenever the half-lives of the consequences are long, *every trial counts*' (Rittel and Webber, 1973, p.

163, emphasis original). Iterative grammars use questions to learn and develop new knowledge, and see so-called 'failures' as opportunities to understand more deeply. A flexible approach recognises that the 'unfolding of the process itself changes the problem': the purpose of the design is discovered in-use (Garud, Jain and Tuertscher, 2008, pp. 351, 364)

One formulation of iterative policy designs is the idea of 'design experiments' (Stoker and John, 2009), which are deliberately iterative: a creative policy option is generated and tested. Conscious reflections and evaluations on the experiences of the previous phase, coupled with data on outcomes, are then used to amend further iterations. Garud, Jain and Tuertscher (2008) provide an 'architecture' for both genuine reciprocity, and for iteration through the idea of a 'design trace'. A design trace helps make transparent how a policy has come about, what assumptions underpin it, who was involved, what ideas have been cohered to make it. It documents assets and resources, deliberative and problem-solving activities and outcomes. Documenting this 'trace' is important – not only in terms of accountability and continuous learning (Fung, 2001, p. 80), but also in providing an understanding of: who contributed what, when and why. In doing this, the trace makes it easier for actors to understand how a design has emerged over time and 'makes it possible for co-designers to engage in the present by building on the past in anticipation of a new future' (Garud, Jain and Tuertscher, 2008, p. 366).

Borrowing from anthropologist Levi-Strauss, Lowndes and Roberts offer 'bricolage' as another technique for supporting iteration in policy. Bricolage is the piecing and patching together of disparate materials or different forms of expertise and contribution (Lowndes and Roberts, 2013, p. 155). Both Lowndes (2005) and Newman (2012) have talked about different strategies, which can reconfigure practice repertoires and support iteration. Lowndes and Roberts (2013, p. 184) describe the strategies of 'remembering, borrowing, sharing, forgetting', explaining: 'if remembering is about looking backwards and borrowing is about looking sideways, then sharing involves looking outwards'. Remembering involves 'bringing back old ways of working, which have fallen into disuse, to address new problems; borrowing involves the transfer of resources and practices from elsewhere; sharing involves learning from the experiences of others (Lowndes and Roberts, 2013, pp. 181–184); and forgetting is 'deliberate neglect' of existing practice (Thelen, 2004 cited in Lowndes and Roberts, 2013, p. 184). These approaches can be creative (Newman, 2012) and 'lead to specific outcomes that are unusual, remote, flexible, numerous and generally non-zero-sum' (Fogg, 1985, p. 331) which are able to 'disrupt' established and conventional practice (Light et al, 2013; Pearce, 2011).

Conclusion

Advocating co-production rests on the recognition that there are complex, 'wicked' and 'squishy' (see Agranoff, 2007) policy problems that cannot be solved without governments, but that governments alone can never solve. This chapter has drawn on the rich lineage of co-production to inform the vision and grammar of co-productive policy design. It has set out an alternative to conventional policy design by articulating a revival and reinvigoration of democratic politics, which draws on a synergy of different contributions and expertise, including that of citizens. Delivering this vision depends on an encouragement of reflexivity and iteration that allows for policy design to be palpably affected by the participation of citizens. While doing so, there is a recognition that co-production will not 'occur spontaneously simply because substantial benefits could be achieved' (Ostrom, 1996, p. 1082) and that designing successful co-productive strategies is 'far more daunting than demonstrating their theoretical existence' (Ostrom, 1996, p. 1080). Grounded attempts to generate, exemplify and prefigure co-productive policy design are therefore useful in meeting this daunting challenge.

The next sections of the book take up this challenge by offering a series of contributions from policy makers, researchers, practitioners and activists who are all interested and actively engaged in different aspects of policy design. Each contribution offers a short, grounded reflection on these experiences and provides a means of challenging and advancing the conversation and heuristics. The authors provide a framing and reflection for each of these contributions.

Contributions are divided into three interrelated and overlapping sections. It is hard to separate out the powerful insights across all of the issues provided by these examples. However, broadly we structure the contributions in the following way. The first section, 'challenge and change within conventional policy design' considers the conventional policy process, its internal critiques and recognition of the need for and possibilities of change. Both Katy Wilkinson and Paul McCabe reflect on the impact and handling of contentious policy issues at the national and local level. Each considers the opportunity, appetite and space for change in conventional systems and processes. Simon Burall and Tim Hughes, and Robert Rutherfoord and Lucy Spurling offer different perspectives on efforts from the centre to develop more participatory and exploratory forms of policy design. Toby Blume considers the challenge of cultural change through the involvement of local communities and citizens.

The second and third sections continue the conversation by advancing the debate set out in this chapter, exploring the vision and grammar of a co-productive policy alternative. The second section, 'Vision in co-productive policy design', focuses on the principles and values that underpin a co-productive vision. Teresa Cordova and Moises Gonzales outline the principles that inform their value-driven practice and strategic interventions in the policy process. Jess Steele shows us the importance of using politics in order to advance a more co-productive approach. The Morris Justice Project provides a further example of how to institute and instil co-productive values into a significant policy issue.

The third section, 'Grammar in co-productive policy design', focuses on the grammars of a co-productive alternative. Phil Jones, Colin Lorne and Chris Speed explore how technology can be used to begin renegotiation of the power dynamics of the policy process. Amina Lone and Dan Silver identify ways to generate community conversations on issues of policy significance and controversy. Michaela Howell and Margaret Wilkinson take us inside an example of policy co-design. Maura Rose addresses how to mediate and resolve conflicts.

Challenges and change within conventional policy design

Can crisis ever be good for policy design?

Katy Wilkinson

This contribution draws on insights into the policy process gained by the contributor as part of a research project – an organisational ethnography of a central government department – and later from working as a policy adviser in the same department. It focuses on the Department for Environment, Food and Rural Affairs (Defra) and the crises that arise around animal health. The contribution shows how these crises introduce new rhythms and uncertainties into the policy process, disrupting the usual way of doing things, but also challenging the perception and usefulness of seeing the policy process in a linear, stagist way, where the role of different forms of expertise is clearly demarcated and proscribed.

Rather than focusing on where policy making went wrong during these crises, the emphasis here is first to see that crisis does not amount to failure. Instead, the crisis allows the recognition of the messy and chaotic nature of the policy process and the unforeseen and/or uncontrollable contingencies that affect policy outcomes. Second, it shows crisis as an opportunity to allow a more diverse range of voices and different forms of expertise into the policy process. The contribution concludes by exploring how the shifts in the policy process during a crisis have acted as a driver for more sustained change in the Department.

Defra's wide remit covers the kind of policy areas that have earned it the nickname 'Department for Biblical Disasters' (Rothstein and Downer, 2012): flooding, animal and plant disease, pollution, food shortages and so on. I focus on one area – animal health – as an example of how dealing with crisis is not only a normal part of business for policy makers in the Department, but can actually be beneficial for them. Defra has a statutory responsibility to deal with livestock diseases under the Animal Health Act 1981 and as part of the UK's membership of the European Union and the World Organization for Animal Health. Livestock diseases are divided in policy terms into 'endemic' diseases, meaning those that are currently present at some level in the UK, and 'exotic' diseases, which are not normally present in the UK. The government attempts to control endemic diseases (including bovine tuberculosis) and eradicate them where possible, but the emphasis of policy is on reducing the impacts of these diseases on both animal welfare and food production. For exotic diseases, in contrast, the government must eradicate these as soon as possible when they occur because the UK's international trading relationships depend on maintaining national 'disease free' status. Exotic diseases that have previously occurred in the UK include avian influenza ('bird flu'), foot and mouth disease, classical swine fever and bluetongue.

As soon as an exotic disease is confirmed as present in the UK, officials are compelled to adopt a crisis mode of policy making. There is no in-between state; either the country is disease free, or else a biological agent is loose, prompting the initiation of a complex policy process involving testing livestock, drawing up exclusion zones, imposing movement standstills and coordinating culls on infected premises. Animal disease outbreaks are characterised by uncertainty, as it can be very difficult to establish how the disease entered the country, how it is spreading, how many animals are already infected, and how many may be incubating the disease but not yet showing signs of illness. Policy makers are constantly faced by the dilemma of overreacting, and causing unnecessary disruption to food production and trade (and perhaps unnecessary slaughter of healthy animals), or failing to react and being blamed for the spread of disease to an even greater area.

In this sense, then, a state of crisis is something that Defra officials encounter frequently in their working lives. As opposed to many government departments, where a crisis represents an aberration to be avoided at all costs, for Defra they are a regular occurrence: there have been 14 exotic disease outbreaks in the last 10 years, in addition to dozens of suspected outbreaks that turned out to be false alarms. Although the academic literature considers crisis to be a failure of good decision making, and therefore damaging to departments, for Defra these states of emergency can be extremely important catalysts of change within the policy process. In this contribution, I argue that crises present an opportunity for the normal routines and inefficiencies of policy making to be overturned, for experts who are ordinarily marginalised within the decision-making process to be consulted on an hourly basis and for bureaucratic conventions to be ignored and overruled. This state of turmoil has benefits both for policy makers (whose attempts to be effective are often stymied by excessive bureaucracy in their work) and their advisers (who have little means of influencing policy making outside of these crisis periods).

Crisis and the science-policy relationship

Owing to the technical nature of the policy areas it deals with, the Department is heavily reliant on expert advice, and this is especially true in the animal disease division. Scientists and veterinarians (and, to a lesser extent, economists and legal experts) are routinely consulted. The usual practice, when there are no outbreaks of disease, is for scientists and veterinarians to meet as 'expert groups' convened around specific topic areas, with the intention of keeping policy discussions and scientific discussions separate. The remit of these groups is to consider issues such as the likelihood of outbreaks and strategies for disease prevention or vaccination, without taking into account political factors such as cost or public acceptability. While acknowledging that such practical issues inevitably do arise at experts' group meetings, the sense of objectivity is maintained by the practice of keeping policy and scientific discussions separate, with reports and papers traded between the two sides. While there are advantages to this division of labour – the scientists can give their advice without needing to become experts in the policy process and can feel they have not compromised the objectivity of their findings – it also perpetuates some of the more problematic aspects of evidence-based policy making. The experts may not be consulted early in the policy process, when the key questions are being defined, and as a result their advice may be sought to bolster existing policy prejudices rather than allowing alternatives to be seriously considered. Ministers seeking to place the resulting policy decisions beyond political criticism may overstate the neutrality and certainty of their advice.

When a serious disease outbreak is declared, these protocols are radically disturbed. The feeling inside the Department changes, as officials and scientists are united in their efforts to eradicate the disease. Such is the difference in organisational culture during outbreaks that a language has developed to reflect this, with disease-free periods being known as 'peacetime' and outbreaks as 'wartime'. This practice dates from the 2001 Foot and Mouth Disease (FMD) crisis when many practices and terms were borrowed from the military, including the habit of holding meetings standing up (so business was dealt with faster) and with everyone grouped around a map showing the latest infected areas. Known as 'bird tables', these meetings are designed to allow rapid communication of key details, a far cry from the officials' normal routines where meetings can last for hours and be accompanied by reams of paperwork. The drama of wartime is recreated through regular full-scale contingency exercises that are held to simulate an outbreak, such as 'Exercise Walnut', a mock Classical Swine Fever outbreak that was run in 2013. In these exercises, over 500 people including Defra officials, vets, publicity officers and local authorities spend several days running through their responses to an outbreak as if it were happening in real time. They have no prior information about the outbreak, to simulate the uncertainty and confusion of a real event. People are even sent out to farms to check that communication between remote locations and the disease control centres is possible. All of this activity takes place according to a 'battle rhythm' – the sequence of tasks that need to be completed and communication that needs to be undertaken as the outbreak progresses.

The role of the expert adviser during these periods of 'war' on disease is necessarily very different to the disconnected, arm's-length approach described during peacetime. Policy makers may need scientists' advice on the areas where movement restrictions should be imposed, or whether thousands of livestock need to be slaughtered, and have to implement that advice on the very same day. The separation of science and policy becomes far less distinct as officials rely on their advisers to analyse outbreak data and provide support on a daily, if not hourly, basis. The formality of expert group meetings is exchanged for ad hoc teleconferences and officials dispensing with the usual bureaucracy of agendas and reports. There is no time to sit and discuss an issue from every possible angle. The traditional hierarchies of the Department are temporarily suspended, and bureaucratic policy making abandoned in favour of whatever methods will bring about the fastest, most effective decisions. As a result, the scientists can give more relevant advice because they are better informed about the practical implications and are also able to overturn entrenched approaches to solving policy problems. Major changes in the types of evidence sought by the Department can be traced to particular disease outbreaks, such as the rapid expansion of epidemiological modelling after FMD in 2001.

The role of social science in policy making

The central importance of the scientific advisers during a disease outbreak is evident; they offer the information and analysis necessary to make practical decisions about the slaughter or quarantine of infected animals. Nevertheless, others who seek to influence policy making also benefit from the disruption that crisis brings, particularly social scientists and economists, who have historically played a very minor role in animal disease policy. The turning point for social scientists seeking to influence Defra came during the FMD crisis, when officials greatly underestimated both the significance of non-agricultural activities within the rural economy and the impact of the outbreak on the public perception of government and the farming industry. When the outbreak began, policy makers relied on their usual combination of vets and scientists to advise on a strategy for controlling the spread of disease. A culling policy was pursued; Defra followed the advice of its epidemiological modellers who suggested slaughtering ever greater numbers of livestock to prevent the virus spreading out of control, despite growing opposition within both farming groups and the media. Images of burning pyres and stories of children's pet animals being slaughtered reduced public support for the policy and a campaign for an alternative vaccination strategy was launched. Moreover, tourists were discouraged from visiting the countryside, partly through warning signs and appeals from Ministers to avoid affected areas, but perhaps more importantly through a fear of the horrors they might witness there. At the end of the outbreak, it was estimated that the losses suffered by agricultural producers was £355 million, while the tourism industry lost between £2.7 and £3.2 *billion*. These outcomes prompted reflection on what Defra's remit should be and challenged the view, dominant for the previous century of policy making, that the needs of the farming industry should take priority over other sectors of the rural economy.

More recently, Defra's policy of culling badgers in order to control bovine tuberculosis has likewise revealed the deep interest that the public take in rural affairs and emphasised that animal diseases can no longer simply be treated as veterinary concerns. Concerted, organised campaigns of resistance have undermined Defra's attempt to implement the badger cull. Even the farming industry is divided as to whether the policy should be pursued, with some farmers joining in the resistance and refusing permission to cull badgers on their land. As a result, Defra has begun to put a greater emphasis on understanding the social dimension of policy making. There are now a greater number of officials with a social science background employed within the Department. In 2012, an Animal and Plant Health Evidence and Analysis team was created, with Defra's Chief Social Researcher as deputy director. In 2012, Defra and the Department of Energy and Climate Change (DECC) created a joint advisory panel consisting entirely of social scientists, a development that represented a move away from the traditional scientific advisory groups. Numerous knowledge-exchange placements and fellowships have been created to bring academic social scientists into Defra and they themselves have worked to create further mechanisms for officials to interact with non-scientific experts, such as stakeholder forums and citizens' juries. The Department has funded many studies into the social aspects of disease outbreaks, including public perceptions of disease risk, farmers' attitudes towards biosecurity, and barriers to adoption of disease control methods. Although social scientists may never find themselves telephoned for advice in the heat of a crisis, it is undoubtedly the desire to avert further outbreaks and to minimise the damage of control measures that prompts this interest in social research.

Sustaining co-production of policy

Despite the opportunities that a crisis affords for policy makers and their advisers to subvert normal decision-making processes and experiment with new, collaborative ways of working, when peacetime resumes these innovations are once again replaced by bureaucratic norms. Scientists continue to work in their separate experts' groups, and social scientists find that the demand for their knowledge is reduced. There are many reasons why this occurs. Gains that are made during wartime in bringing a wider range of experts into the process can be lost in peacetime as government, under fear of public scrutiny of their reasoning process, favours evidence that can be marketed as objective and definitive, not qualitative and ambiguous. Deviating from the evidence-based policy model carries risks of negative attention from external commentators, particularly in the media. The value of the social sciences is not universally recognised, and committing significant amounts of funds to qualitative, 'soft' science can backfire. The *Daily Mail* ran a feature on examples of the government wasting taxpayers' money on apparently frivolous research, and singled out a study of farmer preferences commissioned by Defra as one of their examples. Despite the fact that the social research funded by Defra falls mainly within a narrow range of quantitative disciplines, it remains an easy target for a hostile media looking for evidence of wasteful spending.

The affordance of greater political power to scientists can also be problematic. During the Foot and Mouth outbreak, the leader of a group of epidemiologists seriously embarrassed the agriculture minister Nick Brown by appearing on *Newsnight* despite an agreement not to speak to the media, and publicly disagreeing with his statement that the outbreak was 'under control'. This prompted a desire within the Department to improve their own, in-house, expertise and reduce the dependence on external academics, who could prove unpredictable. While Defra's reliance on scientific information and analysis remains heavy, it is by no means agreed that scientists themselves should be given a greater role in policy making. Moreover, increasingly sophisticated pressure groups, notably the National Farmers' Union and the Badger Trust, have begun to commission their own research to challenge that relied on by government. Evidence is becoming overtly politicised in some of the more contested policy areas, and this further increases the scrutiny that officials face regarding their use of advice. When the crisis passes, and the need for information becomes less pressing, officials regain a sense of caution over the extent to which they involve scientists in the discussion of policy and politics.

Conclusion

In this contribution, I have described two quite different cultures of policy making: that of 'wartime', when expediency overrules bureaucracy and experts are closely involved in decision making, and that of 'peacetime', when these same advisers are viewed with caution and kept separate from policy discussions. Is there any evidence to suggest that policy making in Defra may eventually become more open to outsiders, and that those seeking to influence decisions will not have to rely on a crisis to achieve political influence? There are two major drivers of change in animal health policy that may help to bring this about.

Firstly, although recent outbreaks have not been on the same scale as the FMD crisis of 2001, there is much evidence to suggest that new diseases are a significant threat to animal health, and the spread of a previously unknown pathogen could lead to another countrywide epidemic. Climate change and the globalisation of trade are two forces that increase the likelihood of major disease outbreaks in the UK. Global warming in Europe means that diseases once confined to hotter climates can increasingly survive at more northern latitudes. Scientific research has shown that climate change is particularly likely to increase the spread of vector-borne diseases (those transmitted by ticks and insects) that can be more difficult to control than viral infections where the slaughter of the infected animals prevents further spread. The globalisation of trade in plants and animals also increases disease risk as novel pathogens are introduced to the UK. For example, one hypothesis on the 2008 outbreak of Bluetongue virus in the UK was that midges had been present on cut flowers imported from Africa by air. These factors combined suggest that more frequent, and more serious, outbreaks of disease could occur in the future. It may become untenable for Defra to keep its advisers at arm's length in the face of such sustained and widespread disease threats.

Secondly, the political context for animal health policy is changing, with farmers and producers now expected to bear greater responsibility for preventing disease, and receiving less financial support when an outbreak occurs. The responsibility and cost-sharing agenda prompted both by cuts to Defra's budget and public criticism of the amount being spent on compensation to farmers following outbreaks has been an attempt to shift the funding of disease control away from central government. The farming industry is expected to play a bigger role in promoting good biosecurity and developing insurance schemes rather than demanding recompense from the public purse. However, if farming groups are expected to implement government policy, it follows that they will demand a greater say in how that policy is decided. Defra officials may be forced to pay more attention to incorporating the opinions of its different publics into the policy process, rather than relying on social scientists to 'sell' the policy after the fact. Opening the policy process to social researchers and the public requires a significant cultural change for Defra officials, but it is a change they may be forced to make in order to avoid insurmountable resistance to frontline implementation of their decisions.

This contribution, along with those of Paul McCabe and Robert Rutherfoord and Lucy Spurling, gives us an insight into some of the features of conventional policy designs. It highlights the contradiction between a 'peacetime' approach that espouses the separation of scientific advice from policy making, but at the same time uses this advice to avert political flak or to bolster an existing policy direction. It demonstrates the gap between rhetoric and practice. The insights shared here also illustrate the limitations of this conventional take on the policy process: not only is the policy process unable to deal with the dislocating nature of crisis, but the linearity of conventional thinking is self-perpetuating; because crisis deviates from the rigid ideal, this model is unable to consider and explore the possibilities which crisis opens up.

The nature of the policy areas that it deals with means that Defra is reliant on scientific and technical expertise in its policy making. While this may be co-productive in a descriptive sense – working with scientists is the usual way of doing things – it is not co-productive in a more transformational sense of those in the policy process challenging their perceptions of themselves, their roles and each other. Indeed, in 'peacetime', scientific contributions are kept distinct and separate from policy making, with the aiming of ensuring the objectivity of scientific advice and clearly demarcating it from political decision making or influence. While scientific expertise is high on the hierarchy of evidence sought by policy makers, it is clear where the power lies. Scientists are only able to exert their influence within the parameters set by the conventional system. In seeking influence in the policy process, the example of Defra shows us that in peacetime the influence is open to the chosen few, those occupying the peak of the evidence hierarchy and established lobbies.

Yet the policy process depicted here is also characterised by uncertainty, not only in the sense of not knowing when another disease outbreak may strike, but also of how to react to it. Crisis is not an aberration but a regular occurrence. As such, this contribution serves to demonstrate the cracks and fissures within the policy process that enable the possibility of different influences to be exerted. Indeed, during 'wartime' policy makers are able to realise their own efficacy, are less inhibited by bureaucracy, and voices which in 'peacetime' are at arm's length, if not marginalised or absent, are able to be heard.

When outbreaks occur and the Department moves into the 'battle rhythm' of wartime, the clear and rigid separation of different forms of expertise is breached. Policy making becomes more dialogic, power is more fluid and dynamic. While the distinction between peacetime and wartime still holds – there is 'no in between state' – there are instances where the practices of wartime seep into peacetime as preventative or damage limitation tactics. For example, the tentative recognition of the value of social scientific research, the challenge made to the dominance of the farming lobby and the use of mechanisms to engage with non-scientific experts and draw local knowledge – for instance of geography, trading patterns – into policy design.

As the complexity of policy challenges increases and evidence becomes more contested and politicised, as disease-threats grow and austerity bites, the fissures and cracks exposed in 'wartime' may widen. Looking at Defra illustrates the value of what Jess Steele calls 'doing politics', continuing the military metaphor: acting on several fronts. Media scrutiny and overt resistance are also tools used to effectively challenge policy design in Defra. Crisis may offer a moment of dislocation but it can also serve to consolidate the power of those privileged within the existing processes. As noted by Simon Burall and Tim Hughes, scrutiny and dissent from policy can prompt a defensive reaction from those holding power, serving to reinforce existing ways.

Challenges in policy redesign

Paul McCabe

Writing as an officer for an English local government organisation, this author explores the policy-making challenges of urban planning and housing to accommodate growing populations in a context of argued land shortages, growing expectations and more diverse communities. It presents serious challenges on the feasibility and implementation of ideas of co-productive policy making where there is neither consensus nor respect for pluralism. As the contribution makes painfully clear, the nature of the challenge is partly about whether opening up policy to the public is consistent with social justice and other strategic concerns.

The contribution is based on hard-bitten experience in one city of attempts to have an informed conversation about the use of land and provision of housing across the whole area, and across many different population groups. York is at once a very special case, as a historic city and world tourist destination, but also illustrative of many other cases. There are similar debates in other places, over other scarce or contested resources, and in other policy fields. Paul McCabe documents the city's many, and often fraught, experiences of asking citizens to think about growth, and being rejected. Undaunted, he outlines new efforts to create a sense of shared vision and common purpose between policy makers and hundreds of thousands of citizens.

Policy makers and politicians of all shades recognise the urgent need to plan strategically for the accommodation needs of new and growing populations, including the needs of vulnerable and marginalised groups. The UK government, in its 2011 national housing strategy for England, set out plans for a significant upturn in housing supply, in response to projected growth of 232,000 households per year up to 2033. For decades, the UK has seen a growing gap between housing demand and supply, fuelling what is now widely regarded as a national housing crisis. Most know that the provision of good quality housing in sustainable communities is a key enabler of economic growth and underpins a range of other outcomes such as improved health and wellbeing. Despite this, existing communities have often reacted negatively to proposals for growth and real tensions can emerge between strategic goals and the concerns people have about new development.

Few places are immune to such tensions, including the historic city of York. With its charming medieval streets, iconic world-class heritage, strong economy and low crime the city has long been a popular place to live, work and visit. While still a relatively small city, York's population has grown significantly in recent years, to just under 200,000 inhabitants. This growth is ongoing, and in 2012 York was named as one of the UK's fastest growing cities. Such growth is not universally popular. York is seen by some as a special city, whose outstanding built and natural environment needs protection. While most residents recognise that high house prices, high rents and poor access to accommodation for marginalised groups are increasingly problematic, proposals to address them, such as more new homes, can often be met by stiff opposition. Countless examples abound. In 2010, plans for a small affordable housing scheme in York's rural hinterland drew strenuous opposition from residents despite a village survey showing clear evidence of local housing need. The fact the proposed homes were to be prioritised for local families did little to quell concerns. In 2011, proposals for a state-of-the-art homeless hostel led to well-organised and sustained opposition from residents and local traders. In 2012, concerted opposition was mounted against proposals to provide six additional Gypsy and Traveller pitches on an existing council-owned site on the edge of the city. All these schemes were subsequently approved by City of York Council.

One of York's most high profile housing schemes in recent years is the Joseph Rowntree Housing Trust's (JRHT's) Derwenthorpe development. In 1998, the York-based trust and City of York Council came together with plans for a modest 540-home mixed tenure community on an urban extension site adjacent to three existing suburban neighbourhoods. The ambition became linked to commemorating the centenary of JRHT's 1000-home New Earswick village, which remains to this day a recognised exemplar of good planning, presaging the acclaimed UK 'garden city' movement. Rather than starting on site in 2002 as intended, Derwenthorpe spent some 10 years in the planning stages largely due to a concerted process of objections by local residents. Stated concerns included increased traffic, perceived loss of 'green belt' and the impact on local wildlife (two great crested newts were discovered on the site). The scheme was eventually granted planning permission by the Secretary of State in 2007, just as objectors applied to have the site designated as a 'village common' under the Commons Act 2006. Such designation would have protected the site from development but the application was rejected at public inquiry a year later. Despite the delays, City of York Council remained committed to Derwenthorpe and the first phase of construction was completed in 2013. The scheme went on to win a prestigious 2014 Civic Trust award.

Derwenthorpe's 10-year delay is not untypical, with other landowners reporting developments taking 12 and even 14 years to come to fruition, mainly due to planning delays. Strategic plans setting out longer-term ambitions for housing in York have often been another key target for opposition. Over the summer of 2013, York's draft Local Plan covering the period up to 2030 was launched for public consultation. It contained proposals for up to 1090 new homes each year across 61 new housing sites including urban brownfield, a number of village sites and a new 5000 home settlement beyond the city's outer ring road. It also set out modest proposals for new Gypsy, Traveller and Show People pitches in accordance with the city's housing needs assessments. The plan built on consultation undertaken as part of the earlier draft Local Development Framework and sought to reflect agreed priorities contained within other city plans, such as the economic development strategy, transport strategy and climate change action plan. All households, stakeholder groups and businesses in York received details of the consultation, a dedicated web page was launched and an extensive programme of public exhibitions and events was undertaken in the city centre and within each of York's 22 wards. Over 16,300 responses were received, representing 8% of the population, with 11,400 of these coming via petition. Of the 25 petitions submitted all were of the 'Say No To' variety. Despite the plan containing chapters on transport, green infrastructure, economic growth and community facilities, the vast majority of responses related to concerns about the overall level of housing development, specific housing sites and proposed sites for Gypsies, Travellers and Show People.

So why is planning for strategic housing needs so often a process fraught with difficulty? Must citizen engagement regarding new housing supply always lead to conservatism? Why, when York's housing problems are so well known do we find so little demonstrable citizen support for proposed solutions, such as an increase in the supply of new homes? Occasional exposés in the local press highlight the difficulties that marginalised and vulnerable households can experience in securing a roof over their heads yet, there is often a reluctance to accept proposals that address this. One thing is certain; this pattern of opposition is not unique to York. It is replicated pretty much on a national scale.

One of the key lessons to emerge from Derwenthorpe was the importance of political leadership in strategic planning to provide a context for effective site development. Carley and Baley (2009) in their evaluation of the development emphasised the role leadership must play in fostering broad-based participation across the local authority for sustainable development, including housing in new communities, taking into account future needs, including those of coming generations. They identified the need for leaders to build community consensus on a vision for the city as a foundation for development planning, to ensure that minority objectors do not dominate debate about critical planning issues. Despite JRHTs model approach to resident engagement at an early stage, Derwenthorpe's Achilles heel remained an absence of such an agreed strategic vision for the city.

City leaders and policy makers in York have continually sought ways to widen citizen and stakeholder participation in the policy process, though with mixed results. For many years the council was a trailblazer authority when it set up a city-wide framework of ward forums with their own devolved budgets. The committees were a direct response to the emerging local government modernisation agenda that aimed to give residents a stronger voice and strengthen the community leadership role of locally elected representatives. The framework sought to deliver ward-based action planning built around locally identified needs and accessible forums for presenting and exploring wider issues. Elected ward councillors made decisions about the content of ward plans and the allocation of local funds informed by resident's views. Attendance levels varied, often related to the socioeconomic profile of the ward. Overall numbers were relatively low, with a narrow demographic profile towards the older age range. For many years ward committees remained the principal mechanism for engaging local communities in decisions about their local area and city.

One of the ongoing challenges of the ward committee framework was engaging local residents in discussion about higher-level policy goals, such as the city's strategic housing, transport and economic development needs. Generally, residents would be less inclined to engage on these broader strategic issues, though participation would increase significantly should an explicit and real threat to the local area be perceived. Some wards had resident-led planning panels, commenting on local planning applications but rarely participating in wider matters affecting the city as a whole. The extent to which strategic policy issues were discussed at these forums depended on many factors; ward councillors decided what was on the forum agenda and the choice of items was often influenced by perceived local relevance and the ward members' appetite for and skills to successfully facilitate a potentially contentious debate.

City of York Council is continually developing its approach to citizen engagement, driven by emerging challenges facing local government and perceived shortcomings in current arrangements. This is a time of considerable change in the public policy context and the council, like many others, has recognised its traditional role is changing. Funding pressures are forcing a reassessment about how services are designed and delivered. The Localism Act and National Planning Policy Framework contain new rights and powers for communities. Central to the council's renewed approach are the concepts of co-production and co-design of services. A new programme of 'Community Conversations' is currently being trailed to help reposition the council's relationship with citizens and stakeholder groups, designed to bring them much closer into the policy-making process. This is supported by measures to engage more people through a wider set of channels, such as the award-winning GeniUS open innovation platform that seeks to generate solutions to some of the city's biggest challenges.

Effective co-production at this level will require the development of a sustained iterative relationship between policy makers, stakeholders and local residents with effective engagement at an early stage in the policy cycle. It means building a shared vision and identifying the kinds of problems to which policy responds, rather than just giving people a say in the answer to predefined problems. In practice, this will entail effective dissemination of key housing needs data to underpin and enable genuine conversations about the strategic challenges facing the city and the sorts of solutions that might address them. It will involve wider discussions and agreement about what sort of city residents want, to help frame later debates including the development of a strategic vision and associated plans.

Neighbourhood Plans are a key element of the new national planning policy framework and City of York Council is committed to supporting communities in preparing them. The plans are designed to allow communities to develop a vision of what their area should be like and make decisions on where certain types of development should go. The council has seen growing interest in these plans, aligned in part to housing site proposals contained within the draft local plan, most notably a small rural settlement currently proposed as the location for a new Gypsy and Traveller site. It will be interesting to see to what extent these local plans align, as they should, with the strategic needs and priorities of the wider area and draw out links between local aspirations and those at the strategic level, including the needs of marginalised and vulnerable groups.

NIMBYism (an acronym for the phrase 'Not In My Back Yard') is a popular, though often pejorative, term sometimes used to characterise opposition by residents to a proposal for development because it is close to them, with the connotation that such residents believe the developments are needed but should be located further away from them. Such positions can be particularly evident when planning for the needs of vulnerable or marginalised groups, but they can also dominate the process of citizen engagement, no matter how wide-ranging the process is. With new housing, often the very people who would benefit from the policy intervention cannot be involved in the early stages because they do not yet exist. Interestingly, the evaluation report into lessons from Derwenthorpe asked how far JRHT itself may have fuelled opposition to the development by its decision to consult so intensively with local residents. JRHT estimates it spent an additional £2 million above expected development costs in order to get the site approved.

The extent to which these new approaches succeed in harnessing citizen participation on strategic policy issues remains to be seen and will depend on a range of factors, not least of which is ensuring citizen engagement on issues they do not feel an immediate or direct connection with. It will depend on the capacity/skills of local leaders and policy makers to support and effectively facilitate more sustained, complex and resource-intensive levels of community engagement at a time when local resources are increasingly stretched. It will also depend on how effective these new approaches are in getting behind some of the stated concerns expressed about new development such as loss of green belt, increased traffic or flooding when these can often be proxy concerns masking a range of other worries such as falls in house values, lack of amenity and 'fear of the other'.

There is no question that the nation needs to improve its ability to plan, design and build new communities. Equally, there is no question that improvements can be made to ensure more people are engaged much earlier in the policy cycle to build greater consensus around new development and help improve the often fraught process of planning for the country's burgeoning housing needs. City of York Council, in line with its statutory duties, must plan to meet identified housing needs including promoting social justice for vulnerable and marginalised groups. In light of the many challenges and complexities highlighted above, maybe there will always be a role for dispassionate strategic decision makers in the planning and provision of new homes.

Political scientists have reminded us that politics, at its most basic, is about who gets what, when and how. This contribution deals with a policy area in which local government has a statutory responsibility and where choices are heavily contested. It acts as a reminder, should one be needed, of the complexities and tensions in managing large-scale public policy processes. It is honest about equity considerations, with potential conflicts between the interests of those who are already housed, and those in need of housing. But, in addition to self-interest, citizens also state concern for sustainable urban infrastructure. The author tells us that the experience in York is that people are more tolerant of the needs of others as a general principle than in meeting them, but suggests also there may be an underlying primal fears of 'others' with which to contend.

In this story the policy process is a site for protest, where the citizen's voice is heard by policy makers via angry and distant lobbying groups. There is evidence of citizen mobilisation, successful on numbers, and seemingly successful in winning the arguments to hold back development, at least temporarily. However, for the policy makers who wish to support sympathetic development, this is unwanted mobilisation. On these big policy areas, everything is on a large scale, including the opposition. A set of fractious relationships and debates is coupled with citizen opposition and objections to the needs of those with fewer resources, and to some marginalised groups. All of this has added to the drive to create alternative policy designs. For some policy makers, their response to similar experiences has been to retreat even deeper into a hierarchical and paternalistic style of decision making.

However, in this city the politicians, encouraged by their officers, have instead chosen to experiment with an advance into the unknown of more co-productive policy designs. The author does not make any claims for whether these moves are driven by deep beliefs in the values of asset-based co-productive approaches, or more instrumentally using these approaches as tools, out of necessity. In one sense, this may be irrelevant; if a 'community conversation' is initiated, it may have its own momentum. However, as Paul McCabe points out, effective co-production will require conditions to be in place; citizens may sense if attempts at co-production are not genuine, or lack the supporting factors.

The author shows us how City of York Council is attempting to change the nature of its policy design approach in this controversial policy area. It wants to move towards re-establishing more 'human' connections with its residents, and having more sustained, reflexive and reciprocal relationships. It is doing this through a focus on more dialogue at a more granular scale, and constructing different spaces for dialogue. Dialogue is seen in a more iterative way, as part of a wider shift to engaging people earlier in policy design. This does represent a potentially risky approach – estimated costs for consultation for just one housing development at Derwenthorpe are around £4000 per new home built – but some research argued this additional spending simply 'fuelled opposition'.

Community conversations are new ways to bring in citizens' expertise, but this does not replace other forms of expertise and knowledge crucial for strategic planning decisions. Here, other knowledge includes complex statistical data about projections on predicted future population change, housing growth, and demands on water, sewerage, refuse, education and health provision. Such a complex conversation requires leadership (vision) and sophisticated levels of facilitation (grammar) to build a shared sense of the vision for the city. Dialogue and leadership are mediated via local politicians, for whom this is a shift in role, and challenges their perceptions of their roles.

The hidden politics of policy design

Simon Burall and Tim Hughes

This contribution reflects on the experience of being involved in an attempt to collaboratively develop and model proposals for open government. The contributors thoughtfully and carefully set out a range of challenging issues for more collaborative forms of policy design, reflecting on the interests and experiences of different stakeholders from both government and civil society. In doing so, they show how politics and values are central, if often hidden, in policy making. In particular, they show that seeking to make policy differently raises questions of legitimacy, representation, the exercise of authority, how trade-offs between competing interests and values are made, the allocation of risk and accountability and the interplay between different processes and cultures. This contribution demonstrates that failing to recognise these political dynamics risks undermining the legitimacy and viability of new forms of more co-productive policy design.

> [We have] consistently made clear our commitment for the UK to become 'the most open and transparent government in the world'. Our resolve has not weakened. Indeed, our engagement with civil society to develop and agree the stretching and ambitious commitments in this second Open Government Partnership UK National Action Plan has strengthened, not lessened our commitment to open government. The result of this partnership is a set of commitments that take important steps towards increased openness. (Rt Hon Francis Maude MP, Minister for the Cabinet Office and Paymaster General, 2013)

This contribution draws on an example of open, collaborative policy making which took place over the course of 18 months. Looking back on the process and therefore with the benefit of hindsight, we feel we have learnt a number of lessons about what makes for successful, open and collaborative policy processes. Collaborative policy making can only flourish when it has the political space to do so and this can only be opened, and kept open, by senior politicians. Without 'senior' permission to act differently, those within the process are unable to develop the creativity and flexibility required to identify and reach a commonly defined goal.

Politics, in the sense of shifting power balances and individual interests clamouring to be heard, churn just below the surface of any collaborative process. However, these politics are rarely talked about. Successful collaborative processes will require at least some actors to be highly aware of these politics, to acknowledge them and work with them to create the right incentives to keep all the actors within the collaborative space and heading towards a common goal. Doing so requires those moving the collaborative process forward to be mindful of the politics implicit in the decisions that are taken. This sense is most obvious in terms of who is invited to join the process and how the issue of representation is understood and discussed. However, there are more subtle ways in which decisions, such as where and when to hold meetings for example, can influence the politics of the process overall.

Such collaborative processes do not happen in a vacuum. They will be most appropriate in areas that are less well defined, where neither government nor other actors have clear solutions. This means that they happen in a sea of other policy processes, many of which will be more traditional, closed and un-transparent processes. The politics of the interplay between the different processes will often be hidden to many of the participants in the collaborative space. These kinds of hidden politics represent significant risks to both more collaborative but also more closed policy processes.

Exploring collaboration through a specific example

The example we draw on is that of the development of the UK's 2013–15 Open Government Partnership National Action Plan. The Open Government Partnership (OGP) is a global effort to make governments more effective through securing commitments to greater transparency, participation and accountability. The OGP was launched in 2011 in New York by eight governments, including the UK, but now stands at 64.

A central element of the Open Government Partnership is the development of an open government National Action Plan (NAP), outlining specific, measurable and time-bound open government commitments. These action plans have a two-year lifespan and are reviewed on a yearly basis through an independent process. It is this element of the OGP that gives it bite and opens up potential for significant reforms in the way member governments do business. The process we describe centres on an open and collaborative policy process established to develop the UK's second NAP. This process involved a network of civil society organisations (CSOs) and officials from the UK Government Cabinet Office and other government departments.

Co-creating open government commitments

The OGP has a number of characteristics that distinguish it from similar international institutions. Importantly, each member government commits to produce their open government National Action Plans through a 'multi-stakeholder, open, and participatory process'. The UK published its first OGP NAP in September 2011, at the launch of the initiative. The preparation of this plan in the early days of the OGP meant it was developed with little civil society engagement – a point acknowledged by the government in its self-assessment of the plan. When the time came to begin to develop the UK's second NAP, civil society representatives and the lead government officials were determined that the process would be very different.

In September and October of 2012, members of the CSO network and officials from the Cabinet Office began to meet to discuss how CSOs could be involved in the development of the NAP. By the end of October 2012, these discussions had culminated in agreement about a very different way of working: the NAP would be jointly drafted and submitted by officials and the CSO network for sign-off by ministers. The principle of a joint National Action Plan formed the basis for the subsequent collaboration.

What followed was a series of working lunches between the CSO network and government officials to begin to scope out the narrative and contents of the NAP. The focus of these discussions was framed to a significant extent by a vision document prepared by the CSO network (Cabinet Office, 2012) which outlined a set of issues and policies those CSOs wished to address. This document and initial round of working lunches subsequently informed a series of meetings on a set of themes, which sought to bring in relevant officials from other departments where possible.

A 12-month process of discussions between the CSO network and government officials culminated in the launch of a co-created NAP at the OGP Summit held in London in October/November 2013. The NAP contained 21 commitments, the majority of which had been collaboratively developed by the CSO network and government, along with forewords from the lead minister (Francis Maude) and the CSO network. The process has since been recognised as one of the best examples to date of a genuine partnership between government and civil society to develop an OGP NAP. A number of things distinguish the process:

- The process was established with the principle of open by default. Invitations to meetings were published, the CSO network was open to any CSOs or individual citizens to join, notes of meetings were published and regular updates were posted on the CSO network blog.
- The CSO network was involved from the start in defining the terms of the collaboration and the principles by which it would work.
- CSOs were involved in defining the overarching vision for the National Action Plan as well as the detail of commitments.
- Officials were open about what they were communicating across government and to ministers.
- The process had high-level political and official commitment.

The politics of representation and legitimacy

Claims and counterclaims about exactly who is represented by a particular group of people or organisations engaged in a collaborative process with government are often near the surface. And it was no different for the OGP National Action Plan process. The CSO network has always been relatively small and composed largely, but not exclusively, of London-based organisations working on issues of open government such as open data, transparency, public engagement and accountability. It includes few organisations working on issues of which citizens are likely to have had direct experience, for example health or education.

The network and its members were at great pains never to claim to speak on behalf of 'civil society'. However, questions about the extent to which network members in particular debates represented wider views were a very present, but largely unmentioned part of the conversation. These moments occurred most sharply at times of disagreement about the inclusion or not of particularly contentious commitments. However, where collaborative processes are addressing significant differences between different actors, questions about legitimacy can be used by one group to challenge another. Often these challenges will reflect existing power structures leading to the legitimacy of those with less power to be challenged as they gain more power and influence over the process and its content. For the OGP process, clear explanations, restated at frequent intervals, that the network represented depth of skills, experience, knowledge and energy around open government issues but not wider civil society, were an important part of insulating the network and NAP process from people inside and outside government playing the politics of legitimacy.

Where do collaborative processes fit with parallel policy processes?

Both government and CSOs in the network believed the success of the OGP process depended on ensuring the final NAP had one or two eye-catching and significant commitments within it. However, the OGP process was not the only game in town. There were parallel, but disconnected, policy processes (OGP, G8 and the Extractive Industries Transparency Initiative, for example) discussing and, in the case of the G8 only months before, announcing related policy commitments. In addition, CSOs inside the OGP network were also active within those other forums. All of this meant that it was very unclear to most of those actively involved in the OGP process where political conversations about specific commitments were, or should be, happening, who might claim credit for the final outcome, and whether the final NAP would have significant commitments in it or not.

Where collaborative policy processes overlap with more traditional policy-making structures the lack of transparency risks spilling over and negatively affecting the political dynamics of the more collaborative process (and probably vice versa). However, the nature of these processes, and the speed at which they happen, means that politics and power are often obscured. The negative implications of this spillover were minimised within the NAP process as a result of strong, trusting relationships between some of the key actors in the CSO network, enabling those who were acting in both the collaborative process and the more traditional G8 process to act as honest brokers.

Collaborative processes focus risks on individuals

The lead officials from the Cabinet Office demonstrated a strong desire to develop an open and collaborative process with civil society. This required them to make the case to ministers and take on a significant amount of personal risk. The same was true for some of the individuals most deeply associated with the process from the CSO side. The personal risk on the government side was evident to the CSOs close to the process and undoubtedly contributed to the growing trust between key CSO members and the Cabinet Office.

Open and collaborative policy processes require the carving out of political space by ministers in which officials, CSOs, citizens and other stakeholders can define their own process, terms of reference and outputs. This is potentially quite countercultural for the civil service because most officials are used to operating within a more or less tightly defined brief set by ministers. It requires mid-ranking and junior officials to develop a public persona and step out from the cover of relative anonymity, increasing their exposure, which may have benefits as well as risks to their careers.

Contradictory timeframes can hide the politics

With only weeks to go until the publication of the NAP, a number of commitments were suggested by different government departments for inclusion in the plan. These commitments came into the process with no CSO involvement and with limited time to debate the implications and make clear decisions as a network. The inclusion of these commitments was primarily due to the contradiction of timeframes between typical policy processes and what is needed for a partnership process.

Such contradictory timeframes will normally be a part of policy making. However, the NAP experience demonstrates the need for a clear timeline with a cut-off point beyond which new (particularly controversial) elements to a policy cannot be added, backed up by high-level buy-in to the partnership process and its implications (i.e. no last-minute surprises). An important working principle is that any new policy must have sufficient time for consideration of its implications and is subject to a rigorous approach.

Power, politics and the limits of collaboration

There was some disagreement during the latter stages of the process about the nature of the collaboration. Cabinet Office officials and some members of the CSO network took to calling it a partnership. However, others in the network found this a challenging description due to the imbalance of decision-making power between government and civil society. At all times it was understood that ministers held the final decision over which commitments the government would agree to include. In turn, civil society held a veto over whether the process was considered a partnership or not, based on the principle that a partnership required joint ownership of the plan. This principle provided some leverage for ensuring commitments were not included that CSOs considered to be damaging.

However, the asymmetry between the two parties continued to be a source of concern for some, particularly when government added the new commitments referred to very late in the process. The question about how to describe the nature of policy collaboration will be an ever-present issue because the policy will be, quite rightly, the site of tensions between what civil society wants and what government is prepared to do.

In parliamentary democracies, government ministers must obviously always have the final say over whether a policy is agreed and implemented. However, working on the basis of partnership and co-ownership should mean that robust discussions are had in order to find compromise on the tensions inherent in the process. It is the working through of those tensions which delivers strong and robust policy. The overriding principles, from the CSO perspective, should be: no regression and no surprises.

The politics of driving policy processes forward

The OGP NAP was due to be published at the international OGP Summit at the end of October 2013. This deadline proved very hard for the process to meet. The Prime Minister was expecting to make a significant announcement at the Summit to capture global media attention and demonstrate his government's commitment to openness. This opportunity provided an impetus for some of the commitments, which otherwise may not have been made at all or at this time. These included the public register of beneficial ownership,[1] a timeline for a commitment on greater transparency within the extractives industry and a commitment to develop a cross-departmental anti-corruption plan.

The presence of an external, hard deadline aligned the incentives of both government officials and ministers to the objectives of CSOs to secure the most stretching OGP commitments possible. While such significant external events will rarely be present in collaborative

---

[1] Simply put, the concept of beneficial ownership refers to a person or company which gains the benefits from an asset, but does not formally own the asset. The UK NAP commits the government to creating a public register of company ownership, making it possible to identify the ultimate owners of companies. In the context of the debate about tax avoidance, the public nature of this register was of critical importance to the CSOs of the network.

policy processes, it illustrates the need to understand where individual incentives within a system lie and ensuring that a process plays to these to secure the most robust policy possible.

Conclusion

This process was a credible attempt by both the government and the CSO network to develop policy collaboratively. It had demonstrable effects, including the inclusion of some more demanding open government commitments that, all the indications are, would not have been included without the process. The OGP NAP process has set a precedent for a new way of working – itself modelling open government in action. That said, the process highlights a number of issues that practitioners of new open and collaborative models of policy making will need to be mindful of. These include the need:

- for ministers and senior officials to establish and hold open a well-defined space in which officials can collaborate with other actors to develop policy;
- to ensure transparency in a collaborative policy process to boost its legitimacy, but recognising that this requires officials to take on significant levels of risk;
- to recognise that in practice there is some level of trade-off between collaboration and transparency; intensive collaboration demands high levels of trust and openness between parties, which can require a certain degree of privacy from the outside world;
- to ensure that open and collaborative forms of policy making are not captured or dominated by small groups – the obligation of ensuring wide and diverse participation becomes that of all those involved;
- to be mindful of the interplay of open and collaborative policy processes with other policy processes and cultures.

This contribution takes us inside a credible attempt at collaborative policy making involving government and civil society organisations. This collaborative process centres on attempts to formalise a plan and series of commitments around open government. Not only is open government an issue of significant contention, but exploring the process by which policy on this issue is constructed shows us the possibilities, challenges, opportunities and perhaps most centrally the politics of open government. The contribution seeks to model open government in action.

While often hidden and masked in conventional policy making through the privileging of particular, often technocratic forms of expertise, this contribution shows how politics is at the core of the policy process. Bringing the political 'clamour' of different interests and the 'churn just below the surface' to light also serves to bring the policy process to life. It illuminates how hidden value rationalities can be surfaced. This contribution shows that hidden hierarchies in the policy process are sometimes about the subtleties, such as where and when a meeting is held and those hidden dynamics – what is unsaid perhaps more than what is articulated publicly.

This contribution also recognises some of the important political realities. Attempts to forge a more co-productive policy process do not exist in a vacuum. Constituted, ordered, closed policy making will be happening all around: at times interacting, but also subverting, subduing and generating cynicism which can then inhibit more meaningfully co-productive alternatives. Policy actors need to be acutely aware of the politics and dynamics of power in the policy process and may be able to leverage, negotiate and navigate through them in order to shape the policy agenda and forge policy commitments. One of the most striking reflections in this contribution is the stark comment that the political space needed to create co-productive alternatives can only be opened and kept open by senior politicians.

An awareness of the realities, but also the rhythms of the policy process – 'manifestos, big speeches, set-piece agenda-setting opportunities around the budget or the Queen's Speech or other much more low-key developments' (Stoker, 2013) – is important. The mobilisation and marshalling of these rhythms is crucial: for example, a deadline can be used to stretch and push government as much as civil society partners. However, an understanding of the realities and rhythms of policy making can also be used to disrupt them. While government held the final decision over commitments, civil society organisations were able to leverage their veto over whether the process could be considered a partnership, which was important to the reputation of government but also the external legitimacy of the process.

Indeed, the contribution raises important points about the 'politics of legitimacy'. Debates about accountability can be a 'red herring' in attempting to forge more collaborative attempts at policy making. Where non-governmental partners in policy making are evaluated against traditional forms of accountability then this evaluation is sometimes used to undermine collaboration. The legitimacy of civil society organisations in this process is underpinned not by a representative claim, but by the articulation of the different forms of skills, experience and knowledge that they contribute.

The construction of this second plan for open government demonstrates a learning curve in how to collaborate. In reconvening the network, the credibility of this process as meaningfully collaborative is boosted by the role of the civil society network in determining its vision, priorities, terms and detailed commitments. Civil society organisations are not an afterthought or a rubber stamp, but integral to the process. Importantly, the process was 'open by default' and an explicit effort was made to make the process transparent. While 'open by default' could prompt a critique of de jure but not de facto openness, it is nonetheless hugely significant. But it also alerts us to quite how countercultural working in this way is for some parts of conventional designs. The contribution echoes Archon Fung (2001) in warning us of the potential risks of a more open, co-productive approach to policy making – capture, domination, stagnation – and the importance of working to mitigate them. But it also alerts us to the risks for those in government – the loss of anonymity and cover, and risk to their future career.

This contribution argues that policy actors can seek to mediate contestation in a more open policy process: echoing Teresa Córdova and Moises Gonzales' contribution, Simon Burall and Tim Hughes recognise that 'strong trusting relationships', which are both reciprocal and reflexive, lie at the core of a more open policy process. 'Honest brokers', individuals who can span boundaries, work in different organisations and environments to effect change in different ways, are crucial in enabling the process. By focusing on issues where no one has a 'clear solution', or which are 'less well defined' and working to reveal the hidden politics of the policy process, this contribution is able to state the obvious, perennial but often avoided and important point that a more collaborative approach to the policy process is, at its core, a contestation between 'what civil society wants and what government is prepared to do'.

Designing policy for localism

Robert Rutherfoord and Lucy Spurling

Both of the writers of this contribution are social researchers in the UK civil service, working alongside civil service colleagues developing policy proposals. They are based in the central government department that works with local government, planning, neighbourhoods and housing, as well as encouraging decentralisation, community rights and devolved decision making. As social scientists operating within a politically oriented policy-making organisation, they are well placed to trial new ways to bring multiple forms of expertise into policy. These contributors present an overview of the Neighbourhood Community Budgets pilot programme that aimed to devolve decision making about local public spending down to neighbourhood level. The programme can be seen as striving towards integrating some elements of co-productive policy making, such as the emphasis on community intelligence and co-design of policy, into institutions. Its programme was also shaped by what happened in local areas in a series of iterative processes from which central government learned as the programme developed. Ambitious in scope, the programme showed how there was enthusiasm for a change at a local level, which was tempered but not diminished by all too familiar barriers. It also illuminates how policy researchers and evaluators are attempting to live out some key principles of more iterative and incomplete policy design.

This contribution gives an account of the Neighbourhood Community Budget (NCB) pilot programme. NCBs were introduced by central government in England to stimulate and support innovation in local communities and play a role in the transfer of power to neighbourhoods. Government aimed to transfer more power for decision making over services, community assets and planning.

The UK coalition government of 2010 embarked on a programme of decentralisation, which reduced the control that central government has over local delivery and embodied the principle of localism and community action. The principles of this were set out in HM Government's 2010 *Decentralisation and the Localism Bill: An Essential Guide* (HM Government, 2010). The Localism Bill (now Localism Act) therefore embodied the principles of a particular form of decentralisation aiming to transfer power to the lowest appropriate level, putting communities in control through the introduction of a set of community rights – the Community Right to Bid, Community Right to Challenge and Community Right to Build. In addition, it introduced significant reforms to the planning system involving new powers for communities to lead Neighbourhood Development Plans to shape the nature of the built environment and enable communities to benefit more directly from development.

Localism in England has had a significant impact on the way central government works with local communities. Innovation, to help speed the process of change, has been nurtured by support of local initiatives to develop more efficient and effective ways of working. The idea of Community Budgets, for example, evolved from attempts to move away from central government directing or managing change at the local level. This is to be achieved through performance management, monitoring and scrutiny to create situations where it is local partners that are seen as best placed to drive transformation of public services, improve outcomes for citizens and realise efficiencies in service delivery. This is also seen as an effective way of responding to the challenges posed by increased demand and reduced public budgets. Thus the *Whole Place Community Budget* programme emerged, whereby local authorities, or groups of local authorities and their partners, came together to develop business cases for doing things differently. In parallel, the Department for Communities and Local Government (DCLG) supported a neighbourhood-level version of this process – NCBs – specifically to test the proposition that co-production and community engagement at the neighbourhood level would also provide opportunities for empowerment and innovation in service delivery. This was underpinned by the rationale that a better understanding of local needs, a clear focus on outcomes, and the contributions of local people in service design and delivery would improve services and outcomes. The invitation to join these programmes was set out in the prospectus (HM Government, 2011). Neighbourhood Budgets had ambitious aspirations and the programme as a whole set out to explore:

- the level of influence or control wanted by communities
- which services should be included, given existing commitments
- the right spatial level for the approach to be effective
- balancing community 'demands' against wider area considerations
- the scope for matching the cash element of the Community Budget with community

- resources like volunteers, tools, equipment, secondments, use of local buildings etc.
- the potential to develop new funding arrangements like community shares
- governance and accountability
- what sort of community capacity is needed
- the cost effectiveness of the approach
- developing a mechanism for areas to benefit from the best information and case studies on very local control of budgets and services
- how a 'right to a neighbourhood-level Community Budget' could be defined (HM Government, 2011, Annex A).

This was a radical departure from previous ways of developing policy. In particular, the role of the 'centre' was not to direct but to enable innovation. The move toward co-production requires community and local leadership and consent, so that local priorities are developed and implemented through dialogue. The new approach to policy making is also expressed in the Civil Service Reform Plan published in 2012, setting out the principles of open policy making, which are clear about policy making needing to be more explicitly strengthened by co-design, iterative development and user and frontline engagement (HM Government, 2012, p. 15).

The dynamic of localism, encouraging innovation, decentralisation, facilitating co-production and iteration sets up a number of challenges whose delivery requires a quite new set of skills and practices. There needs to be a move away from 'top down' direction and performance management to a more facilitative approach from civil servants and community leadership. How active a role the centre needs to take in stimulating change is also an important question. Implicit in the programme name was a goal of establishing a shared, pooled neighbourhood budget, which would come under local control, and could be directed toward activities which are more efficient, effective and met local priorities better than those which would be determined at local authority or national level. This is a challenge to manage. It required the pilot areas to develop their own plans, with the centre's role of providing some seed-corn funding, often to pay for some initial staff time, additional community development and partner engagement. DCLG also provided relationship manager support and structured some milestones so that the neighbourhoods would deliver 'Operational Plans' by April 2013. The department also facilitated learning and networking, and social researchers led an in-house evaluation supported by ESRC PhD interns (DCLG, 2013).

The NCB pilots therefore had few explicit constraints, and had innovation as a central theme. The evaluation could be conducted in the spirit of developmental evaluation (Preskill and Beer, 2012) where activities sought to capture and support learning and development, rather than measure predetermined impacts.

Neighbourhoods in the programme

The 12 pilot areas are described in more detail in DCLG (2013). They were neighbourhoods selected from over 40 who applied to join the programme. They were neighbourhood focused, led by different types of bodies and pursued different ambitions. Four examples follow which illustrate the variety in the programme:

1 Town council: Ilfracombe

Ilfracombe is a small, relatively isolated town in the rural district of North Devon with a population of 12,000. The project was led by the Town Council (a third tier civil parish), which sought to gain more control over services to improve outcomes and coordinate services through a joint partnership board with greater community representation. An innovative aspect of this proposition was to identify public spend going into the town and publicly monitor it over time, to provide an online 'virtual bank'. An operational plan was created, centred on decentralisation of services from the district council, development of key actions to join up services to tackle social isolation of the elderly, get long-term unemployed youth into employment and to act on illegal tobacco in the town.

2 Housing association: Poplar

Another of the pilots was led by an established housing association in the London Borough of Tower Hamlets – Poplar HARCA. This housing association manages the majority of the social housing stock in two of east London's most socially disadvantaged electoral wards. This pilot took as its starting point an extensive community consultation exercise and developed a project designed to help communities and services providers work together to tackle diabetes and support healthy lifestyles through social prescription and community-led interventions such as health volunteers. The project had a robust cost–benefit analysis which made the case that investment in this way of working had the potential to produce substantial health outcomes, which would in turn reduce demand on the core health services.

3 Community: Balsall Heath

The Balsall Heath Forum has been an exemplar of community-led neighbourhood-level action for more than two decades (for more information, see Atkinson, 2012). This organisation sought to use the opportunity of the pilot to create a neighbourhood-level pooled budget derived from core service budgets – through partners identifying spend locally, the neighbourhood evidencing that they provided 'better for less' and negotiating the transfer of budgets. The Forum has worked with residents on community safety and street scene initiatives for some time and used the opportunity to develop their business cases and support sustainability planning since core funding from local partnership sources had become scarcer.

4 Local government: White City

The London Borough of Hammersmith and Fulham, working closely with the White City Neighbourhood Forum, sought to engage with communities and develop new approaches to local issues in the White City Estate. This area of west London, with a large local authority-owned social housing estate, has been seen to be characterised by high levels of social need, despite being adjacent to areas of high employment demand. The pilot created a new organisation, Team White City, to engage communities, support volunteering and develop new initiatives. Key activities were the parent–mentor network – encouraging local parents to mentor others who had parenting challenges. White City Enterprise, a social enterprise using local residents to provide public services, has also been developed.

What did they do, and what did we learn about policy making?

It quite quickly became apparent that the process of community and partner engagement changed the focus of many of the pilots' initial plans. This is entirely consistent with the ethos of the programme, which was to remain locally led. In some cases the pilots were quite surprised by the level of community appetite for engagement. In Poplar the housing association commissioned community engagement about priorities, surveying over 1100 residents which resulted in over 100 residents stating that they would be interested in developing a volunteering role shaping decision making in the neighbourhood. As a result of partner engagement, however, ambitions in many areas were scaled back as the decentralisation was seen to be difficult to operationalise in practice. For example, where local priorities were in a policy area where partners were not able, or willing, to cede control, neighbourhoods typically ended up shifting to dialogue with more willing partners and developing arrangements for working in partnership instead.

The development of co-production as a principle was an important dimension to the pilot. Co-production implies that public bodies, service users and residents come together in new ways to deliver activities which meet citizen needs. As commentators have pointed out there is always some element of co-production evident in all production of services. All the pilots used the opportunity to develop resident and service-user input to the service design and priority setting process. And many successfully identified ways to develop user involvement in the delivery of services. Balsall Heath, for example, has a history of resident action in 'safer, greener, cleaner' type of activities, deploying street patrols with the police and engaging volunteers to maintain green space (Atkinson, 2012). This type of community co-production was nurtured and developed in other areas. Poplar and White City developed health volunteer roles which would help engage residents at risk of health morbidities, and encourage them to become involved in local activities which would reduce risk, social isolation and need for medical interventions. Residents got involved not just by having a say in priorities, but by actively co-designing the services that local people felt were important.

Overall there was an energetic response to the attempt to foster new ways of working with communities at a neighbourhood level. Partnerships came together to shape a vision and priorities for the neighbourhood. Business cases were developed which showed that changing priorities could yield long-term efficiencies.

Among the findings of the evaluation it was clear that there was *potential* for neighbourhood level budgeting to offer significant efficiencies through service redesign. This was evidenced by many of the community-led business cases for new ways of working submitted with the Operational Plans. These business cases, however, need further development and testing in practice. The most common motivation for taking up this approach in neighbourhoods and communities was to gain local and community control, and make decisions based on local priorities and local knowledge. Efficiencies on their own, therefore, did not mobilise communities into action.

There was no single path that the areas took in developing their operational plan; areas very much built on the conditions in their locality. Local bodies took different approaches to community engagement. One of the most common issues to be reported back from local areas was that budgets were seldom pooled. More often, the neighbourhoods succeeded in achieving better alignment of activities and what were sometimes described as 'virtual budgets'. Moving towards a truly pooled budget may therefore be overambitious without further work to create financial instruments and governance arrangements which generate confidence, incentivise those who can realise savings and provide appropriate levels of accountability.

It was also reported, that culture change was a key issue when negotiating new ways of working at a local level. Further, a change of structures, priorities, incentives, and assumptions and expectations of all parties (local authorities, public sector organisations and other partners, and communities) is required at the local level. There are, therefore, indications that neighbourhood budgets are taking communities on a journey toward greater local control, improved outcomes and developing the ability to do 'more with less', stretching neighbourhood spend.

Barriers

During the course of the programme, the areas flagged up a number of issues and challenges which impeded progress. These were also confirmed by those areas which undertook their own local process evaluations. These issues should be borne in mind by other areas pursuing a neighbourhood budgeting approach and those assisting them.

1. Areas found it a challenge to get meaningful data at a neighbourhood level. Often a starting point to negotiating with public services locally is evidence on the pattern of spend at neighbourhood level.
2. Areas needed to ensure they got the right partners on board at the start. The pilot process particularly demonstrated the importance of having the Local Authority (LA) either on board or at least supportive of the work.
3. The reorganisation of public services can inhibit progress of such initiatives. At the time of the pilots, for example, public health was

being reformed at local level. This creates uncertainty about budgets and operating models.

4. It was important that there is clarity about the extent to which some potentially high cost policy areas are within scope, as it has often proved difficult to gain data and engage partners on these areas. This led to a lessening of ambition in some pilots, which altered their focus.

Areas need to have access to skills and methods related, in particular, to community engagement and business case development. If these do not exist in the local partnership, they need support from elsewhere. Future support and sharing of learning in these areas appear to be clear priorities should this strand of work progress further.

Concluding comments

The NCB programme was a flexible but relatively ambitious way of government stimulating innovation at a local level. Given the programme was about stimulating innovation and local control, the centre played a role in structuring a pilot process, providing some resource in sharing learning and collating evidence. Each area took a different path and achieved different outcomes. The relationship between centre and localities was not directive in the sense that there were predetermined targets or outputs, so the programme developed in an iterative and co-productive way. The initiative is a promising example of co-production as the project attempted to join up centre and localities, local government, citizens and community organisations in productive partnerships. Incremental steps have been taken to develop new relationships in public service delivery.

The fact that the major obstacles remain centred on the changing culture of service providers, and the willingness to devolve budgets, suggest that a key condition – the alignment of incentives to support decentralisation at a local level – needs further attention. Having persuasive business cases for pooling or shifting resources on their own may not be sufficient if the local government and the local bodies of central government services are not incentivised to decentralise to community level. This is all the more important when resource constraints are forcing agencies to decommission services – potentially, this is the time when the gains from community co-production could be greatest, but the obstacles faced can also be intensified.

The pilot of neighbourhood budgets was rolled out to a further 100 areas in 2014 under the name 'Our Place'. The lessons from the pilot have been considered and it is expected that many of these areas will be able to follow the example of the pilots and provide more exemplars of decentralisation of decision making and services to neighbourhoods.

In this contribution, the authors signal that approach taken in the Neighbourhood Community Budgets pilot programme was a radical departure from earlier policies. Central government is described as making a deliberate effort to move away from the performance management-driven levers of predetermined outcomes. Instead, the idea is for locally driven change based on the values, or what has termed vision, of co-production, citizen engagement and collaborative local leadership.

Robert and Lucy note that, in some local pilot areas, there was surprise at the level of latent demand for engagement, which was generated simply by a different form of 'ask' of citizens. Expressions of initial interest and appetite do tend to dissipate, leaving a smaller number who go on to participate. But the point is partly about getting different responses from citizens simply by using new or different mobilisation techniques – something that community organising and other approaches have also shown. It also suggests that the many assumptions made about how far and how many citizens want to co-produce may need to be unpacked or re-examined.

Some of the policy discussed in this contribution is set out explicitly in the context of the major public policy challenges, focused here on the limits of traditional public welfare and service models, such as those which are deficit rather than asset based. Implicit here is also recognition of pluralisation of spaces for political dialogue, which mean that citizen voices and actors from organisations outside the public sector need to be brought into a policy conversation. Of course, all administrations state their desire to shift the policy paradigm. Where this contribution goes straight to the heart of matter is its recognition that genuine co-production is ultimately about control over resources, particularly cash resources. Equally illuminating is the level of explicitness about some organisations' resistance to handing over control and power to citizens or even outside of their own organisation to other professionals. An old story, but instructive still.

This is one of three contributions written by professionals employed by central or local government – that is, institutions with formal power holders and electorally mandated decision makers. At first glance, the contributors in this vignette might be described as the technocrats of Chapter Two. However, a closer look at their contribution shows that they are attempting to overcome unbalanced forms of expertise in policy and draw in a wider range of forms of knowledge. These policy evaluators conducted their own in-depth evaluation of the process. They did this using a combination of qualitative methods, including observations of local initiatives and face-to-face interviews. Drawing on insights from the pilots gained from their research, the evaluation therefore balances their technical input with direct experience from the local areas. As civil servants, they also situate these two forms of knowledge alongside an acute awareness of the political priorities for the programme. Their roles are to gather data from local policy pilots, and translate this into lessons for policy officials, who also may add a layer of translation. Arguably, they are boundary spanners between these groups, functions and types of expertise.

The volume as a whole tries to deconstruct the notion that policy making is confined to a small group of nominated decision makers. In the context of a co-produced knowledge base, the notion of 'a' decision maker becomes extremely hard to maintain. In practice, decisions are made jointly, with some people having more authority than others in that process. The contribution offers us an example of the value of creating policy designs which are incomplete, and allow for flexibility and local learning. This is evident in the local pilots themselves, which opened up spaces for citizen expertise in policy design, development and delivery. Their iterations in approach showed how they adjusted for higher than anticipated levels of citizen interest, but tougher than hoped for resistance to pooling resources. For central government, their learning was based on respect for different forms of knowledge within the formative evaluation, and the desire to allow detailed policy formation to be partly created in a co-designed and co-produced way within local areas, and in the relationship between the centre and localities.

Creative disruption for cultural change

Toby Blume

The author of this contribution is an experienced advocate for the community and voluntary sectors. Here he reflects on his experiences working with local government. Writing as an independent commentator, Toby Blume occupies a position as what could be thought of as a boundary spanner but what he calls a 'view from the boundary's edge'. This clear-sighted view gives us insight into the human dimensions of working with more incompleteness in a complex policy and delivery environment; business as <u>unusual</u>. This contribution illuminates the scale of change required to translate a co-productive vision into a three-dimensional reality. It puts forward examples and ideas of creative disruption techniques used to generate more co-productive relationships.

The case study is of the London Borough of Lambeth, and a story of groundbreaking work to reorientate its work along cooperative principles. It shows an attempt to introduce an explicitly asset-based approach into its decision-making processes about what local public services should provide, and how. Toby Blume's reflections on the process document just how much of a cultural shift co-production can be for large public institutions. It illustrates difficult choices about managing large-scale change processes internally and with citizens. The author makes a cogent argument that Lambeth Council's experiences suggest that co-production will need radical transformation not just in new forms of citizen vision and mobilisation – a participatory civic economy – but also across a huge and complex bureaucratic machinery.

Lambeth Council has made clear its intention to become a Cooperative Council – an ambitious plan to redefine the relationship between citizens and the state and place people at the heart of decision making. 'Sharing Power: A New Settlement between Citizens and the State' (Lambeth Council, 2011) set out a series of conclusions, principles and recommendation that aimed to fundamentally transform everything the council does and how it does it.

Focus on citizens

Lambeth's Cooperative Council is reframing the way we relate to our communities, by reflecting the untapped potential and latent resources that exist in all communities. This strengths-based approach (or 'Asset Based Community Development') seeks to unearth the talents, ambitions and assets within the community. It is an essential requirement of the Cooperative Council vision, where power and decision making is shared and improved local outcomes are achieved through co-design and co-production. As one report put it:

> It is about putting the resources of the state at the disposal of citizens so that they can take control of the services they receive and the places where they live. More than just volunteering, it is about finding new ways in which citizens can participate in the decisions that affect their lives. (London Borough of Lambeth, 2011, p. 2)

If a Cooperative Council is to truly redefine the relationship between citizens and the state, then it must shrug off the traditional deficit-based approach that has inhibited regeneration programmes of recent memory. From 'sink estates' to 'troubled families', the language behind targeting resources to areas most in need has created a perverse incentive to be 'the most deprived'. This approach fails to recognise the strengths and assets that exist within our communities and distorts the relationship between citizens and the local authority: 'creating a false dialogue that sees citizens only as problem-bringers and providers as problem-solvers and gate keepers to resources' (London Borough of Lambeth, 2013a, p. 6).

The Cooperative Council Citizen's Commission invited citizens and interested organisations to submit their views on the Council's White Paper. The Commission instigated a programme of engagement and consultation to gather opinion – using public meetings, focus groups, survey, road shows and social media to reach out to people who do not traditionally get involved in public service consultation exercises. Around 3,000 citizens contributed their views.

Whole systems change

Being a Cooperative Council, it was recognised, is dependent on whole systems change. Since then the organisation has been singularly focused on realising this goal. Shifting perceptions, culture, expectations and practice towards a co-production-based approach is no simple task. As Peter Drucker is alleged to have said, 'culture eats strategy for breakfast'. So considerable effort is needed to change the culture and overcome traditional expectations and norms – within the council and among citizens – and this has been recognised from the outset. Despite the effort and thought that has gone into supporting culture change and embedding co-production into practice across the council, there remain considerable challenges in achieving this.

For an organisation as large and diverse as Lambeth it is incredibly difficult to specify clearly what co-production means for each and every individual role. Setting out some clear principles can help, but it does not guarantee that they will be accurately or consistently interpreted by everyone. Finding ways to translate the big picture – the Cooperative Council vision and co-production principles – into practice as a default way of working is hugely complex. People want to know, quite understandably, how to reflect the new approach in their day to day roles; but the very nature of co-production makes it practically impossible to set that out in detail in such a prescriptive way. This poses something of a managerial conundrum. And of course some roles lend themselves more readily and more obviously to co-production. Roles focused on delivering frontline services might be easier to transform to be more citizen-focused and cooperative than more internally focused business functions that help the organisation to operate effectively, such as IT support.

Co-production requires very different skills and capabilities from those that have traditionally been required within local government. The very suggestion that the experience and expertise that has served people well are no longer valid or as important as they have been in the past can easily be seen as a threat to people's livelihoods. When set in a context of massive budget cuts and inevitable reductions in staffing, the likelihood of this fear manifesting itself in the form of resistance to change is increased.

Breaking down the delivery silos

One of the ways of encouraging culture change is to alter structure. There was, from very early on, recognition that if the council was to radically transform how it operated, there would need to be changes to the way it was organised. Lambeth, like most other local authorities, had evolved into a series of discrete departments with responsibility for specific service areas: Housing, Regeneration and the Environment;

Children and Young People's Services; Adult and Communities Services, along with the corporate backend of the Office of the Chief Executive and Finance and Resources. These departments were tasked with overseeing the commissioning and delivery of services; and that is what they did. They sometimes collaborated but often operated in isolation to each other. What other departments did, while relevant in the broader scheme of things, was not the metric on which they would be judged. Their performance was measured on the basis of how well they were delivering the services they were responsible for. An unintended consequence of this approach was a lack of coherence across the organisation and relatively few incentives to work more closely together. They were for the most part autonomous silos.

People, and communities, do not work in this way. We live our lives in the round, and any inconsistencies and lack of coherence are felt acutely by citizens. Any meaningful effort to move to co-production with citizens therefore required these silos to be broken down and reassembled in a more coordinated and coherent structure that enabled – rather than hindered – genuine community participation.

Cooperative commissioning

Possibly the most significant manifestation of becoming a Cooperative Council is the development of a new commissioning model that places citizens and elected councillors at the heart of decision making. Commissioning is, according to the Audit Commission, 'the process of specifying, securing and monitoring services to meet people's needs at a strategic level' (Audit Commission, 2003). However, within the standard commissioning cycle, involving citizens can be peripheral to a fundamentally top-down process. Merely consulting citizens on how services are delivered and who delivers them fails to rebalance the relationship between citizens and the state that is central to realising the Cooperative Council ambition. Lambeth's new approach to commissioning involves citizens working alongside council employees and elected councillors throughout the commissioning process, allowing citizens' priorities and preferences to lead, with professional expertise and support being provided by officers.

Within cooperative commissioning, co-production is explained as 'service users and service providers working together at every stage' (London Borough of Lambeth, 2013b, p. 19). As shown in Figure 5, this extends from deciding what outcomes should be, how resources are allocated, which activities will be provided and how services will be reviewed and monitored. Co-production will take place at every

Figure 5: Lambeth's Cooperative Commissioning cycle

step of the commissioning cycle; with continuing dialogue between citizens, councillors and professionals not just when new activities are introduced, but throughout delivery and review. Given the importance of co-production to the Cooperative Council, it is clear that only through a fundamental reworking of the traditional commissioning model can Lambeth realise its ambition.

Co-production takes time

Many of the changes needed to deliver the Cooperative Council take time. Lots of time. Time to think through the highly complex set of relationships and dependencies in pursuing whole systems change. Time to plan and implement the reorganisation of structures to better align with the requirements of a Cooperative Council. Time to understand and define the new culture and capabilities that are required to deliver the vision and then establishing an organisational development plan to support this. Time to translate the high-level vision into practical actions that can guide what people do on a day-to-day basis. Time to deliver things in a radically different way.

And of course, because so much of what a council does is providing vital services that people require, it all needs to be done without unduly disrupting services and maintaining high standards of quality assurance. This all places incredible stress on a system that is grappling with massively reduced budgets and growing demand pressures. These myriad internal changes taking place are often practically invisible to local people, who rightly question what is being done differently when much of how they experience local services remains for the most part unchanged. Like a swan gliding through water, the council can appear from outside to be far more static than it feels on the inside, as beneath the water line the legs paddle furiously to deliver change. Politicians, ever conscious of citizens' perceptions, are keen to ramp up the pace of change, while recognising that the changes they want to see take time.

Doing things differently

Human nature has a habit of reverting to what we know – even the most ardent 'change junkie' is drawn to the familiar. We are also incredibly adept at being able to rationalise our behaviour in ways that fit with new ideas or beliefs. When our behaviour and our self-beliefs are in conflict it is often our beliefs that get adjusted, rather than our behaviour (Festinger, 1957). I have, on numerous occasions, seen officers put their own slant on the Cooperative Council in ways that appear to justify them doing precisely as they have in the past. Part of the reason for this might be due to the high degree of uncertainty of what the future holds. Embarking on a journey whose eventual destination we cannot predict – without pre-empting where citizens will want to go – can be unnerving. Overlay this with a period of deep budget cuts and it is perhaps unsurprising that many people cling to the familiar. To put it crudely: 'How will I be able to prove my worth if I don't know what I'm doing?' There was a pressing need to shake things up, to encourage the questioning of business as usual. This needed to be 'business as *un*usual'.

The Work Shop and Open Works (www.theopenworks.org/about) are a deliberate attempt by the council to prototype this new way of working in one neighbourhood, by disrupting normal patterns of behaviour and encouraging us to question how and why we do things and shaking us out of our preconceptions about business as usual. We started to think about how we could begin to disrupt our normal approach to engaging residents in discussions, to develop a different, more 'cooperative', conversation. The result was the Work Shop – a pop-up shop on the high street which ran for a month.

A programme of talks, hosted conversations and workshops were held by the council, public sector partners and local voluntary and community groups, on a wide range of topics. In addition to these more 'formal' elements, there were plenty of more informal opportunities to engage, and passers-by were invited in to have a cup of tea and chat. There was information about things going on in the area, inspirational examples of what can be achieved through collaboration, and space to capture people's ideas of how things might be changed for the better. We also undertook some asset mapping – gathering community views of services, buildings, people, talents, ambitions and passions the local community has and values.

The Work Shop was an experiment in the 'art of the possible' and an attempt to test a new way of working with citizens that can be applied to other parts of the organisation. A shop on the high street in one part of the borough for a few weeks is not, by any stretch of the imagination, a panacea for the myriad challenges we need to overcome in order to realise the vision of the Cooperative Council. The Open Works built on assets identified through the Work Shop, to support local people – in collaboration with the council – to develop new ideas and projects that can deliver positive outcomes for the community. Local people were invited to put forward ideas for projects and then supported to develop their proposals by capitalising on the countless resources within the community and the council. The sharing of local skills and knowledge was encouraged through a Trade School[1] and the council embarked on an iterative programme that sought to reframe the relationship between citizens and the state.

The approach was distinctly bottom-up, building on the day-to-day realities and aspirations of the local community, to define and deliver the future they wanted for their community. It extended well beyond the traditional role of a local authority – to commission and deliver public services – by placing citizens at its centre. 'These initiatives are not building new public services or more consumer-orientated markets, but are reframing our everyday local experience toward a new type of practical and participatory civic economy.'[2]

These initiatives have successfully inspired residents with the vision of a future they collectively create and unearthed the desire of the local community to participate in realising this. But despite, or perhaps because of, this success the experience of Open Works and the Work Shop has thrown into sharp focus the challenge of connecting community assets with how decisions are made. Supporting embryonic

---

[1]   Trade School is a global movement of alternative, self-organised schools that run on barter. See http://tradeschool.coop/

[2]   See www.theopenworks.org/about/

community initiatives to develop and grow is fine but if it does not align with decisions about commissioning and delivery then it is going to fail to radically transform the way the council operates.

While the experience of the Work Shop and the Open Works has been overwhelmingly positive, the organisation's appetite for risk and experimentation varies. Involving citizens in co-production requires very different ways of working and so there is a need to experiment, innovate and trial new approaches. However, the very nature of innovation is that we do not know what will happen before we do it. It is therefore inevitable that some things will not deliver their anticipated goals (and others will over-achieve). Failure is a word that some find unpalatable or even unacceptable, but if we are serious about doing things differently then we must accept that sometimes we will experience failure. The organisation's appetite for risk taking is critical to realising the ambitions of being a Cooperative Council, but local authorities are not traditionally known for taking risks. There are obviously good reasons for this; scandals and high profile service failures have left their marks on the local government psyche, and rules develop in response to these problems. And yet there must be some appetite to take managed risks if the traditional ways of doing business are to be effectively disrupted.

Conclusion: view from the boundary's edge

Despite over a decade's experience of working with local authorities, I am not a typical council officer. My background has primarily been working in the voluntary and community sector to support marginalised communities to influence decisions that affect their lives. Though I had gleaned considerable experience of working with numerous councils across the country from my time at Urban Forum, this was quite different to the experience of actually working within a local authority.

As a Cooperative Council Implementation Lead, my role gave me time to look at the big picture – as well as focusing on specifics and details. The role requires a degree of boundary spanning – looking across and beyond the organisation – but as a local government 'outsider' I also bring the perspective of someone looking in from the boundary's edge to the heart of the machine. I sometimes feel my four-year-old son would be as well equipped as I am to do my job: question everything and ask 'Why?' repeatedly, until satisfied with the answer.

I never truly appreciated quite what large, and sometimes unwieldy, institutions local authorities are. Even from my centrally positioned role within the Office of the Chief Executive, I found it an incredible challenge to 'get a handle' on what was happening across the organisation. Keith Joseph is alleged to have said he wanted to get his hands on the levers of power, but when he became a Minister he realised they were not connected to anything. This possibly apocryphal quote has some resonance for me working in local government. The ability of any individual – whether a politician or an officer – to effect change across a council is more limited than I ever imagined. However strongly and clearly one articulates a vision or direction of travel, there remains considerable scope for things to be misinterpreted or disregarded. I had, perhaps naively, assumed that the democratic mandate of a council's political leadership would provide the 'golden thread' for the entire organisation. What I had not appreciated fully was the challenge of translating that vision into practicalities. Even if I understand where we are headed, that does not mean I know what it means for me and my job on a day-to-day basis. Throw in some complex and unfamiliar concepts such as 'co-production' and 'community-led commissioning' and the challenge of becoming a Cooperative Council becomes even more acute.

London Borough of Lambeth is an ethnically diverse inner-London borough with over 300,000 residents. Its neighbourhoods range from tourist destinations on the Thames river, to leafy suburban residential areas, to the urban cool of the edgy and gentrifying, and urban chic of the gentrified. It is a long way from its old reputation as a struggling 'basket case' in local government. Indeed, it has now been cast by some in the media as the hero defending a future vision of socially just, more co-productive local government. In this sector, one binary framing of debates about co-production has been the battle between the 'John Lewis' council (referring to a UK department store known for being an employee-owned mutual), pitted against the neoliberal villain of the 'easyJet' council (where local public services use the airline model of low-cost tickets with options to purchase extras like baggage allowances or meals).

As with the contribution from Bradford seen later, this is an attempt to reshape services by starting from existing citizen and organisational assets. This vignette describes work on a large scale. Being confronted by the sheer scale of operations, as well as the need for fairness and equity, might help to explain why these processes seem to lend themselves more to large-scale hierarchical mechanical bureaucracies than tailored approaches of co-production. In this contribution, there is a live example of a rejection of a conventional approach. The articulation of the deep thinking behind this change attempt is an analysis of the negative consequences of deficit-based technocratic ways of developing policy locally.

The author makes it painfully clear that shifting from existing ways of doing things to more co-productive alternatives is incredibly difficult. However, Toby Blume offers some glimpses of ideas for creating change. One set of techniques might be loosely termed creative disruption, where the council deliberately tried to 'disrupt normal patterns of behaviour' by constructing and modelling possible progressive alternatives. The contribution has practical examples of a temporary 'pop-up' space for dialogue on a high street, and a skills and ideas sharing project. Questions remain about how far these experiences can be scaled up, or rather scaled out across the whole area. However, these experiments in dialogue and mobilisation of citizen assets have, the author reflects, been helpful in refocusing on the institutional elements of this radical transformation. Another creative idea raised by this contribution is the 'repetitive why' or 'five whys' technique. Effective in the hands of small children, it has also been used in the private and public sectors to challenge and re-problematise issues. Problem framing and problem definition is a critical factor in policy decisions; 'repetitive why' is one practical way to open up conversations about problem definition.

Finding ways to conceptualise Toby Blume's position as a practitioner in Lambeth raised many issues with the notion of boundary spanning. As was explored in more depth the practice example, it became less clear what might be being spanned, and who and what he might be spanning between. However, the core notion of a boundary remained. This boundary is linked to the experience and perspective of the practitioner, in this case from other fields outside local government. It may be partly linked to simply being new to a situation. This contribution is written from the perspective of someone who feels they are an 'outsider' to local government culture. Individuals' roles within structures are not static but fluid. One classic 'co-option' dilemma this contribution illustrates is how to apply skills in understanding the norms of the institution, building reciprocal and reflexive relationships to effect change, without becoming unduly absorbed by them, all the while maintaining a sense of the outsider perspective.

Finally, this contribution illustrates what the reality of 'institutional stickiness' (Pierson, 2002) might look like. Some of the tensions of co-production are highlighted here, including a strategic desire for flexible iterative design that competes with a very human desire for structure, certainty and specificity. Structure also emerges as a potential tool for generating cultural change, in what the author cautions us may be a longer process that needs time to emerge fully.

Vision in co-productive policy design

Establishing principles for value-driven practice

Teresa Córdova and Moises Gonzales

This contribution from New Mexico-based planners and researchers – working as part of a broader collective involving students and traditional communities – demonstrates how the explicit statement of principles informs value-driven practice and contributions to policy. Coupled with the intent to make strategic interventions in the policy process, the Resource Center for Raza Planning (RCRP)[1] was able not only to influence policy decisions, but to challenge those decisions which may prove problematic for traditional communities and provide a platform and method to propose more inclusive, progressive alternatives. Starting from a position informed by identity and emotional connection to place, the RCRP drew together different forms of expertise: an understanding of the rhythms and dynamics of policy making, technical planning expertise, skills in participatory resources and experiential knowledge. This expertise, guided by clarity of purpose, was then mobilised in order to make successive and sustained interventions in place-shaping.

Over the span of the Resource Center for Raza Planning's (RCRP) nearly 20-year history, students have worked alongside researchers, professionals and community residents on projects and programmes related to land use and zoning, economic development, the provision of infrastructure, urban design, water quality and availability, transportation, employment, cultural preservation, youth development, agriculture and neighbourhood change. This contribution is a brief description of some of those activities and how a set of values and principles were employed to influence the outcome of planning and policy decisions and their impacts on the shaping of place.

---

[1] The term 'raza' has roots in a concept, *raza cosmica*, developed in 1925 by Jose Vasconcelos, a Mexican intellectual. During the Chicano Movement of the 1960s and 1970s, the term came to symbolise the bonds among Mexican Americans as a people. The continued use of the term signifies the embracing of an historical and interconnected identity of the Americas.

Statements of purpose and principles

A deep-seated love of place and concern for its future was the basis for commitment to the work of Raza Planning. Students understood growth policies as a continuation of historical patterns that exacerbated economic, social and cultural inequalities. They believed that the field of community and regional planning offered a vehicle to both challenge problematic development decisions and propose better alternatives. Thus, RCRP exists to contribute to the efforts towards wise development decisions. Such a statement was a call for engagement and insertion into planning and policy making. This decision to engage was accompanied by a conscious and explicitly stated mission and principles that provided the beacon to guide the purpose and direction for action:

> Resource Center for Raza Planning was formed to contribute to the community development efforts of traditional communities in New Mexico. The goal of RCRP is to maintain the sustainability and survivability of our traditional communities. We promote integration between higher education and our traditional communities through the application of planning processes and techniques. RCRP conceives planning as multi-disciplinary, intergenerational, directly responsive to community needs, and developed through ongoing, long-term relationships.[2]

The principles were developed in the late 1990s during a weekend retreat. From the laughter and commitment emerged the following 10 principles of *Raza Planning:*

1. Sustaining future generations through cultural preservation, ecological conservation and economic development
2. Ensuring planning processes that foster active community participation for just and effective decision making
3. Forming mutually beneficial relationships based on honor,[3] respect and trust so that work within our communities results in positive contributions

---

[2]   See http://saap.unm.edu/centers-institutes/rcrp/guiding-principles.html

[3]   US spelling retained to honour original document.

4. Providing information and analysis with the intent to educate and clarify the implications of development policies on our traditional communities

5. Promoting integration between higher education and our traditional communities through the application of planning processes and techniques and through linking resources

6. Advocating for planning processes and development policies that ensure economic equality, political self-representation, cultural preservation and ecological conservation for social and environmental harmony

7. Standing against development which displaces and impoverishes communities and destroys local ecology

8. Challenging processes and institutions which continually deny communities their given right to land, natural resources, human services, economic wealth and environmental health

9. Creating a community among ourselves, thereby supporting the personal, academic and professional growth and leadership of our brothers and sisters with whom we laugh and break bread

10. Holding one another accountable to act with integrity, respect, honesty, responsibility and confidence; and to maintain a balance between pride and humility[4]

The commitment to this mission and to these principles became the basis for *values-informed practice* that positively affected the ability of the RCRP to influence planning and policy decisions. The approach was somewhat systematic: equip ourselves with knowledge and skills, obtain a deeper understanding of the issues and seek ideas for possible solutions. In knowing the issues, we could then identify key decision moments and particular points for strategic intervention.

In any given set of issues we determined the key actors, what we would need to do to make a difference at these key decision-making moments and what skills, resources and strategies we would need to employ to make that difference. Then we inserted ourselves – got ourselves to the table and with our intentions clear we engaged in the planning and policy-shaping process. The result is that in many instances our work had an impact on the direction of development whether it was through affecting economic development policy and projects, land use decisions, infrastructure provision or urban design (Córdova, 2011; Simon et al, 2004). In the remainder of this

[4] See http://saap.unm.edu/centers-institutes/rcrp/guiding-principles.html

contribution, we briefly describe examples to illustrate how explicitly stated values and principles can provide contours for action.

Small business development

An example of RCRP's long-term ongoing relations was its work in the South Valley, an unincorporated area of Bernalillo County, southwest and adjacent to Albuquerque, New Mexico. Struggles for identity, survival and economic vitality date back centuries and are ongoing. After strategically and successfully writing the economic development language for a County planning document (Córdova, 1999), RCRP partnered with a local community development corporation to help them realise their vision of a small business incubator and commercial kitchen.

The purpose of the project was to increase 'household wealth and community health' by stopping leakage of money from the area, building self-employment options to counter the high rates of unemployment, providing local access to goods and services and by building markets and providing means for value-added processing for agricultural goods. The values that we brought to this project stemmed from economic development workshops that we had sponsored. In the workshops with community developers, we defined community economic development as 'a process for mobilising physical, financial, natural and human resources to produce marketable goods and services. Essentially, it is a process for creating "quality" jobs, increasing incomes, and expanding access to wealth for those who need it the most.' For Raza Planning, this meant development that did not harm or destroy existing natural resources or community structures. Other criteria for judging community economic development included:

- recirculation of dollars invested or spent;
- a process that includes the community in planning, design, and implementation;
- real community representation and community governance;
- a process that empowers the community politically;
- organising as a key component;
- meets retail and service needs of community;
- if the proposed development does not reflect or benefit the real interest of the community then stop it (when possible).

When we partnered with this community group, we understood its connection and commitment to the vitality of this community and that it presented the opportunity for a university/community partnership that could make a difference in the shaping of this community's future. Our goal was to supplement the work of the Rio Grande Community Development Corporation and assist them to reach their goals.

Over the period of the three-year grant, RCRP built on its relationships to identify possible funding sources and subsequently did the necessary work to raise $1.8 million dollars of the $2.2 million that was necessary for this incubator. We wrote the business plan, conducted a community assessment, and staffed a community advisory group. We also brokered the relationships which underpinned the incubator as a three-way partnership between community, university and local government. The South Valley Economic Development Center (SVEDC) is today a small business incubator – individuals and groups have access to a certified commercial kitchen that allows them to produce goods for sale in and outside the area – and a lively centre of community activity.

Infrastructure and neighbourhood change

As planners, we understood issues such as urban infringement, annexation and the connection between infrastructure, land use and economic development. Thus, we strategically made the decision to get ourselves to the table at a time when roads, drainage and water and sewerage systems were being designed and built in the South Valley. While county and contract engineers may not have immediately understood why residents might have strong opinions on the level of intensity of infrastructure development, we understood large-scale development could jeopardise the cultural fabric of this community. At the same time, we knew that infrastructure provision and improvements were long overdue after years of political neglect. We wanted to have a role in shaping the design, particularly by facilitating residents to participate in engineering decisions.

By being informed and aware of the timing of decision-making points, we were able to obtain contracts to provide the public participation processes for various infrastructure projects. In some cases, these contracts were directly from the County and in other cases we obtained subcontracts with engineering firms. By understanding the National Environment Policy Act (NEPA) regulations for environmental impact assessments we knew both the process and the logic of its requirements. In several cases, we conducted public participation processes that extended over several months, convincing engineers and public officials that involving the public in design decisions was in everyone's interests. As a result, we were able to create win–win agreements that addressed community concerns and vision while still meeting the criteria of engineering givens, fiscal constraints and project justification.

We were very conscious about the kind of process that we established. We used food as a good way to get people out and involved but we used other strategies in our mixed-method participation process. We always had well-attended community meetings and managed to broaden the interest in infrastructure planning and design. We did more than just advertise the meetings; we conducted outreach strategies, such as follow-up postcards and reminder phone calls. We created a method of tracking issues raised at the meetings with a question and answer matrix. After every meeting, we added any new questions to the matrix; engineers added to the answers and revised matrices were made available to the public. We employed organising skills that brought community voices to the decision-making table. RCRP frequently employed the random sample survey as a tool to supplement the other public participation tools. The surveys were a means to access the generalisable opinions of the wider community, including those that did not attend community meetings. We did not just throw these together. Every questionnaire was carefully designed with feedback and input; we thought it through and went through a collective process.

As a result of our efforts, instead of five-lane roads that destroyed historic corridors, roadways were built that protected small businesses, were pedestrian-friendly, cost less, added additional facilities such as pocket parks and enhanced the cultural landscape. As a result of RCRP efforts, drainage ponds were built with sustainability features and neighbourhood amenities. Water and sewerage systems were built based on community preferences for a long-range pace of growth. Through our work on infrastructure, we enhanced stakeholder dialogue connecting infrastructure, cultural landscape and long-term implications.

Community-based economic development planning in North Central New Mexico

In the summer of 2013, the Resource Center for Raza Planning received a grant to conduct an intense summer research school in Rio Arriba County to assist rural communities in developing community-based economic development initiatives. The objective of the Indo-Hispano Rural Planning and Design Field School (I-HFS) was two-fold. First, to provide graduate students in the University of New Mexico

School of Architecture and Planning with a community-based learning experience by working with traditional Chicano communities of Northern New Mexico. The second objective was to offer research-based technical assistance to communities in the Rio Arriba region in the areas of natural resources planning, physical design and community development (RCRP, 2013). The primary goal was to partner students with community leaders from Land Grant and Acequia Communities[5] in an effort to advance the development and implementations of community-based catalyst projects.

Rural traditional Chicano villages that have maintained a land-based agricultural economy for over four centuries uniquely populate the Rio Arriba Region in North Central New Mexico. After World War Two, the development of Los Alamos National Laboratory and the development of extractive industries began to transform the agriculture-based culture of Rio Arriba. However, in recent years, the budget sequester of federal government support in the region has compounded the out-migration of youth to seek jobs in urban areas. The region is struggling to develop a culturally based economic strategy that can create jobs while protecting the unique cultural landscape of Northern New Mexico.

Over a week, students, alongside community members, conducted qualitative research to understand the local context of community conditions and economic complexity. For example, community members set up meetings for the students with a cross-section of actors involved in the development process, which helped students understand the local community context. The field study was then followed up by two weeks of quantitative data analysis in order to develop the economic assessment and findings based on the understanding framed for the field experience.

In autumn 2013, RCRP presented an economic development report to local community partners and county, state and federal agencies. The report lays out short and longer term strategies for economic development that build on rich community cultural assets, including sustainable agritourism and ecotourism sectors in a region worthy of a UNESCO world heritage designation. Since the completion of the study, Rio Arriba County has requested that RCRP assist it in developing a culturally appropriate branding strategy to promote ecotourism. RCRP will continue to partner with local community

---

[5]   Land Grant and Acequia Communities are local community governing entities that manage communal land and water resources on behalf of the community. The governing entity has existed since the time New Mexico was under rule by Mexico.

leaders on the ground in Rio Arriba for years to come, to see the implementation of catalyst projects identified through the field study.

Place-making in the International District, Albuquerque, New Mexico

The International District, located in the south-east quadrant of Albuquerque, was constructed in the 1950s during the post-World War Two boom. The neighbourhoods in this district were developed 'overnight' to fulfil the immediate housing needs of workers supporting the Kirtland Air Force Base, providing compact apartment housing, but very little mixed use zoning and virtually no public parks. By the 1960s, the permanent workforce moved into newly planned suburban areas. Since the 1980s, the area has become an immigrant-majority district. In the past decade, community members have been organising to transform this community from its decaying post-World War Two worker housing units and hard urban landscape into a vibrant immigrant district.

RCRP began working with community leaders to transform this neighbourhood, starting with the rebranding from its label of the 'war zone', which portrayed the community as a high-crime neighbourhood, to the International District that could celebrate the community's immigrant diversity and community assets. Based on RCRP's values of community practice, our engagement framework was to build the capacity of community leaders to lead community development efforts through immediate projects while transforming long-term land use and economic policy through formal planning efforts by the City of Albuquerque. Through a series of community workshops, RCRP trained community leaders in formal community development planning while developing small catalyst projects to empower community leaders in the planning process. In the summer of 2009, the work of RCRP began with an Urban Design Studio class focused on assisting the community in a branding strategy and vision for community redevelopment. We began with a number of workshops focused on the vision for new housing development, improving park space and creating walkable streets, and creating economic development opportunities from local assets.

Later that year, another studio class continued to work with the community on formalising some of the goals of the summer studio into a community redevelopment effort. The success of these studios has led to formal redevelopment plans as well as rebranding efforts, such as the International District Sector Plan and the International District Trail

110

Scoping report, which targets improving trails and pedestrian safety in the community (Bernalillo County, 2011; City of Albuquerque, 2012).

In addition to RCRP's role in developing community capacity to impact on long-term planning policy, we felt it was important for communities to develop small community projects that would further build community participation and support of the community vision. Formal policy planning efforts often take years to realise, while community support in shared vision is lost due to the frustration of implementation. For this reason, RCRP developed several community urban gardens and public art installations targeted on keeping community members excited about the rebranding efforts in the community. Since 2011, two community gardens have been designed and contracted, along with a community park space with a small playground.

Currently, RCRP along with the School of Architecture and Planning at the University of New Mexico has received a grant from the National Endowment of the Arts entitled 'The Stories of Route 66: Creative Placemaking with the Albuquerque International District Community'. The purpose is to further develop community engagement in public art and community gardens that will help define the character of the district while enhancing the urban landscape (City of Albuquerque, 2014). Students in Community and Regional Planning recently worked with RCRP to design and construct four public art installations as part of an International District Fair held in the summer of 2014. In the spirit of building community, RCRP is vested in the International District for years to come by leveraging small catalyst projects today while formulating institutional change in the long term.

Concluding thoughts

The Raza Planners understand the needs of the communities described, primarily because they were *from* them, and carry a committed value of *place*. A university education became a vehicle to build skills and capacity to serve their communities, which faced uncertain futures but could benefit from their conscious and strategic intervention. The primary vehicle was to use planning knowledge, processes and techniques to facilitate a wider range of voices into decision-making policy choices.

Each intervention involved some initial assessment – being in there and analysing what is really going on. By 'getting in there', forming relationships and by being vigilant and aware, we knew: what decisions were imminent, who the actors are, what the various structural factors are, such as fiscal constraints, geological or geographical issues, political dynamics. We knew about the development decisions because we were there; we knew about the infrastructure because we were there.

Each case involved the use of planning skills and/or research. Planners, we suggest, are better when they incorporate research into their planning. Each case study involved knowing actors and building relationships and then each one involved a commitment beyond itself – a larger purpose that we had in mind. We were not just worried about a water system, for example, but our larger purpose – as set out in our principles – always influenced what we did.

You have to know the issues, build and institutionalise relationships. We cannot emphasise enough the importance of relationships, which are key to the success of effectively intervening in policy formation. The quality of relationships matters. Figuring out what will be useful and doable is key. Many times we might start out thinking we are going to do one thing, but quickly figure out what we can actually do. What is feasible to accomplish in the amount of time that you have. You do what you can do in the time that you have to do it, but you do it well. Pulling your team together is important, as is getting your resources in place. Awareness, strategy and focusing on what is useful and effective are important. You always have to evaluate what you are doing and you have to set up that evaluation for protracted engagement.

Values matter, as does thinking through the potential impacts of development decisions as they relate back to those values. Applying knowledge pools and skills becomes a basis from which to contribute. Accuracy and analytical rigour are essential. The values described are not an excuse for not having analytical rigour and methodological rigour – quite the contrary. The quality of the work really matters. Never at any point did anyone ever question the quality of our work. You want to make sure that what you are doing is tight. Incorporate experiences and voices. You learn by actually engaging in the process. The process of engagement is what teaches us how to engage. Which also means that sometimes you are going to make mistakes. However, the set of values and principles provides the guiding light for action as well as the basis to care. Skills and methods can then be applied to make a positive difference in how a community develops. What we describe, we would argue, is good community development practice.

We can have an impact on shaping the outcome. It may not be the full impact that we want. However, the difference that we can make is better than if we had not done anything at all. It may not be everything we wanted it to be, but the difference we made expanded possibilities while reflecting use values that contributed to the long-term protection of culture and place.

By bringing together forms of expertise given some recognition in the policy process – professional planning practice and robust and rigorous research skills – and allying them with expertise which is usually marginalised – the experiential expertise of traditional communities – the Resource Center for Raza Planning demonstrates how critical interventions in the most legalistic and technocratic aspects of the policy process can be made. Drawing in experiential expertise enables Raza Planning to challenge policy decisions and put forward 'real' alternatives which represent the lived experience of traditional communities.

Each of these forms of expertise is marshalled and mobilised through the statement of explicit principles in order to make a difference and shape interventions in the policy process. These principles serve to inform, sense-check and guide action. While these stated values are central and necessary to this intervention, they are on their own not sufficient. It is the creative process of bringing together these principles with explicit intent and different forms of expertise which is crucial.

A notable aspect of how Raza Planning was able to make these interventions and generate alternative planning futures was having the stated intention to do so, but also knowing how to play the game. The contributors make repeated reference to the decision to intervene, an awareness of the risk of co-option. They employ of a set of informed tactics and get a 'seat at the table'. Like Jess Steele's contribution, they recognise the importance of 'doing politics'.

It is important to note other factors which are critical in the success of Raza Planning. Three stand out from the contribution. First, the planners were able to understand the needs of traditional communities because they were 'of them': there was a shared identity and emotional connection to place. Second, they were 'in there': they were situated and embedded in the places which they were seeking to shape: 'we knew ... because we were there'. Third, the planners themselves were able to act as intermediaries, as 'boundary spanners' working the spaces between different organisations and communities, in order to build relationships and generate change. But recent work has drawn attention to their specific practices, what they do and how they do it: their ability to listen empathically, build and sustain reflexive and reciprocal relationships and manage conflict. In this way, they emphasise the centrality of these 'soft skills' to planners working in complex environments.

The principles set out do not work simply to inform local action and interventions, but also situate the work of Raza Planning in broader social debates, giving it a larger purpose. The principles serve to link Raza Planning to wider struggles for cultural, environmental and economic sustainability but also embody a more participative form of democracy and nested form of accountability. In this sense, Raza Planning serves as a 'boundary space' where the ideas of mutual learning, reciprocity, reflexivity and creative synergy between parties with distinct roles and claims to knowledge can flourish. Building this inclusive, nested and deliberative 'boundary space' takes time, which can work to generate trust but can also fuel frustration.

Among the many important messages of this contribution, the sense of this being crucially about relationships is perhaps the one that sounds loudest. These relationships draw from shared experiences and common connections, but are also mediated and sustained through public art and the sharing of food and broadened through the explicit tactics of community organising and outreach. In the midst of principled idealism, the Raza Planners are pragmatic about the limitations of their work; they recognise the continuing struggle to bring people with them. They see, too, that meeting these challenges needs principles, together with a range of strategies, tactics and tools– working with the policy process and challenging it.

Doing politics to build power and change policy

Jess Steele

This contribution shares a personal story about navigating the changing landscape of regeneration in the UK over the last 25 years. It is an inspiring journey showing how people can gain a sense of agency and make change happen, but also a cautionary tale on how being right is often not sufficient to win the day and that knowledge does not mean power.

Jess Steele relates a number of stories of how local communities have galvanised themselves in order to save and reimagine the public purpose of neglected physical assets in their communities. These buildings often became catalysts for action in the community, motivating and mobilising others. Repeatedly, local communities came up against public institutions – particularly local councils – which acted, to use Sirianni's (2009) term as a 'civic disabler'. Rather than supporting these community initiatives, they actively worked against and stifled communities' efforts to take control. But the contribution also shows a process of learning – from experience and elsewhere – about how to mobilise a community, challenge the established ways things go by 'doing politics' and developing an alternative way of making decisions and managing public assets and resources.

This contribution is fundamentally about power and what can be learned from experiences of working outside, within, against and with holders of established power in policy making. Government at different levels is able to use its power to advance its agenda and in doing so often divides, disenfranchises and frustrates communities. The response in this contribution was to generate community power through the tactics of community organising: realising the power of numbers, conducting power analysis, listening emphatically and doing politics. It concludes that in order for the potential of co-production of policy to be realised and the risk of co-option to be avoided, disruption and challenge to the usual way of doing things, acting entrepreneurially and realising the agency and power of communities is vital.

For the past 25 years, I have been a highly critical 'regen-watcher' and an independent community activist. This contribution is the story of a personal journey to some provisional conclusions. It has to

115

stay tentative, because I am deepening and challenging my learning every day. But my passion for community organising, rooted in lived experience, both shapes and reflects my enduring values. Community organising is a systematic process of consciousness raising that starts with people where they are and the world as it is. It helps people to clarify the issues that matter to them; to ask questions about *why* things are as they are, and to ignite the impulse to act to protect and enhance collective self-interest. It builds networks of trust between large numbers of people because numbers bring power and relative safety. It encourages individuals to take up leadership roles through taking action collectively. It turns the world upside down, take a moment to refocus and then exclaim delightedly 'but that's how it's meant to be!'

In the early 1990s, a group of friends and acquaintances squatted the semi-derelict Lady Florence House (Lady Flo's) in New Cross, South East London. They cleared the building out, redecorated, replumbed, rewired, reglazed, patched the roof and installed a coffee bar. The group of performers, clowns, jesters, bands and dancers ran arts workshops, offered rehearsal space for local groups and organised a series of performance events and parties. I watched in April 1992, as they were evicted by bailiffs after the Council ignored their proposal to legitimise the use of the building as an arts centre. Lady Flo's was sold as warehousing, its windows breeze-blocked up. The people of Lewisham were bought off for £80,000, three-quarters of which went straight to central government, as was the policy for asset disposals at that time.

An even more precious building, Old Town in Deptford was a 1926 Carnegie library, a pretty building constructed in a human scale dwarfed by its brutalist surroundings. Wasting away on the disposals list for years with a derelict public bathhouse next door, it suffered arson, flooding, squatting and neglect. In 1992, local people (truly local tenants from the housing opposite) took over. With the help of the estate's community worker (a 'detached' worker who had 'escaped' from the local authority), they got a temporary licence and a small grant and undertook the refurbishment themselves, working with offenders on community service. They made something truly wonderful at Old Town: a multicultural youth and community centre entirely run by volunteers.

However, a local Indo-Chinese community group was looking for premises and the local authority decided that this was the only available site (which was blatantly not true in an area at that time littered with derelict public land and underused buildings). What was at stake here? The council was concerned about money for the borough as a whole (despite only getting to keep 25% of the capital receipt), serving the needs of minorities, subduing challenge and avoiding risk. Local activists' interests were in saving a local asset, DIY self-help, whole community integration, serving diverse majorities, challenging authority and embracing risk (since they had little left to lose). The Indo-Chinese group's values were about DIY self-help, achieving stability and profile, serving their own constituents and managing risk (to their funding and hard work).

Each player was trying to get what they wanted because they believed it was right. Of course, as always, those with power were able to play out their values in the real world while those without power became angry and disengaged. Though the council was vendor, surveyor, negotiator, funder and planning authority, it did not see that it had a conflict of interest. The local regeneration agency, Deptford City Challenge, failed to mediate or take a strategic view.

Despite a vociferous public campaign, an oral history project and exhibition and a lot of work to identify other sites, the planning committee – with its back to the public – decided, literally, by two votes to one, in favour of demolition. Perhaps if we knew how the decision-making world worked we would not lose so viscerally again and I could stop crying with frustration on the council steps. It never occurred to me to become a politician, though I was approached often enough. That felt like condoning the outsourcing of policy to a tiny group of people motivated by electoral gain.

Instead, I concluded that 'knowledge is power'. A group of six of us came together at a summer school hosted by Goldsmiths in 1995. We each had large collections of paperwork (often in such controlled conditions as under the bed or on top of the bookcase!), each with a different specialism: heritage, environment, regeneration, planning, funding. We decided to collectivise our knowledge. In our various meeting places, we often came across left-behind board papers – the detritus of power – and gathered them up eagerly (inspiring the name Magpie). Magpie began as a 'community planning resource library', but over time, it specialised in creative outreach – recognising that it is not enough for a few people to be empowered through knowledge.

Meanwhile, the regeneration wagon continued its inexorable process. By 1995, there had been 18 different local programmes in Deptford, spending a total of more than £150 million. Deptford Community Forum commissioned a local research company to explore the impact from a community perspective. This research concluded that the cycle of regeneration failure was due to the lack of pre-bid community involvement. People were not shaping 'policy' – that is, the statement of intent on how 'we' want to affect the real world. So their agency was constantly and fatally submerged. They were being 'done to', over and over again.

In response, Magpie's New Cross Research and Training Project helped local people learn to be their own regeneration managers – able to make both policy and practice to create social and economic change in their own neighbourhoods. Interestingly, it was clear from the start that the participants were less interested in accreditation for their learning than in power – they wanted to be 'on the board' and 'in the driving seat'. Long before I understood community organising, I was training people to be out and about in the neighbourhood – to know it intimately, to build networks, to be visible and to listen, listen, listen. We used all kinds of engagement techniques and learned how to undertake robust participative research.

The more we listened, the clearer the message: 'We don't want any more money until we know we can control how it's spent.' So instead of a major solution-focused regeneration master plan, the bid that got written on the streets of New Cross was the process and relationship-focused 'Get Set for Citizenship', a community-led programme to end the cycle of regeneration failure, change hearts and minds, find creative, citizen-led solutions to 'impossible' problems and prepare for a new millennium of active local citizenship.

There was a huge amount of good in the Get Set programme. It won awards and the independent evaluation was very positive, noting that large numbers of people had become meaningfully involved and the programme had built unprecedented skills, structures and citizen-led strategies. But it also highlighted the other side of the coin: 'they' were still not listening. Looking back I realised two failures – we did not use the resource to buy assets that could have sustained our independence and we did not activate the power of the network. Having gathered a database of many thousands,we never actually asked them to flex their power. Conclusion: it is not enough to just be knowledgeable!

It often takes several hard lessons before the learning properly sinks in. In 2004, I moved to Hastings, for two years I stayed away from community life, but in November 2006, Hastings Pier was closed after its delinquent offshore owner abandoned it. I spent the next seven years working collectively with others to solve this 'impossible' problem. For the first three years we worked hard making the case for Compulsory Purchase of the pier – still believing that being right would be enough. But the council were waiting for a fairy godmother to turn up (in other words someone with recognised agency, the ability to impact on the world). In 2009, we changed tack and began the 'Battle for

Hastings Pier' campaign. As if by magic, we came across a small fund to support community groups in campaigning. They agreed a grant of £4000 just in time for a march we had planned. We used it for posters, flags, hi-vis jackets, collection boxes and a very expensive copy of the complete Compulsory Purchase Order Handbook which we tied up with ribbons and presented to the council at the end of the march!

Amazingly, the grant was withdrawn a few days later, not specifically to do with us, but because No. 10 had found out just how 'unpopular' most of the campaign causes being supported were – transgender, asylum seekers, gypsies and travellers and so on – and forced the Office of Civil Society to pull the fund. Perversely, this gave us a real boost! We got onto Twitter to make a fuss and began to feel the buzz of social media campaigning. We already had 500 fully paid-up members and had built up over 4000 people in the Battle for Hastings Pier Facebook group. But, we were about to find out just how important numbers can be.

The council still was not listening – or maybe, with hindsight, they were moving towards the brink, becoming more directly disrespectful – and things were getting desperate for the pier. It was time to do politics. Two weeks before the pier closed, back in 2006, a surprise election result had kicked out the Labour administration and put in place some classic provincial Tories who had never expected to win and were bewildered by it. By the autumn of 2009, the council was very nearly hung. By chance, one of the Tory councillors died and a by-election was called. We considered putting up a candidate, we even talked to the Lib Dems about the possibility of them not standing a candidate so that a pier-supporting Labour candidate could win the seat with our help. No chance! So instead, we crafted a campaign around 'Vote Pier', encouraging voters to ask the candidates what they would do about the pier. It was crucial to get across that the future of the pier was a political decision.

We distributed leaflets and postcards to 2000 households twice, using volunteers (and their families). Around this time, we began to get support from the Re:generate Trust. Their approach of genuine, systematic listening changed the way we talked to people. Instead of trying to 'sell' the pier message, we asked what they cared about – what they loved about the town, what made them angry, sad, frustrated, what they would like to see. We also put this out as a survey to our members. The results gave us a depth of insight that councillors can only dream of.

Just before the by-election we held a Candidates' Debate at the local primary school. Rather than giving the candidates a platform to give speeches we managed the whole thing to focus on the pier, establish the Trust's credibility and then give the public a chance to question the candidates on any issues that concerned them. By the time we were done, the candidates were leaping up to sign the Compulsory Purchase pledge!

When the vote came in, the Tories had lost over 400 votes, holding the seat by a mere 48 votes. The very next day we were invited to the town hall to discuss our plans for the pier with the Leader, Deputy Leader and senior officers. We presented our approach and worked out a way for them to save face while backing down – taking little steps on both the ownership and the funding in parallel. It helped enormously being awarded a £75,000 feasibility grant later that month. At last we were in 'active partnership' with the council and we had some real money to spend. There was still a long way to go but we had made something happen, changed the powerful; we had found our agency. Now I always advise people: take politicians to the brink. They'll respect you for it.

In 2009, working for the Development Trusts Association (DTA), I was seconded into the Department for Communities and Local Government (DCLG), taking over the role of promoting community assets. It was an eye-opening experience. One day a memo came round asking if we had any ideas on policy for town centres. I rushed around getting pictures of empty shops and knocking up a two-page suggestion called the Meanwhile Project, aiming to facilitate the temporary use of empty properties. A fortnight later, it was part of the announcement of town centres policy by two Secretaries of State (Hazel Blears of DCLG and Andy Burnham of DCMS [Department of Culture, Media and Sport]). I headed back to DTA with a sigh of relief: I had a £500,000 Meanwhile programme to deliver. Obviously this was great: I believe we squeezed every penny of value from the grant and we also began to establish 'meanwhile' as a philosophy rather than just a programme. But how shocking that we spend so much time trying to influence policy from the outside, while those at Whitehall desks have such opportunity for agency yet use it so little.

All the lessons described here, and many more, went into the Locality[1] bid to run the national Community Organisers programme to train 500 full-time community organisers (Cos) and 4500 volunteers. Community organisers are dedicated, motivated people who build

---

[1]   Locality was formed in 2011 from the merger of the Development Trust Association, Bassac and the Development Trusts Association, two national networks of community owned and led organisations.

trust, respect and networks through a systematic broad-based local listening process that ignites the impulse to act. COs go to people where they are, they knock on doors. They bring no specific message and seek no specific outcome. But we can see from the stories that we have gathered since the first trainee COs went out in September 2011 that there are nine types of outcome from community organising, shown in Table 1.

Table 1: Nine types of outcome from community organising

1	Individual possibility	Moving individuals from apathy to agency, building a sense of possibility
2	Early wins	Immediate action that inspires and invigorates
3	Community spirit	Sense of community spirit, coming together, overcoming isolation
4	Activating networks	Using the network to solve problems, either one-to-one connections or by mobilising numbers
5	Neighbourhood housework	Extending the tidying up and caring work that goes on in households into the wider neighbourhood
6	Influencing decisions	Influencing decisions about resources and plans for the neighbourhood
7	Assets & services	Community takeover of assets and services
8	Enterprise	Starting up new businesses, services and projects
9	Democracy	Inspiring/transforming democracy

The necessity of having the power to make change is as true of the policy world as it is of any other campaign or action, whether policy is seen very broadly as a statement of intent to change the world or more narrowly as the direction in which government funding flows. If policy is the way 'we' achieve rational decisions in the service of specific public objectives, that tiny word 'we', which litters academic and political conversation without explaining itself, hides all kinds of co-options. 'We' needs to be made genuine and that can only happen through community organising: an explicit and systematic focus on relationships, voice, action and power.

But where does power come from? Money, land, control of resources, control of the discourse and norms? Lacking all these, the power that 'ordinary people' have is all about numbers. It is about voting (at any and every level of democracy), striking (not just labour strikes but rent, tax, sex or housework strikes – refusing to do what you are expected to do), mass challenges (marches, occupations, sit-ins) and coordinated consumer choices (boycotts, switching, community investment). And since 'power is what they think you have', in all these cases the threat/

promise to take action (vote, strike, occupy, buy) can be as powerful as the action itself.

How do you achieve policy change through people power? The action depends whether the aim is to get rid of bad policy (for example the Poll Tax – polarise, focus, strike, riot) or introduce good policy (for example the Living Wage – testimony, pledges, alliances, sustained campaigning). The vast majority of people do not feel any connection to or ownership of policy because it takes such a strong sense of agency and entitlement to believe that we can affect the real world. One of the most sinister aspects of established power is the control of the discourse. Thus is the status quo sustained. Community organising tries to disrupt that 'magical reality' in which things could not be any different, so that people can clarify what matters to them, become conscious of their own agency and know that it is possible to take action. Co-production of policy can only work where the values of the co-producers can somehow interlock and complement each other. People can only co-produce if they have agency. As Alinsky said, 'If people don't think they have the power to solve their problems, they won't even think about how to solve them' (1946, p. 4).

Jess Steele's contribution is, in part, about saving assets that are important to local communities and can act as examples of and catalysts for what she has in other places called the 'self-renovating neighbourhood: people looking out for their own, regenerating their own neighbourhoods on their own terms' (Durose, Justice and Skelcher, 2013). In telling the simultaneously inspiring and depressingly similar stories of different community attempts to reinvigorate and take control of public assets, the contributor is able to make a number of salient points about power. How established power holders in some cases have worked to subdue challenges to it, but more importantly, how power is not 'zero-sum' and how communities can gain a sense of their own efficacy, and generate power in order to disrupt and challenge established power.

Jess Steele challenges and unmasks the casual use of the word 'we' in the policy process and the easy consensus it suggests, instead demonstrating that 'we' often hides co-option of those without established power. The stories that she shares show the different and contradictory interests of parties involved in or seeking to influence a policy. Rarely are these different interests reasoned or deliberated on, but rather power comes into play: 'those with power were able to play out their values in the real world while those without power became angry and disengaged'.

In one sense, Jess' recognition that people feel disconnected from policy shares the starting point of this book. But her analysis of 'why?' pushes ways of thinking. This disenfranchisement is not simply because of apathy generated by poorly designed opportunities for participation which are effectively 'empty rituals'. It is also caused by a repeated undermining of citizens' sense of agency and efficacy: 'they were being "done to", over and over again'. This undermining is illustrative of the constituted power (that of the state, here local government) over the constitutive power of the people. Those in power are detached from the lived experience of local communities and so policy feels like it is 'outsourced ... to a tiny group of people motivated by electoral gain'.

Jess Steele relates how she learnt – repeatedly and the hard way – that knowledge in itself is necessary but not sufficient to gain power. But rather – echoing Teresa Córdova and Moises Gonzales' contribution – power comes from mobilising that knowledge. In part this is about being value driven – a critique of how policy making is going wrong and a sense of how it could be done differently. But also a sense of how to play the game: an explicit intent to 'get to the table', to be willing and able to 'do politics' to get there, and to take action when the opportunity presents itself.

'Playing the game' and 'doing politics' is informed by the community-organising tactics pioneered by Saul Alinsky in the 'back of the yards' area of Chicago. This approach is continuing to have influence now, notably in the 2008 US presidential election where former organiser Barack Obama built a campaign from the grassroots, but also in organisations such as the Industrial Areas Foundation and Citizens UK. This form of community organising is based on the recognition that local communities have power in numbers and on a valuing of the often unrecognised and hidden assets they hold. Activating this power is about building local knowledge through empathic and repeated listening, not only to what people hate and feel frustrated about, but to what they love and want to take action on. This local knowledge is important in directing power analysis, understanding where power lies, what are its rhythms and how to disrupt them. This vignette reflects on the importance of doing politics, 'activating' and 'flexing' power by utilising specific tactics – voting, protesting, striking, occupying, buying – to 'push politicians to the brink'. Its contribution draws attention to the significant impact which individuals outside and within public institutions can make in the policy process, for example, as active citizens, activists, community organisers and policy entrepreneurs. By narrating a personal story, Jess Steele shows how an individual can transition between different ways of making a difference in communities and to the policy process. These individuals are vital and necessary – if not sufficient – to effect change.

This contribution refocuses and reminds us of the centrality of power in thinking about co-production. There is potential for co-production to fall into the trap of 'big tent' politics, assuming that consensus not contestation lies at the heart of politics. The 'dark side' of co-production lies in its potential to be co-opted, and an acceleration of 'common sense' orthodoxies of marketisation. An alternative and more emancipatory rendering of co-production relies on shared values but also in realising economies of scope, reconciling timelines and sharing agenda setting. Jess Steele reaffirms that the process of policy making is and should be about contestation and challenge, as easy consensus is often anything but.

Participatory action research and policy change

*Brett G. Stoudt, María Elena Torre, Paul Bartley,
Fawn Bracy, Hillary Caldwell, Anthony Downs,
Cory Greene, Jan Haldipur, Prakriti Hassan,
Einat Manoff, Nadine Sheppard and Jacqueline Yates*

The Morris Justice Project (MJP) works in an area of New York City that is internationally renowned for its place in urban music and culture as much as the stigma that is associated with its reputation. MJP is an informal collection of collaborators and, through its members, is connected with an academic institution. The Project engaged in research-driven activism which attempted to change aggressive community policing methods. One core idea was to use participatory action research methods to generate fresh data on the official policy of 'stop and frisk' of residents who were seen as suspect by police. This data was then discussed with a wider set of local people, and used by MJP as part of a city-wide movement for reform of New York Police Department's 'Broken Windows' and 'zero tolerance' policies. Theirs is a powerful and uplifting story of community mobilisation for social justice.

With 12 authors actively involved in producing and editing, this writing team is itself an example of co-produced knowledge from the start of the inquiry through to and including writing this contribution. It is an illustration of what it could mean for all parties to take seriously multiple forms of expertise. This is not only about elites or professional experts respecting lived expertise, but includes community experts advocating the value of research, or what one participant in the MJP describes eloquently as 'coming from a place of knowing'.

My first time in the neighbourhood was also my first introduction to Jackie and Fawn. It was quickly interrupted because two of their friend's sons were just taken to the 44th police precinct for no apparent reason and another friend's son had a court date, in which the attorney forgot to show. There was a sense of urgency and frustration but also a basic lack of surprise. I remember how impressed I was with how highly coordinated and responsive the mothers were. In minutes, over texts and phone conversations, some went to the court and some went to the precinct. It all suggested this was not their first time. Of course, we found out later it wasn't. (Brett)

The Morris Justice Project brought together a diverse collective of academics, lawyers, artists, activists and residents of a South Bronx neighbourhood outraged by New York Police Department's (NYPD) aggressive use of 'Broken Windows' policing. Designed as a critical participatory action research (PAR) project in 2011, our aim was to systematically document the local impact of these practices, including the controversial use of 'stop, question, and frisk' that led to nearly 700,000 stops of overwhelmingly innocent Black and Latino men the year the research began (Jones-Brown et al, 2013). Together through PAR we designed a survey taken by 1030 residents in what we have come to call the Morris Justice neighbourhood: 42 blocks cut down the middle by Morris Avenue, bound by three wide-laned streets and a commuter rail corridor, four blocks south-east of Yankee Stadium, and in the shadow of the Bronx Supreme Court. This, 'our' neighbourhood, had 4882 recorded police stops the year we met; 59% of which involved physical force and 91% were 'innocent' (neither arrested nor given a summons). The NYPD's rationale for these stops was to reduce gun violence, yet for all those stops only eight guns were found. Our hope was to produce data that would be useful in igniting a broader community conversation as well as contribute to education, advocacy and activism efforts towards police reform.

Our work is rooted in that long, international tradition of critical activist scholarship known as participatory action research. PAR produces research *with* community members for the purpose of informing policy and countering inequality. Participatory researchers hold the belief that expertise is not solely concentrated in sites of political-cultural power (such as universities, government, lawyers) but is instead widely distributed, particularly among those disproportionately affected by the policies or social issues of concern. From this position, those who bear the greatest burden not only have the ethical right to conduct research on issues important to their lives, but their situated knowledge is necessary for the highest quality research and most useful activism (Cahill, 2007).

Just as we conducted our research collaboratively, we also wrote this contribution collaboratively. We first assembled a long list of questions to help us focus our reflection on the project. We organised these into a set of topics and then discussed each in pairs. A draft was written from the conversation themes, discussed and revised by the group. At first, quotes were used heavily throughout to best represent our many voices. As drafts and discussions about the article accumulated, many of the quotes dissolved. While those that remain may appear individual, they reflect the ideas of the entire group. Our essay is written in three parts: the first briefly describes the context of our research, the second explores *doing* participatory research for public policy change, and the third discusses *using* participatory research for public policy change.

Context

As cities and states swell their prison/incarceration budgets at the expense of education and social welfare (Torre and Fine, 2005), police stand as the point of contact between citizens and entrance into the criminal justice system (Gilmore, 2007). The NYPD's nearly two-decade emphasis on order-maintenance policing is legitimated by a theory known as 'broken windows', which argues that community 'disorder' invites serious crime (Kelling and Wilson, 1982). The NYPD's expression of this theory has been to flood police into 'hotspot' neighbourhoods and then encourage officers to aggressively police low-level, 'quality of life' violations and misdemeanours (such as riding a bike on the sidewalk, sitting in a park after dark, public drinking, smoking marijuana) (Greene, 1999). This has produced high volumes of police stops known as 'stop and frisk' on individuals (particularly young people) who are suspected of having committed, are committing or are about to commit a crime (Stoudt, Fine and Fox, 2012). The basic tenets of 'broken windows' policing have gone largely unsupported by empirical evidence (Harcourt, 2001).

The South Bronx, birthplace of hip-hop, has long been described as 'dangerous', 'burnt out', a 'ghetto'. But 'this *is* OUR home', as residents within our group have pointedly expressed. "The feeling of safety when it is your home is very different from how it is perceived in the media. Those who call this neighbourhood a 'hotspot' or 'full of crime' haven't come here to visit or talk with people" (Einat). "I enjoy the neighbourhood. It is not a bad area, it is just that the police were harassing the kids and it got overbearing" (Fawn). Entire communities of colour like ours are targeted, harassed and assumed suspicious by police simply because their/our neighbourhoods have been labelled 'disorderly' and unsafe. While some say this is a small price to pay for safety (MacDonald, 2013), we strongly disagree. In order to speak back informed and with authority, we needed to "come from a place of knowing" (Anthony). We decided to engage in collective, community-based research.

Doing participatory research for public policy change

A family of a different kind

We are a group with different backgrounds, experiences and motivations. Most of us live in the South Bronx neighbourhood we studied. Some joined us right away and others joined at various stages along the process. We got tired of "the police harassing our sons and the other kids living in the neighbourhood" (Fawn) and "wanted them to know it doesn't have to be like this. You can make a difference if you just try" (Jackie). So we joined the project "to see what we could do about it" (Nadine). Others of us joined because of our personal experiences of being detained by the police and realising "there's a lot of people in there who don't deserve to be there" (Anthony) or growing up and getting stopped by police "every day, all-day – hallway, courtyard, corner – so many times I can't even count" (Cory). Others had less personal experience and "became convinced about the need to do something about the police by doing the work involved in the project" (Prakriti). Some of us are students who "have always been involved with criminal justice issues" (Jan), "witnessed some stops that have been really upsetting" (Hillary) or drew connections with their "work in Israel/Palestine" (Einat). Two of us are professors from the public university who "had done participatory research with people who were incarcerated or formerly incarcerated" (Maria) and learned from their projects that "something was beginning to boil in NYC around policing" (Brett).

If you get to know us, we'll surprise you. We are not easily stereotyped. We are elders, mothers, fathers, youth, professors and students of multiple intersecting races/ethnicities, nationalities, sexual identities, genders and religions. We play the lotto and like a drink (or two). We are authors and orators. We dream big but work local. "We believe in the justice possibilities of 'public science'; of democratising social science so that everyday people can engage their right to research" (María). We have each lived lives that have sharpened countless skills and expertise that enrich and inform our project. "We didn't always trust each other – why should we? [W]hen we first met I thought, 'Oh boy, we ain't gonna do too much good.' I thought it was just going to be a lot of bullshit to be honest" (Fawn). Ours is a research collective that experiences misunderstandings, frustration and disagreement – and that's okay. Unpacking these tensions helps us establish stronger relationships and enriches our analysis (Torre and Ayala, 2009).

Ours is also a collective that provides ongoing opportunities to broaden our perspectives, stretch beyond what is comfortable and learn from each other. We are not shy of expressing what we think to the group. If there is something we don't like, we say it: "'No I don't think that's going to work' or 'I don't think we should do that' or 'maybe we should do it a different way'" (Prakriti). We cultivated a space that was respectful and responsive so that each of us had a sense of ownership and responsibility.

> 'When I first joined, the group really listened to me. I was actually able to voice my thoughts and the key thing was, the group started to work out ways to incorporate them into the survey. I felt like I was not only speaking for myself but for my community. I was a channel, a mouthpiece so to speak.' (Paul)

Together, with and across our differences, we work in solidarity. Our work has become a space for hope, a space to imagine change, and the possibility for collective action. We are a family of a different kind – a family of researchers and activists who want something different for our children, our neighbours, and all residents of NYC.

Learning from each other

We spent our first summer in the basement of the local public library exchanging knowledge in a 'research camp'. We learned that research is fundamentally about asking questions and many of us were surprised that we already had some of the skills needed to become effective researchers – we were already asking questions, we already had theories, we already were close listeners and observers. We spent time describing what it was like living in the neighbourhood and sharing personal stories, struggles, joys, similarities and differences. Our assumptions about each other, policing and research were challenged and complicated. Guests came to educate us on the criminal justice system, our legal rights, NYPD policing policies and the stop and frisk statistics. Gradually, we began reframing the themes of our discussions into theories, interview questions and survey items. With more than 20 drafts, a survey and a set of open-ended focus group questions were born about experiences with and attitudes towards police, as well as perceptions of the neighbourhood. "It was cool knowing that we really created the survey from the bottom up. We just created it from scratch as a group. It wasn't just some symbolic activity – it was real" (Jan).

"Trying to get the survey itself done, figuring out the right questions, and imagining how people would respond to it. That was kind of tough. We're just a few people trying to represent 42 blocks" (Jackie). We *were* just a few people trying to represent the neighbourhood, which is precisely why we sought input from our neighbours by distributing the survey block by block and later for help with analyses. Sampling was fundamentally through neighbour-to-neighbour interactions and it was important that our co-researchers who lived in the neighbourhood were the survey creators, not simply giving it their stamp of approval. "I think if I handed out the survey without standing next to Jackie, Paul, or Prakriti there might have been a lot more suspicion" (Brett, who is White and lives outside the neighbourhood).

Taking a self-reported survey is certainly an individual and self-reflexive experience – that is part of its methodological value. However, our process was designed to encourage the relational part of community sampling: feet to the ground, on the blocks, clipboards in hand, person to person. Many of us were surprised by how willing people were to take the survey, often forgoing the incentive of a free Metrocard for the opportunity to have a conversation about police. "We were surveying up and down the blocks. I loved it. You got to meet different people and people got to meet you. You'd be surprised how many were interested. And you got to hear other people's battle stories of the street" (Jackie). "I remember an older gentleman who was recently stopped for the first time and wanted to tell me the story. I couldn't believe he would tell me, a complete stranger, but hearing stories like that from people really made me see things differently" (Prakriti). "When we handed out the surveys some would say no but then you would get in this long conversation after they read it through" (Nadine). Our survey produced moments of community engagement and a sense of connectedness, validation and solidarity grew.

We analysed the data collaboratively using a set of interactive, flexible and inductive participatory analysis techniques we call 'stats-n-action' (Stoudt and Torre, 2014). Data, numbers, survey items, graphs, cross-tabulations – all took on different significance because they were derived from OUR survey in OUR neighbourhood.

'To me the stats-n-action part was so amazing because it wasn't just numbers and charts thrown up on the wall. *Now* I knew what that number meant because it was *my* neighbourhood that we did it in. I knew that little kid that I watched grow up and now's in that 16–21 age group we were analysing. I knew each group and somebody who was in that group. Even I fit under a category. It wasn't just a chart now; I'm somewhere up in those numbers.' (Jackie)

Running analyses together in real time helped us understand the neighbourhood more deeply and beyond our personal experience.

In addition to our survey data, we also reanalysed and mapped the NYPD's publicly available data. Juxtaposing our research with their numbers allowed us to examine the extent of the issue while also demystify the justification and power they claimed from the data:

> 'I definitely learned the issue is bigger than the Bronx. I learned data can be manipulated sometimes. When I looked at the police data and then looked at the data I actually participated in collecting, I saw disparities. When we ran some of NYPD's statistics we realised they couldn't be right. I was surprised at the amount of stops on the street versus the amount of crime actually committed or weapons uncovered. The numbers seem to be very off. Somebody has to realise in the police department, somebody at headquarters, somebody has to realise that something is wrong here and it needs to be corrected as soon as possible. They have to open their eyes and take light of our data.' (Paul)

Alongside our quantitative data we analysed the qualitative data we collected by a series of methods including focus groups, interviews, the open-ended questions on the survey, and the photographs of responses that residents wrote on white boards to the question, 'What does community safety look like?' Our multi-method data gave us varied results but dominant patterns emerged. Residents in the neighbourhood overwhelmingly reported having frequent and negative interactions with the NYPD. The consistent unfavourable attitudes, frustration and concern about current conditions pointed to strained community–police relationships. There was a general sense of feeling profiled for who we are or where we live and wanting the police to respect our community as more than just an alleged 'high crime' neighbourhood.

Using participatory research for public policy change

The Morris Justice Project was intentionally designed to deeply engage a small neighbourhood that had been affected by aggressive policing methods, so the research and action would be grounded in a local community even as it spoke across the city. As we conducted the research we established strong, reciprocal connections with a host of citywide police reform activities including grassroots activism, legislation and lawsuits. The following are some of the strategies and paths that we pursued as a way to speak back to, and out from, the neighbourhood.

Back-pocket report

Traditionally academics speak first and foremost to other academics. While we understood the academy to be a worthy audience, our primary commitment was to our South Bronx community and the urgency of our findings led us to produce a 'pocket report' as our first method of dissemination. Rather than a lengthy technical report that might be tossed away without reading, the pocket report unfolded into a colourful and informative poster of the story of the Morris Justice Project and the results of our research. It easily slipped "into a back pocket so we can have a conversation and inform them what other people think in the neighbourhood" (Cory). It felt important to "let the community know this came from you all. Without your input we wouldn't have had this. Remember last year when you took the survey? Yes? So now you get to see" (Jackie).

Sidewalk science

An enactment of public science, 'sidewalk science' creates ongoing opportunities for residents throughout the 42 blocks to learn about our findings, immerse themselves in neighbourhood data, connect with the police reform activities and, most importantly, engage in face-to-face discussions about policing and safety (Stoudt and Torre, 2014). An example of sidewalk science involved the Morris Justice Project's partnership with an activist art group called 'the Illuminator'. A van outfitted with a giant projector, the Illuminator beamed our survey results and two documentary/educational shorts about stop and frisk onto the side of a 20-storey public housing building in the neighbourhood. The event began with drumming and dance, to gather an audience, and ended with a 'know your rights' training:

> 'It was right in the heart of my neighbourhood. People were getting off from work, looking – you couldn't help but stop. You had to STOP. Even the police had to STOP.

LOOK. And the people gathered weren't only just Black and Latino it was White, it was different nationalities, all standing for the cause. They never even met us but they came out to back us up.' (Jackie)

Amidst a sizeable crowd vibrating with the sounds of solidarity and public conversation, the NYPD broke us up and sent us home.

While the Illuminator was a single event, we have held ongoing sidewalk science sessions in different sections of the neighbourhood. Using fences to hang display boards we share the story of our project, information about the relevant lawsuits/political activities, 'know your rights' pamphlets, ways to get involved and voter registration forms. We also share maps of our findings, encouraging viewers to share their interpretations; layering their ideas onto our analyses. We hand out data-driven t-shirts and buttons and chalk our findings onto the sidewalks. All of these activities are designed to generate public discussion, facilitate critical engagement with policing and the underlying issues of community investment, and inspire activism. "When I'm out on the sidewalk I tell people that stop a little bit about what I've been through. I feel it opens them up once they hear what you've been through or what you've done" (Fawn).

Linking to the police reform movement

During our entire project, the NYC police reform movement came together powerfully as a large collective known as the Communities United for Police Reform (CPR), ultimately authoring language incorporated into the reform legislation that was passed, organising grassroots activism and supporting several landmark class action lawsuits (in fact, two of us were co-plaintiffs in one of these high-profile cases). The Morris Justice Project participated with this movement in multiple ways. We were invited to speak about our findings at local town halls, rallies, block parties and academic conferences as well as through various media outlets (such as journalists, documentary shorts, television). These events provided opportunities to speak with mayoral candidates, city council members, other local politicians and, ultimately, the newly appointed police commissioner. With our data-driven signs, banners, t-shirts and buttons, we sat in on the trials and attended important votes, rallies and press conferences. One City Council member – the co-sponsor of the police reform legislation – grabbed our sign with a quote from our qualitative data – "It's not a crime to be who you are" – and later folded the language into his speeches and blog. The project also developed an active social media campaign that included twitter, tumblr, video data shorts and a daily blog from inside the courtroom. In addition, we contributed to an Amicus Brief submitted by CPR. Our activist work continues however, each of these actions wove strands of our data into the citywide debates that were challenging existing policing policies.

Reflecting back but moving forward ...

'For me it has been really interesting seeing how this project has been part of the police reform movement. The NYPD has acted like a gang in many ways – ruling through intimidation and above the law. So it's been interesting to see how things have begun to change over the course of a few years, in large part because of the advocacy and activism that has grown and developed and strengthened. This is one of the areas of policy that I think has changed the most in this city in terms of urgent social justice issues. So it has been really interesting and exciting to be part of. Especially because the data and the experiences of this project have helped the coalition directly: The people directly affected by the problem have done this research – a really different way of doing research. When you ask us, you're not just asking one person, you are asking a group that has systematically asked 1000 of their neighbours. This is a great example how research can be involved with a social movement in a really strong way.' (Hillary)

Though we are cautious, we have noticed changes in our neighbourhood and citywide.

'There are less than 200,000 stops now from the peak of nearly 700,000 when we started this project. We have a new commissioner and new mayor who were elected on a police reform platform. While things might change, many things remain. The underlining policies of broken windows and order maintenance policing continue, maybe even more emphatically with our new commissioner. But we now have some legal and legislative wins, and there is a new inspector general to oversee the NYPD. And public opinion has changed quite a bit too.' (Brett)

"When we were surveying, some people questioned us: 'Why are you doing this? How is this going to do anything?' Then when we did the sidewalk science people recognised us: 'Oh you guys were the ones giving out the survey.' And they were like, 'Oh, you're still here?'" (Prakriti). *We're still here.* We know public policy reform does not happen overnight, *but for it to be meaningful it must come from the ground up and through participation.* And as the story of the Morris Justice Project shows, community-based critical participatory action research has a crucial role to play.

This contribution reads like a classic David and Goliath tale, pitting a loose network of people from different backgrounds against the might of the NYPD, city council, police commissioner, mayor and other elite power holders. MJP was the group without formal power and therefore without guaranteed or easy access to resources for policy analysis and evaluation. Several charitable foundations supported the work, and the group received other in-kind support such as free venues. Even from the very abbreviated description of the process, it can be understood that this was an intensive and lengthy process for the core members, with extensive investment of time and voluntary energies. Many people have acknowledged that doing policy differently places demands on citizens' resources. However, the authors frame the lessons of their work in terms of their sources of power and resources, not their lack. So, in place of the usual message of 'involving the public is costly and lengthy', this contribution highlights the assets they gathered together. It demonstrates the mobilisation and effective use of the assets of the participants, including their various personal motivations, professional research skills, local knowledge and neighbourhood roots, links to wider political and lobbying movements, as well as access to philanthropic and research monies. Outside of the discussions raised by the authors, it is not clear whether co-produced knowledge and policy is more resource-intensive than conventional processes, or whether the costs are simply more visible. Resources for conventional policy analysis are often not transparent and therefore hard to quantify. It is not unusual for policy development to see 20 drafts of a document be circulated among over a dozen people in an organisation, or to commission a survey of 1000 respondents.

In some ways, there is no need to go beyond the mainstream policy literature to understand the Morris Justice Project. Some aspects of this process look familiar to conventional policy making, including the emphasis on the value of high quality data and research. The group used a blend of policy analysis and evaluation across all phases of the policy-making process. They were simultaneously evaluating an existing policy, while setting out alternatives, and attempting to set a different agenda by redefining the policy problem. MJP joined the wider city movement, Communities United for Police Reform, in a policy coalition for change. The lobby group network then attempted to mobilise a shift in public attention to the issue of stop and frisk, in order to change policy priorities.

In other ways, MJP represents a stark contrast to conventional ways of doing policy. It is like what might happen in the City Hall, but with the roof blown off. Community anger in the South Bronx had been generated by a default setting underlying NYPD policing policies, which was a pathological view of people living in the area, particularly younger minority ethnic men, as potentially liable to commit crime. Fundamental to their research was to reproblematise the issue from one of 'high crime neighbourhoods'. The group advocated for respecting the neighbourhood in all its complexity and seeing its residents as part of the solution instead of as the problem.

It is an innovative and politically radical piece of co-designed public science. MJP has an explicit aim of opening up social science, as articulated by one participant: "We believe in the justice possibilities of 'public science'; of democratising social science so that everyday people can engage their right to research" (María). As well as democratising social science, they also tried to bring more science and expertise from evidence into the democratic process. As one participant described it, there was some initial scepticism that research could make a difference which was overcome as the Project showed the power of the data combined with other forms of expertise. A staggering number of surveys were completed. The opening up of the research process meant that those involved could build on their personal experiences with additional evidence and intelligence. Participants' personal experience and expertise was used to build theory and shape what questions were tested in the research. MJP's version of public science with its lively 'stats-n-action' approaches is a world away from rarefied methodological terminology, but did not sacrifice methodological rigour. The contribution communicates how doing research was empowering and liberating. For example, the participants give joyful descriptions of the moment that the data started to reveal patterns, and they felt sufficiently in command of data to challenge other organisations' analysis, or 'manipulation', of it.

Finally, this contribution is a salutary tale of where a full co-productive policy process may simply not be possible in some circumstances. Co-productive policy approaches need a sympathetic grammar, and if formal power holders are firmly in constituted mode, then alternatives may need this to change before they are possible. The campaign for policy reform in NYC was confronted by resistance from decision makers, and as a consequence, had to use a combination of lobbying and mobilisation tools to try and create change, including legal challenges. It echoes other contributions in this book which set out deep power struggles where more confrontational approaches are needed, alongside an aspiration to be fully co-productive.

Grammar in co-productive policy design

Using technology
to help communities shout louder

Phil Jones, Colin Lorne and Chris Speed

This contribution from an interdisciplinary team of academics offers an attempt to support communities in 'shouting a little louder' within policy making. It models its own aspiration in reflecting the importance of bringing together different forms of expertise: in planning, interface design, engaging communities. The contribution focuses on the development of an app, MapLocal, which aims to draw in the local knowledge of people who may not usually get involved in neighbourhood planning. The app provides a tool for mapping community assets and contributing to planning by tapping into the fine-grained understanding of a place, which comes from living there, but also providing a way of generating and harnessing community creativity and imagination. MapLocal is an example of the potential of such spatial and visualisation tools to shift the parameters, power and potentialities of policy by enhancing the engagement and interaction of communities for local problem solving.

The UK's coalition government, which came to power in 2010, took a flamethrower to the English planning system. Superficially, the Localism Act, 2011 offers a major transfer of power to communities: you can write a legally binding Neighbourhood Plan and bid to buy community assets or to run community services. The rhetoric is that this enables communities to co-produce their neighbourhoods and shape their own local planning destiny. Looking at the detail of the Act, however, co-production only seems to go so far. Communities can suggest which areas of their neighbourhood should be a priority for development and the kinds of things they would like to see built, but these suggestions have to be in compliance with local and national planning guidance. If they are not, then they cannot be included in a Neighbourhood Plan. Similarly, and perhaps more significantly, communities cannot *prohibit* types of development in their area. Planning that restricts tall buildings, McMansions, chain coffee shops and so on is simply not possible within the new legal framework. Economic growth is everything and planning is not permitted to act as a 'constraint' on this.

Neighbourhood Planning as conceived by the Localism Act, then, allows for co-production of planning so long as communities are happy to co-produce the things that policy makers want. More so, Neighbourhood Plans are profoundly technical, legal documents and thus communities need to muster the expertise and resource to translate aspiration into a formal plan. In the face of swingeing cuts, local authorities are broadly unable to help communities with this job of translation; central government funding meanwhile was restricted to a relatively small number of 'Pathfinder' Neighbourhood Plans. Given the shortage of public funding, if you do not already have the necessary money and expertise within your community you are extremely unlikely to be able to put a Plan together. By the end of 2013, only around 40% of Birmingham's 1.1 million residents lived in an area that had established a Neighbourhood Forum – the local bodies given the power to draw up Neighbourhood Plans. Few of these Forums are actively working on a Plan and to date no Neighbourhood Plans have been approved within the city.

Rather than being frustrated by how the game of co-production seems to be rigged in favour of already well-resourced communities, we chose to think about ways to help communities realise the potential for co-production embedded in the rhetoric of localism. Our approach starts from the position that the people who live in an area have significant expertise, even if that expertise is not necessarily recognised in formal policy-making processes. At a basic level, this can simply be a fine-grained knowledge about problems in the area – the streets that are prone to being used as rat-runs, the parks used by local drug dealers, the empty properties kept in poor repair by their owners. Beyond this, however, suggestions can be made for changes to the area based on this detailed local knowledge – converting an old pub to a new use, turning a long abandoned site into a development opportunity, getting a local artist involved in improving the look of an area and so on.

Gathering this kind of material can, of course, take place in town hall meetings. These can be intimidating for those not used to public speaking, be held at inconvenient times and often require a degree of spatial literacy for discussion around maps and plans. They also take place at one remove from the sites under discussion – being *in* a place prompts people to talk about it more than they might in a meeting room. Even before the Localism Act, Phil had been talking to urban design charity MADE about the possibilities of using mobile technology to help communities take some control over the planning of their neighbourhoods, while Chris has experience in interface design and engaging communities with technology. Together we received funding to produce and pilot a smartphone app to draw together the expertise of community members who might not otherwise get involved with local planning.

We consulted with Chamberlain Forum (a self-styled 'think and do tank' in Birmingham) about the kind of features that should be included in the app. This discussion was followed by discussions with an app developer about what we could practically deliver given our timescale and budget. Phil's recurring refrain was that the app should be simple, intuitive and have 'big, granny-friendly buttons'. It would also be based around a map, so that people could gather spatially located information of the kind necessary when speaking the language of formal planning.

We settled on three core functions:

1. taking photographs, giving them a numerical ranking and the ability to add text-based comments;
2. recording audio clips;
3. marking boundaries by walking around them.

The idea was that you could simply walk around your neighbourhood and use the app to share your understanding of how the area works. Chris put an elegant interface design together and commissioned a former student to write the code for an Android-based app we called 'MapLocal'. Working intermittently, initial design and testing took about six months. Photos, audio clips and boundary marks recorded by users are tagged with GPS coordinates and uploaded to a website hosting the community map.

All of this, however, was designed to happen automatically in the background – from a user point of view you simply walk around your neighbourhood taking photos and occasionally talking into the phone. Simplicity was key.

As a pilot scheme we needed people to try out the app and give us feedback on how it worked. Antonia Layard, one of our co-investigators, pointed out that a lot of the rhetoric around co-production comes with an implicit assumption that people should volunteer their time for free. But this did not feel particularly in the spirit of co-production, particularly when working in more deprived communities. Given that we were asking people to do a piece of work for us in testing a newly developed app, we felt it was important to pay our participants (£100 each) to trial the app and give us feedback – an important symbol of how vital their contribution was to the project.

Colin was hired to recruit participants, undertake training sessions and gather feedback about the experience of using the app. Cheap Android phones were then loaned out to participants. The revolution kicked off by the launch of the iPhone in 2007 has meant that carrying a smartphone has been normalised even in more deprived neighbourhoods. Five years earlier there would have been considerable health and safety concerns about asking people to walk around openly carrying small, powerful personal computers. By 2012, our participants looked unremarkable, chatting into phones and taking photos. A range of recruits, teenagers to septuagenarians from different backgrounds took part, all of whom were very quickly able to get to grips with the app and begin collecting material about their neighbourhood. As an example, Colin's field diary records an instance during a training session where Sanjeer started teaching his friend Abdul how to use the app, despite only having learned it himself moments earlier.

We picked two sites in Birmingham: Balsall Heath, a fairly deprived area which had received central government Pathfinder funds to begin developing its Neighbourhood Plan; and the Jewellery Quarter, primarily a district of small businesses which had not started work on its Plan. Across eight weeks, the 50 participants produced over 1000 photographs, 626 audio clips and 182 boundary marks. The kinds of material generated tell a story about the appetite for sharing local knowledge and ideas. Audio clips accompanying photographs give insights into local histories, suggestions for new facilities, opinions about the problems facing the area and how they might be tackled. Some ideas were fanciful, others less than PC (politically correct), but the majority were thoughtful and grounded in an intimate knowledge and engagement with the spaces of the neighbourhood.

Balsall Heath faces a number of challenges, primarily relating to economic deprivation and rapid population turnover. It is all too easy to dismiss such neighbourhoods as 'failed'. Indeed, prior to 2008 the model for regenerating this kind of area would be large-scale demolitions and rebuilding to the tastes and aspirations of middle class gentrifiers.

> 'it's just an eye-sore at the moment and it's serving no purpose to the community. So it was once a well-used sports centre and astro-turf and a lot of the local residents are worried about what will be built here eventually.' (audio clip, Balsall Heath)

The quote represents a well-founded concern that the people who live in this kind of area tend to have developments imposed on them that are designed to suit the needs of outsiders. Of course, there is a tension between the kinds of developments that would be valuable to residents

– a new health centre, reopened train station and affordable housing were all mentioned – and the kinds of developments that would attract private sector funding. We do not propose that a smartphone app can reconcile these tensions, but it does enable community voices to shout a little louder about the specifics of their neighbourhoods to make it clear that tensions between community and developer agendas *do* exist.

The Jewellery Quarter is primarily a business district with a small, largely white, residential population and thus faces different kinds of challenges. Within the neighbourhood there is a rich legacy of historic industrial buildings that present many opportunities for redevelopment:

> 'Nice little building, empty, no-one seems to want it, loads of homeless people. Okay it's burned out inside but how little would it take to do up and turn into some cheap, liveable accommodation and get some people off the streets. 1916 on the building, not even 100 years old. This is what needs sorting.' (audio clip, Jewellery Quarter)

A hostel for homeless people can be seen as a socially responsible use of a derelict building, although it would not necessarily be something that everyone living and working in the Jewellery Quarter would want, even if the money could be found. This example highlights a critical point in any co-produced approach to neighbourhood redevelopment – attempting to reconcile different needs and desires of individuals living there. Some people do not like what new supermarkets do to local retail, others are desperately glad when they open because of the convenience they bring. Some might be wryly amused by the presence of a massage parlour while others are offended and upset. There simply is no single community voice with a clear agenda for taking forward development in a neighbourhood.

The vast quantity of data generated by MapLocal in just eight weeks highlighted a significant problem with the project. We had deliberately been very conservative with what we sought to achieve on a small pilot: the app was designed to allow people to collect information and opinions, but offered no help with how to analyse these. The danger with this kind of approach is that you turn residents into surveillance drones merely collecting information for more powerful people who then make the decisions – Goodchild (2007) uses the phrase 'citizens as sensors'. In some ways, however, a bigger danger with something like MapLocal is that, faced with a mass of unfiltered and contradictory material about an area, decision makers simply ignore it.

One solution is to provide a means for users of the app to rank the relative importance of different issues that they are concerned about. Such a process would allow hotspots to emerge on the community map where multiple users have highlighted priority issues. Of course, this relies on people's willingness to give a ranking to the materials they and others have gathered – another demand on busy people. Nonetheless, such a facility would start to shift MapLocal from being a mere information gathering tool, to one that helps people make sense of that information.

For this project to operate on principles of co-construction, we needed to draw participants into the process of designing the functionality of the app. Based on feedback as part of focus groups held at the end of the pilot, we significantly improved the web-based interface for viewing the shared community map. Unfortunately, we did not have sufficient remaining budget to develop a revised version, which would add a system for ranking priorities for action, which was a key suggestion from one of the focus groups. We were, however, able to fix the many bugs participants had identified and make the app available for free download via the Google Play store.

A key issue that emerged from the focus groups, however, was a reminder that the expert knowledge of communities can be just as fallible as other forms of expert knowledge. An example of this is the discussion of a pub that had closed down in Balsall Heath. One participant suggested it closed because the neighbourhood is in transition; as white and African-Caribbean populations move out and Muslim residents move in, so a pub business is less viable. When presented with this version of events, however, a local councillor present at a focus group noted that the owner of the pub had refused to pay protection money to a local gang and had chosen to simply close the business instead. This story illustrates the importance of triangulating different kinds of expert knowledge – community, police, policy makers, health professionals and so on – in order to make informed decisions about taking a neighbourhood forward.

Localism seems to offer community empowerment and co-construction of neighbourhoods, but in an age of drastic cuts to public funding the reality appears to be very different. The MapLocal app is no cure for the ravages of austerity, but it suggests ways in which new technologies can be used to help communities find ways of more directly influencing the future planning of their neighbourhoods. Fundamentally, such technologies can amplify community voices in discussions where they are all too easily drowned out by more powerful stakeholders.

The authors repeat the important, if obvious, point that initiatives such as MapLocal do not take place in a vacuum. Rather, they are set against a policy background, in this case the reform of neighbourhood planning set out in the Localism Act 2011. Sharing a critique made in the opening chapters, policy making – here, specifically neighbourhood planning – has been problematic when detached from the lived experience and priorities of those affected by such decisions. As was seen in the vignettes from New Mexico and York, rhetoric of community empowerment through localism is set against the realities of local dilemmas about economic development and growth versus growth which includes local communities. These different, potentially conflicting agendas serve to illustrate the political dimensions of even the most seemingly legal and technical areas of local policy making.

The authors point out how opening up neighbourhood planning policy is done in a 'substitutive' way, rather than with professionals working with communities in an 'additive', synergistic way. This leaves communities to navigate the technical and legal demands of planning alone. It further denies access to neighbourhood planning and shaping the future of the places to all but those communities with access to particular resources. By doing so, the reform of neighbourhood planning serves to reinforce and perpetuate social inequities as well as hierarchies of expertise, rather than challenging them. But the example of MapLocal demonstrates the possibilities of making an intervention into implementation, in a way that offers a different rationality and purpose. In short, while features of conventional closed and complete designs may be rigged against a more co-productive way of doing things, technology can provide a way of giving people voice.

The piloting of MapLocal demonstrates that technology can challenge some of these inequities: opening up neighbourhood planning to people who may not usually get involved or have a voice in policy decisions which affect their everyday lives. In particular, enabling participants to be in a place, not removed or abstracted from it, generates conversation and exchange. MapLocal also challenges the assumption often made, that such technological fixes are only for particular demographics – the young with the resources and know-how to use them – by showing that by providing access and training, they can be open to far wider parts of the community, tapping into a latent appetite to share local knowledge. While an app may be initially perceived as offering an individual form of co-production, the potential for peer-to-peer interaction and collective action should not be dismissed.

While tools like MapLocal offer a way to tap into and value the experiential and local forms of knowledge which are often marginalised and ignored in policy making, the authors make the point that although the inclusion of the significant expertise held by citizens is necessary, on its own it is insufficient. Rather, it should be 'triangulated' with other forms of knowledge, in this case legal and technocratic expertise. By doing so, creative possibilities and ways of doing things differently may open up. Geo-ICT apps provide a different kind of 'boundary space' with the potential to renegotiate power, by offering voice, transparency and accountability (Kurniawan and de Vries, 2015).

Although parts of the app work well – its simplicity and accessibility and the core functions of taking photos, recording audio clips, adding text and marking boundaries on a neighbourhood map – MapLocal is an incomplete design. Two significant challenges remain: first how to draw participants into the design of the app. This challenge reminds us that MapLocal is a tool, not a panacea. The issues of how to motivate citizens while meeting their different demands and priorities, and how to recognise and value the homogeneity of citizen voices, are not resolved. But MapLocal's incompleteness at least offers the possibility for co-construction of its future development. The second challenge is how to filter, order and marshal the material which the app helps to generate. Resonating with other contributions, the authors' critical reflection on their own work illustrates that providing a way of generating and giving voice to different forms of knowledge is not enough to shift how policy is made. This knowledge may be ignored or indeed manipulated. So how this knowledge is marshalled and directed is of crucial importance. Apps such as MapLocal are insufficient on their own, but making such technological tools easy to use and widely available may be an important part of imagining a co-productive alternative to policy making and analysis.

Generating community conversations

Amina Lone and Dan Silver

This contribution is set against the backdrop of the summer 2011 riots in England in two Northern cities, Manchester and Salford. Challenging a policy discourse that centred on the criminality of the participants, the authors trace efforts to shift the parameters of the policy conversation towards a less deficit-orientated view of citizens.

The wide-reaching impact of the riots created demands for the policy agenda to be informed by the views and priorities of a number of different groups, not only politicians, policy makers, the media and those in public institutions, such as the police, but also by voluntary and community groups, residents and rioters themselves. Through a series of community conversations bringing these different groups together, broader 'wicked' cross-cutting social concerns which situate the rioting came to light: not only mistrust and anger at the police, but also poverty and inequality and a wider sense of social exclusion. From these conversations, a different and more complex policy agenda emerged. The example of the response to the riots shows the potential of an event to disrupt policy making as usual.

The August 2011 riots in Manchester and Salford saw street violence that was directed against the police, as well as the looting and destruction of shops within the two cities. Manchester appeared to be more targeted at disrupting the city centre and looting from shops, while Salford was widely seen as a demonstration of anger against the police.

These events brought to the surface deep-seated and complex issues in our society that demanded in-depth analysis to understand why people riot. However, in the backdrop of burning buildings and severe violence, the immediate government response to the riots was that they were the demonstration of 'criminality pure and simple'. This analysis informed the policy agenda that emerged following the riots, one which was consistent with the 'Broken Britain' narrative – that society was breaking down due to a lack of morals. This agenda was chiefly targeted on the poorest communities, but rarely involving people from those communities in discussions about the policies that impact directly on them.

The Social Action & Research Foundation (SARF) believes that communities have capabilities, knowledge and experience that must be more valued within the policy process. To seek to understand the riots is not to condone the actions of those involved. The impact of the riots was felt at all levels in our community, and so reflection on the causes and potential solutions not only provided, but necessitated, the forging of links in order to engage a wide range of people in a debate about complex social policy issues.

As part of the *Guardian* and London School of Economics' *Reading the Riots* project, we interviewed people in Manchester and Salford who had directly participated in the riots. This research involved finding people to speak to who were involved in the riots, but were not caught. We relied largely on trusted community networks to gain access. This research provided insights into what motivated some people to be involved, which included antipathy towards the police – driven by consistent criminalisation through the disproportionate use of Stop and Search, perceived inequality within society and a lack of hope for the future. There were also people who wanted to riot because it was an exciting thing to do as well as those who were 'swept up' within the momentum of the disturbances. Interviewing people who had rioted provided perspectives that had been neglected. But we felt that there was further knowledge from within communities that was being excluded from policy discussions. We felt that the policy agenda was being set by people who had little connection to the communities that had been affected. With the media and government agenda being largely set in London, we felt that there was not enough recognition of the different characteristics and challenges presented by what went on in the North.

SARF hosted the Manchester and Salford *Reading the Riots* Community Conversations. The conversations aimed to explore the deeper social issues that the riots have revealed and to develop some new thinking that might tackle them. They brought together policy makers, representatives of voluntary and community sector organisations, the police, the media and local residents to explore the responses to the riots and provide an opportunity to reflect on the policy responses in a way that neither city had really done. Importantly, they were designed to provide a platform for communities to voice their challenge to the dominant narrative and give voice to those whose communities had been directly affected and whose perspective had been sorely missing.

The conversations provided the opportunity to begin to hear perspectives that have been neglected in the mainstream debates about the riots and provided a starting point to work towards changing the frame of debate beyond the narrow confines of the 'criminality pure and simple' explanation. This alternative framing of the causes of the riots was necessary in order to set the agenda for a more fundamentally social response to the riots. As the government response was largely centred on a punitive reaction against criminals, the policies that followed were of a similar nature. Therefore, before policy responses could be influenced, it was important to change the nature of debate. The Community Conversations were intended to bring community experience and knowledge to the fore. But we felt that it was vital to include decision makers within the Community Conversations. Also, to co-produce policy, it is important to work with the statutory sector, not only because they have the power to make changes, but often because they are committed to the communities they serve and are keen to learn more on how they could achieve more successful results.

The Community Conversations were in essence public meetings, with a panel made up of representatives from the police, politicians and the local community who were invited to speak at the beginning of the conversation and then an open question and answer session. People were invited to attend through our networks and people also turned up on the night who had heard about the conversation through word of mouth. In order to scene-set the local policy response, representatives were invited to speak one by one, to share their views and begin to stimulate a wider debate. These were people SARF had worked with before and knew were well-connected to some of the communities that were directly involved in or affected by the riots. We did invite private sector businesses onto the panel, but the businesses we contacted were reluctant to participate in the debate for many reasons, one being that they wanted to put the riots behind them.

Over 250 participants attended the two Community Conversations in total, with more attending the one in Salford. Participants included residents, voluntary and community sector (VCS) organisations, academics, politicians and statutory agencies. To recruit people to the Community Conversations we used existing community networks, local media and word of mouth. There was considerable appetite from many people to discuss the riots, as it was a conversation which many felt had not really taken place.

The Manchester Community Conversation was based in the city centre near where the riots happened. The panel included representatives from the police, the city council, youth and criminal justice organisations. This diverse panel shared their thoughts on the riots from different perspectives and stimulated a wider discussion from the participants, who were more widely drawn from voluntary and community organisations and the general public. The discussions were robust and many people voiced their concerns about the way the police dealt with the riots and the way young people were potentially being demonised as a consequence. The challenge of re-engaging disillusioned young people was one consistent theme throughout the Manchester Community Conversation, with participants often debating the extent of alienation, its causes, both real and imagined, and the differing effectiveness of official and community attempts to change it.

The Salford Community Conversation was based at St Sebastian's Community Centre, in a neighbourhood of the city that has high levels of socioeconomic deprivation and is close to where the riots took place. The riots in Salford were different in character to the events in Manchester and there was a more explicit antipolice agenda. The panel was made up of the police and city council, along with local community groups. Unlike the discussion in Manchester, the *Guardian* was asked not to film the discussions, and even before the event, it was anticipated that it would be livelier.

There were community participants who had strong views on some of the reasons for the riots and the subsequent response. Participants were drawn more from the local community, many of whom had examples and longstanding grievances against the police and the council. At the event, there were police officers patrolling outside in case there was any unrest as a fatal shooting had taken place just before and the police were cautious on possible tensions spilling over. Strong chairing of discussions was required as many people were keen to talk for extended periods and passions were quite high. Martin Wainwright, who covered the debates for the *Guardian Northerner*, noted the 'very large audience's enthusiasm for a practical debate which would further the process of sorting out problems, causes and grievances' (Wainwright, 2012).

Relations with the police were a major element of discussion. The police recognised that 'previous good relations between local officers and young people had deteriorated and disappeared'. Several participants agreed with this analysis, and provided examples of alleged police heavy-handedness. But a different police perspective contested this view, asserting that organised crime took advantage of the trouble and made it worse. It was suggested that improved detection rates and a steady fall in crime in the last four years in Salford may have fuelled professional criminals' desire to hit back and stated that public support for the police had risen after the riots. This argument caused much disagreement and provoked debate with many people unable to agree on the policing tactics and the motivations or causes of the riots locally.

The Community Conversations framed particular policy agendas that participants felt had been neglected following the post-riots discussions by politicians and the media. However, with the relatively short timescales of the Community Conversations and with such a large number of participants, developing solid and locally focused policy recommendations based on a consensus simply from the Community Conversations was not possible. What clearly emerged from the Community Conversations was that the riots were not caused by criminality pure and simple. There were complex causes which demanded complex solutions. It was clear that certain policy areas required more thinking and a need to engage communities more effectively.

Guided by the issues that were raised through the Community Conversations, we met with communities, practitioners, academics, politicians and decision makers in Salford and Manchester in order to gain critical insights and develop our learning to be able to make policy recommendations that were rooted in practice and build on the knowledge that exists within the community. SARF went to speak more in depth with communities and public sector workers to follow up on the issues that had been brought up, to be able to shape an alternative agenda and provide more solid recommendations.

These Community Conversations showed a more radical approach to agenda setting. By having discussion on existing policy and hearing alternative perspectives, it is possible to change the framework of possible explanations, and in the process begin to shape the agenda in a more community-rooted direction. One participant at the Manchester event noted that these were the sort of debates that the city required, but which had been sadly lacking after the riots. By providing the space for community perspectives to be put forward, we were able to change discussions that had been taking place in the city, and begin to build wider agreement on some of the issues that needed to be addressed

Following the Community Conversations in setting the agenda, we identified five major policy areas:

- Family interventions: it was felt that 'bad parenting' had been blamed and that a more positive approach to supporting parents was required, which built on the strengths of parents and did not stigmatise people who were trying their best.

- The potential of restorative justice: there was general agreement that sentencing was disproportionately harsh, while at the same time recognising that people who had rioted needed to take some responsibility. This discussion opened up the path towards looking at alternative responses, such as restorative justice.
- Providing more opportunities for young people: The lack of opportunities for young people came up frequently. It was clear that a more positive approach to working with young people, which created a greater stake for them in society, was necessary.
- Policing: relationships with the police were clearly a major issue, from individual police–community relations to strategic decisions.
- Policy making: the Community Conversations opened up the space for more democratic debates in Manchester and Salford and there was desire to provide more possibilities to be able to do this.

SARF sought the collaboration of professionals and communities in developing these ideas further, and collected it all in a report entitled 'A Tale of Two Cities'. This was launched in July 2012, with political leaders, police, community members and participants from the voluntary and community sector. Professor Tim Newburn, who led the LSE research, wrote in the introduction that the Community Conversations illustrated:

> the importance of local ownership of the core policy responses to such significant social issues. All too often 'solutions' are imposed by outsiders and however well-intentioned such interventions may be, they are almost inevitably destined to fail. It is precisely the local focus and practically-oriented concern of this report that make it so valuable. (SARF, 2012, p. 3)

We also involved the local and national press in this with a clear message: the causes of the riots were not criminality pure and simple; they were more complex and the policy agenda needed to adapt to be able to provide the responses that were required. This argument has had an impact on changing the framework of the debate to encourage the public to consider responses beyond the immediate government version. In terms of policy, several recommendations have been put into action, such as a review of 'Stop and Search', more focus on literacy and numeracy in primary schools, and tackling youth unemployment. It would be ridiculous to claim that these changes have emerged as a result of the Community Conversations, but it would be fair to say that the conversations helped to contribute to a deeper public debate.

By holding Community Conversations, we widened out the debate and importantly brought the community into agenda setting – something that many had felt excluded from following the riots. As a result of this, we were able to develop a deeper understanding of what had happened, and why – and crucially set the tone and direction for more detailed policy work to be developed.

This contribution focuses on efforts to challenge, influence and reappropriate the policy response to an unexpected event, namely the advent of riots in two of the North of England's major cities. The conventional policy response to the riots – that they were a demonstration of criminality – fitted within a broader policy discourse of moral breakdown and informed a policy response focusing on retribution and punishment of those involved. Different interpretations and perspectives were excluded and pushed out. Bringing the public in helps to illuminate the ways that conventional policy discourses serve to reinforce social pathologies.

What started as an effort to understand the motivations of those who were rioting but also the socioeconomic context and implications of the riots developed into formulation and articulation of an alternative set of policy priorities. By engaging with those involved and those directly affected, the conventional policy response was revealed to be disconnected from the lived experience of those local communities where the rioting took place. While the need for individual responsibility is clear, and without condoning the action of those involved, local communities articulated how the rioting needed to be interpreted through a lens that recognises structural inequalities and violence.

Echoing other contributions in this book, SARF – like the Resource Centre for Raza Planning and the Morris Justice Project – start from a position of principle: that the experiences of local communities should be reflected and valued within the public policy process. But – again reflecting other contributions, for example in the development of MapLocal – that taking such asset-based perspectives on communities is necessary in order to address the scale and complexity of some policy challenges. As such, SARF's approach was to try and bring communities together with different expertise from the media, the police and local councillors.

It is important to point out that even – and indeed, perhaps because – the riots were such a high-profile concern, that there was appetite on both sides to have this conversation. As with Katy Wilkinson's depiction of crisis in central government, a jolting event, such as a riot, can present a moment of dislocation which disrupts the usual way of doing things, opening up the possibilities of mutual learning and the forging of alternative ways of doing. One of the challenges that emerge is how to consolidate and sustain these new relationships once the crisis has passed.

By taking time to build trust and relationships locally, SARF – along with other community and voluntary organisations – are able to act as intermediaries, working with and in the spaces between different stakeholders in the conversation. They are able to bring these different groups together by drawing on their local knowledge and trusted local networks, acting entrepreneurially but also informed by a sense of how they would like society to be: offering a vision. The community conversations were convened as public meetings. They demonstrate that bringing different parts of the community together does not always demand innovation, but simply that such meetings are actively promoted as open and welcoming, efforts are made to mobilise and engage different stakeholders and they are skilfully chaired.

The conversations demonstrate how the active – and vocal – contributions of local communities on an issue of real significance are desirable. Also, that without these contributions there is a very real risk of misinterpreting and misrepresenting the underlying causes, but also the priorities and aspirations of local communities. Bringing the public into policy debates may not produce 'quick fixes' or easy answers. Indeed, they can introduce greater complexity; but doing so does have the potential to shift the parameters of a policy conversation, generating solutions that are informed by the local communities and that local communities can contribute to delivering. What is also important to note, however, is that the co-productive grounding of this policy debate does not ensure its reach or influence within the conventional policy process.

Policy design as co-design

Michaela Howell and Margaret Wilkinson

Drawing on an innovative co-design process, facilitated by the contributors, this vignette explores how practitioners have tried to make concrete the theory of co-design. The example highlights the deep challenges this presented to traditional ways of working and thinking. It concludes that a 'leap of faith' is sometimes needed for practitioners to see the benefits of unusual co-design processes. The illustrative example is of an attempt to redesign public services in one neighbourhood in Bradford, West Yorkshire, in the north of England. The neighbourhood is known by its postcode – BD5 – and is a place, and set of people, that had already undergone many attempts at urban renewal and regeneration. As with other stories presented in this book – in Deptford and in Birmingham for example – previous government-funded regeneration programmes had brought some improvements to the area, but not enough and not as transformatory as was needed. This contribution relates the details of a process used to bring in new thinking to longstanding issues facing local people and organisations.

A case has been presented for 'incomplete design' as a positive feature of alternative policy-making approaches. By presenting a rich and honest picture of the work done, this contribution allows us to glimpse some of the flavour of what incomplete design felt like for those participating in it. These designs lack the security of certainty, or at least old certainties. This example shows us that introducing new approaches is not easy, and may initially feel uncomfortable for participants, and needs facilitators to manage these feelings. The challenge it presents is to be comfortable with uncomfortableness. Fundamentally, it reminds us that creating change in policy and policy processes is often really hard. It offers a methodology to produce better policy outcomes in a more effective and inclusive way. This illustration is of some accessible facilitation tools, which are transformatory in making principles real. At its core, it advocates for reconnecting with citizens' lived experience in policy.

Context

In many areas there is a neighbourhood similar to BD5; loved by its residents, with people who want to make a difference, a vibrant multi-ethnic mix, and all the potential that comes from being close to the city centre. It is also a neighbourhood where there has been a series of government-funded renewal initiatives and regeneration programmes which created many improvements, but not enough. Bradford Trident is a community-owned and run social enterprise which grew out of one of the regeneration programmes. It has chosen to try to play a wider role in addition to providing services, and uses its assets and resources to bring local residents and agencies together to coordinate activities.

The drive for co-design originally emerged out of Trident's work under a government pilot programme (Neighbourhood Community Budgeting NCB – also described in Robert Rutherfoord and Lucy Spurling's contribution) which enabled Trident to focus on the local provision of employment, enterprise and skills services. This was seen as a window of opportunity to improve the involvement of residents in discussing responses to local priorities, in the knowledge that there was still an appetite for change and a determination to improve provision from both residents and local service providers working on the ground. This was an opportunity to use Trident's relationships with residents and providers to do things differently.

Our journey

Based on data about higher than average levels of unemployment and economic inactivity in BD5, Trident initially identified employment, enterprise and skills as a priority. It then established a Community of Practice – an informal network of practitioners providing services related to employment, enterprise and skills. All organisations providing support in the area, whether local or national, and across public, private and voluntary sectors, were invited to join; to better coordinate service delivery; to share ideas and practice; to work together to improve what is on offer. The group identified a series of priorities from their own knowledge of local issues, and from feedback they had received from residents. But they found it difficult to agree practical solutions that could be easily tested. This was in part due to practitioners being focused on the difficult funding climate, the need to deliver 'core business' and ensure their organisation survives, the expectation that national players should take the lead in responding to changing local needs, and the eventual realisation that there were difficulties to this happening.

Trident commissioned the Planning for Real Unit to organise a community consultation, which was coordinated by one of the contributors of this piece. A Planning for Real community consultation process uses visual and other accessible methods to consult local residents, and was vital in involving local residents in identifying their specific needs and gathering their suggestions and comments. Lots of data was gathered which provided the Community of Practice with current information and included understanding what was already known; how budgets and resources could be better used to meet local needs; who the consultation needed to reach; and the best opportunities for engaging local residents of all ages and backgrounds. There was a programme of community engagement events, both open sessions and targeted events, held in different accessible venues and outdoor locations across the area. This delivery combination resulted in approximately 300 local residents participating, representing a good spread across gender, age and ethnicity. Out of the themes consulted on, Employment, Enterprise and Skills generated the highest number of individual responses, identifying this as a priority for residents, which was in line with the other data, and therefore gave a strong steer and grounding for the focus for the next stage, the co-design activity.

Co-design was deliberately structured to make sure that different forms of expertise were incorporated: leadership and leaders' vision for the area; direct experiences of residents who had used, or not used services to help them with work, education or training, as well as the direct experiences of the services themselves; and data on things like levels of economic inactivity, family size, as well as residents' views from the consultation. Vision was developed by a group of local civic leaders who were brought together by Trident. The group included elected local community councillors (from an 'urban parish council'), heads of local public services, senior managers from the local council, and others. This civic leaders' group developed the vision for the co-design work by being encouraged to think differently through taking part in creative, participative exercises, facilitated by one of the authors of this contribution. For example, one exercise was to get the civic leaders to reconnect and relate their own personal experiences to those of local people. They were asked to first think about the sorts of experiences their organisation was trying to help local people have – not what services were provided (job training), or the outputs (completing a CV), but things like being able to ask for help when nervous or scared, having the confidence to do something new for the first time, resolving a conflict, opening people's eyes to misconceptions, learning to trust someone/something, getting answers from someone in charge or righting a wrong. They were then asked to 'think of a time' when they had had this experience themselves, ideally outside of their normal working environments. The group then discussed who was involved? Where was it? How did it happen? Following this, the themes for the co-design work from the civic leaders were: positive community networks; self-reliance; and collective problem solving. This exercise was already a relatively unusual process for people more familiar with sitting in conventional board-style meetings. The authors then proposed to organise a series of workshop events to bring in the other forms of expertise to the process, before agreeing on what would happen practically.

The civic leaders' group had many questions about how this process would work, what difference it would make, and how to manage the process. One condition the group put on their continued support for the co-design (for example, allocating staff time from Trident to arranging it, and funding from the Government Neighbourhood Community Budget pilot programme for the specialist facilitation expertise from Planning for Real) was that it would take place over a relatively short period, and be able to show practical results quickly.

We already had information about the views of local residents from the Planning for Real consultation. The Board had developed its vision. There was the informal network of practitioners in the Community of Practice, which could provide a forum for conversations to take place among the organisations providing the services that were being redesigned. So, the work of co-designing could begin. A programme of three intensive workshops involving both service providers and local residents was delivered. As with the work with the civic leaders to create the vision, it was important that these sessions also were creative and interactive rather than following the traditional meeting format.

Workshop 1 offered the opportunity for participants to undertake a rapid audit of services involving consideration and identification of: key factors to realising potential; generating 'goals' for services; mapping services that were already on offer, by whom (noting who else was offering the same or a similar service) and their level of "importance' to delivering the goals;

Workshop 2 looked at experiences from a user and service provider perspective: a carefully facilitated workshop bringing together residents (users) and practitioners (service providers) to share powerful first-hand experiences of what it is like to search for work and what it is like to help and support those searching for work and/or wishing to develop their skills. Each participant was asked to draw a picture which represented their own 'journey' either as an organisation, or a service user. Everyone then shared their picture and told their story to the rest of the group. The service user perspectives were starkly honest, and illustrated some frustrations – for example, for one person, of feeling like they were going round in circles with their job training. For another resident who shared their story, the group was very moved by their experiences of survival of domestic violence and journey as a single parent into volunteering and using their assets. Through this customer journey mapping each participant was able to draw out one negative experience, one missed experience, and one positive experience and collectively agree the key issues to be taken forward to the next workshop;

Workshop 3 saw practical actions for change developed: an action-focused workshop to turn the talk into action. This session brought together all the learning so far and provided the opportunity for individual input and pooling knowledge and experience in developing an action plan. One of the facilitation tools was to give each small group a large printed spreadsheet, with summaries of all the information, data, consultation, first-hand experiences, mapping and vision that had been collected up to then, under themes. There were blank spaces where different organisations could draw implications from all the material, and make practical offers of what they would or could do in response. This meant the groups had their 'eyes down' on the sheet, focused on action, to avoid the classic problems of inaction, indecision or disagreement in usual attempts at collective decision making in meetings. Everyone had a pen, giving them control and also trying to make sure everyone could offer to do something to contribute.

These workshops were designed to be practical. Their interactive nature was intended to ensure that maximum input and benefit were gained. In the event, for many participants they were a new way of working which they initially found difficult to engage with, finding themselves outside their comfort zone. Nevertheless they were willing, having embarked on the process, to embrace the new way of working and new experiences. It was also important to be clear from the start what the benefits of this work would be both for communities and the partners involved; that they all had something to gain. While they were committed to trying new ways of working in the spirit of improving local delivery of services, they sometimes had to be convinced that tangible outcomes from which everyone would benefit would result – that it was not all just a 'creative process exercise', with no effect on their everyday lives. Creative exercises take people outside of the familiar meeting setting, and in order to overcome concerns about this and about the intended outcomes, we met with individuals outside of the workshops to talk about how they felt, reassured them that the exercises were tried and tested and encouraged them to 'trust in the process'. Their commitment to the goals and vision and their desire to be involved in change ensured they stayed involved. Working together to design solutions was a challenging new experience for both residents and practitioners. We worked with the residents who were part of the process to build their confidence when 'coming to the table' with professionals and to reassure them that they would be taken seriously and listened to. It was important to structure the sessions in such a way as to make sure that this was the case. The workshops enabled members of the Community of Practice and residents to reach a point where smaller working groups formed in order to develop detailed action plans to bring about agreed change in key areas.

In the months following this work, childcare provision has been expanded, with more places in existing settings and a new venue opened. A local training provider has now gained accreditation as an adult guidance provider, the enterprise support service has expanded to offer enterprise support specifically targeted at young people, two volunteer hubs have been opened in local community centres which are supported by a new brokerage service, matching volunteers to opportunities across BD5.

Learning

People and relationship are critical

Bradford Trident has a history of partnership initiatives, working with a wide range of service providers and is proud of its strong relationships with key partners. However, it was not always able to influence these partners to fully participate in this process, particularly as it would mean potentially reallocating resources – people and money. Despite that, we benefited from a flexibility and determination to change things by working with a range of local people and local organisations who have a historical association with and understanding of the area. Co-design focuses on what the people who are in the room can do, not what other organisations are not doing. It 'works with the willing' to get things moving and the outcomes demonstrate that it is worthwhile to pursue the vision and realise the benefits for communities and for partners. By having, in the room, a range of community residents who experience the service delivery at first hand, we were able to share extremely powerful messages about what works well and not so well. The community voices helped service providers to get a deep understanding of the issues, and give our data a 'human face'. We were able to have constructive dialogue because it was facilitated in a way that allowed people to focus on how to make things better and move forward. We found including residents in the process added additional expertise and that this did not lead to running the risk of raised expectations or accusations of blame. It was important to keep the conversations going outside of the workshops as a means of addressing any frustrations and uncertainties that the activists, workers and residents had. As this was a new way of working it naturally generated concerns about 'being outside their comfort zone' while at the same time acknowledging this was powerful in itself.

Using the data

The consultation exercises gave a clear focus for the discussions and enabled the community to be involved in the conversations and interested in what was coming next. Our practical ideas for change which we discussed at the workshops were backed up by all of the evidence from statistics, consultation, residents' experiences and practitioners' knowledge. When consulting or gaining a further understanding of residents' experiences, we were careful not to ask what had already been asked in previous exercises as this would have caused frustration and a lack of credibility in what we are trying to achieve.

Leadership and accountability

The clear vision and framework for the project was created by the civic leaders' group, including timeline and a creative methodology which they had used themselves to create the vision. We were encouraged to take risks by trying new methods and to be creative in the delivery. The group has representation from local and district-wide partners and provided a strategic approach with an interest in learning from this innovative work for future work elsewhere. We identified a named person who organised the workshops, maintained momentum through conversations and work outside of the workshops, followed through the actions and made sure that we remained community led by putting our community residents at the forefront. Behind all of this sat a set of pre-existing local governance and practitioner structures, including the Bradford Trident Board, the elected Community Council and a regular lunch meeting for local professionals, which meant we had access to a range of trusting relationships, ample opportunities for checking the data with on-the-ground intelligence, and established mechanisms for feeding back findings and proposals.

Doing more of the same will result in more of the same outcomes

Integrated into the pilot NCB work was the expectation that cost–benefit analysis exercises would help to make the case for proposed interventions with key partners, as well as demonstrating any economic savings. This is an important step in the process of redesigning services for those who need to be convinced about the need for change and what might be the 'wins' for them. However, finding colleagues with the necessary expertise to complete these exercises and locating the required cost information proved very difficult (authorities do not systematically record service and budget information on a local level). This proved to be a timely and complex exercise which was undertaken alongside the co-design work but did not contribute to the outcomes. The methodology we chose for the co-design exercise was difficult for the participants to believe in at first and many found the process uncomfortable, hence the need to keep talking and motivating individuals in between workshops. Of course, there was the risk that some services may be decommissioned and this added to the sense of uncertainty for some participants as their organisation may be damaged by redesigning provision. However, because they were committed to the local community, were confident in their flexibility, and we had built up their trust over a number of years and they understood that our facilitators were experienced in creative and interactive processes, they had faith in the process and our joint commitment. Our methodology was designed to keep the focus on action, to build consensus quickly and to concentrate on making the greatest impact with who we had around the table. This was important in building the participants' confidence and in maintaining a positive outlook rather than looking at the past or at who was not around the table. 'Eyes down' and hands-on exercises, like the ones used in the workshops, proved to be effective ways to help turn talk into action. Forums for sharing information and good practice can be very useful, but co-design also means that something different happens as a result.

Elinor Ostrom points out (1996) that just because it would be better to do things differently, it does not necessarily follow that people will want to change. In Bradford, they recognised the need to build on an 'appetite for change'. The specific policy context and timing gave a 'window of opportunity', which synced with the rhythms of policy at an opportune moment. One of those rhythms was an 'eventual realisation' by local organisations that they had to take ownership of developing new policy directions for themselves. Even so, Bradford Trident, as the lead organisation, was working against many drivers in the opposite direction, for example with local organisations which felt that the way to maintain viability in the face of public spending cuts was to hunker down rather than use resources to take risks. Throughout the process, the tools used helped to bring in additional data, previously marginalised voices and underexploited expertise. Michaela Howell and Margaret Wilkinson describe how this knowledge was mobilised through the workshops to reinforce and increase appetites for change by iterative reproblematising of the issue, and redefining the policy problem.

The co-design process was very clearly structured into a series of stages that followed logically. One of its huge strengths was that it was also a flexible, messy process which deliberately allowed for looping back on itself. It deliberately planned in flexibility and change. It challenges the neat conventional linear model of stages; at every stage of the process, the co-design asked again – how is the problem understood from different perspectives? Having created some momentum, the authors' account points to some of the deep challenges of incomplete design. There were many things they managed to hold in contention. Incomplete design means outcomes cannot be specified in advance. But there were tensions with the desire of some partners to use the process to achieve efficiencies (or savings to the public purse), while others had the goal of increasing the amount of revenue flowing to their particular group. Some of the way the authors dealt with these tensions was to believe in the efficacy of their methodology, repeating a mantra of 'trust in the process'. At the same time, the practitioners involved in this co-design quite rightly were focused on the prospects for the process, however creative, to lead somewhere. As the authors say, they kept 'the focus on action'. In this, their perspective chimes with Ostrom's conditions for effective co-production, which is the incentive that things will change as a result.

Change is both an incentive and disincentive, depending on one's position. In Bradford, the facilitators 'worked with the willing'. It alludes to the fact that some of the power holders were reluctant to have a conversation about potentially significant shifts in resources, or control of resources. Other participants were willing, but still concerned about their recognition that doing things differently could potentially mean decommissioning of their own organisations or even jobs.

The process illustrates the idea of modelling that is being exemplary in one's own practice of the principles and values you are trying to implement. They modelled uncomfortableness, and iterative processes. It was uncomfortable partly because of the newness of the facilitation techniques, but also because it had lots of uncertainty. Some of the uncertainty came from the responsive and iterative nature of the process. Facilitation was needed to alter existing hierarchies of expertise, including creating space for community experts to speak when 'coming to the table' as other voices could crowd them out.

What was novel about this project was not just the tools, but the process created, which was orientated around a vision which emphasised core values that local civic leaders wanted to strengthen, such as positive community networks, self-reliance and collective problem solving. This replaced the original more conventional document, which largely described services that formal organisations would provide. As the authors describe, the vision was generated by an exercise where local leaders attempted to relate policy goals to lived experiences – their own and residents'. One striking aspect of the project which is clear is that it is a story primarily about relationships and conversations.

Using mediation to resolve conflict

Maura Rose

This contribution is based on two decades of experience of delivering conflict resolution in community settings. Re-engaging the public draws in new forms of expertise to decision making, but also opens up a complex arena for conflicts of interest and disagreements. One of the key challenges is how to negotiate differences of opinion that arise. Mediation is offered as one practical approach to resolving conflicts in ways that respect the participants, and attempts to generate positive outcomes for all parties. Drawing on some illustrative examples, it suggests core principles for conducting constructive dialogue. The lessons from these specific cases and broader principles are applicable across a range of policy settings.

Maura Rose offers a grounded account of what might at first sight appear to be micro-processes of human negotiation. She sets out the seven principles of mediation and demonstrates how these abstract principles might be translated into practice. This contribution starts to flesh out what an alternative approach to dialogue on complex issues could look like. It is one way to understand what might happen within boundary spaces. As with any tool, if used incorrectly then the outcomes are not what are hoped for, reinforcing the idea that facilitation is itself a skilled task. Conventional approaches can suppress or manage conflict, and principles drawn from mediation show how to handle conflicts of interest openly. The contributor also reflects on criticisms of alternative approaches to dialogue that it is an idealistic and marginal activity. She gives us powerful messages about the challenges of people holding themselves open to constructive problem solving, when the legacy of past grievances has a strong hold on emotions.

Mediation, using an independent third party to facilitate discussions between disputing parties, has long been used in the UK for many types of disputes and has largely enjoyed a great deal of success. I began my journey into mediation in 1996 when I trained as a mediator with Bolton Neighbour Dispute Service, the first service of this kind to be set up in the North of England. After studying a degree in Psychology, with very little of it really making much sense, I was thrilled when suddenly I began to hear theories which started to make sense – not only making sense but leaving me feeling optimistic too. Suddenly, here was a process which relied on the fact that people can and will make their own decisions, resolve their own problems with a little help from a third party. It sounded simple but the techniques learned and the results that followed have continued to impress me on a regular basis. The fact that people were recognised as having the skills to problem solve and repair relationships and change their behaviour was and is wonderful to hear and even better to witness. I went on to mediate on many neighbour disputes. I became a board member of Bully Free Zone, the peer support project which was started and supported by Bolton Neighbour Dispute Service, joined the Good Practice Group, and then, in 2000, obtained the post of deputy coordinator with the newly named Bolton Mediation Service. In 2006 I became manager of the whole service. From 2000 until 2012 (when I left) the Service expanded and was not only mediating on neighbour disputes but also on victim/offender cases and restorative justice, special education needs disputes, workplace, intergenerational family disputes or homelessness mediation, family group conferences, anti-social behaviour cases, community cohesion cases and cases involving racist incidents. Over these years I saw many successful agreements made and adhered to and the service is still enjoying success today.

How does mediation work?

"I do mediation every day! It's my job." This is usually what is said on the first day of any training course in mediation. People often share the belief that mediation is only a matter of getting people together and figuratively banging their heads together and problem solving for the participants. Fortunately for the disputants there is more to mediation than initially believed. In order to mediate effectively, most mediation services will generally work to the following seven key principles: independent, non-judgemental, impartial, future-focused, confidential, voluntary and informed choice.

Independent

Mediation should remain independent from other services. What this means in practice is that they do not have their targets set by organisations which may not have any understanding of mediation and its principles. The aim of mediation is primarily to facilitate communication between people or groups in order to improve understanding. Once this is achieved, however, it has an uncanny knack of meeting other organisations' targets. For example, once a parent and adolescent have managed to stay in a room together for two hours and have developed their own agreement, under the guidance of the mediators, they can see a way forward and agree for the child to return home. Once the indigenous family has come face to face with the refugee family it has been terrorising for the last six months the former suddenly realise that they share the same problems and start to see the refugee family as people rather than an article in the *Daily Mail*; it becomes harder for them to post excrement through their door, or throw stones at their children, thus reducing antisocial behaviour and racist incidents. There is a danger that mediation services may get drawn off course by other agencies or organisations. However, with flexibility, communication and good monitoring in place there is no reason why the mediation service should not be able to set its own practices and goals.

Non-judgemental

A mediator isn't a judge! We aren't there to make a decision, nor should we offer advice. When asked what would we do in a certain situation, it is not a good idea to respond honestly. Truly most people in disputes don't want an honest answer anyway, they would rather you took their side. What a mediator should respond with is, "Well this isn't about me, and how I respond, this is about you and your situation. What would you like to happen?" We are not to be drawn into judgements and giving advice, however appealing it is to share our ideas.

Impartial

We need to treat parties equally, offering equal respect, time and choice to the people involved in the dispute.

Future focused

When people are involved in disputes they often lose their ability to see an end to the situation or to see the future unfold. People who are locked into a dispute, whatever that may be, are often held back from finding a solution on their own because they are too focused on the past and who did what and when. Even if they try to move forward there is always that helpful friend, neighbour or colleague, who has been enjoying the dispute so much, who will make a comment and remind them of the past indignities they have had to endure because of the dispute and they are quickly drawn back down the hole again. Mediators are trained in how to encourage the participants to be focused on the future. They use questions to get the disputants to think of how they want things to be in the future, or they may encourage participants to imagine a time four years hence when the dispute is resolved, and ask how they think they may look back on this.

Confidential

Mediation needs to be confidential. Trust is a key aspect of mediation; if a party feels that you are going to be sharing their information with housing or social services then they may be reluctant to open up in quite the same way.

Voluntary

Forcing people into mediation is not a good idea. "Why?", I hear you cry. Well, if you force people into mediation, then you can actually do more harm to the relationship than good. In the case of victim–offender mediation, we would often have young offenders saying they have to do it, they would sit with their arms folded, glaring and saying "I got to say sorry to that no mark whose house I burgled." "If that was your house, would you want that kind of apology or would you prefer to hear from someone who actually was sorry for what they did?" Mediation should be safe for everybody and by forcing someone into a mediation session you increase the risk that one or more of the parties could be harmed emotionally or physically.

Informed choice

All through the process, parties must be given the right to choose. Not only this, but you must encourage them to make an informed choice. It is like offering a holiday in Blackpool and a holiday in Inverness with the decision maker knowing little of either. Therefore saying, "Do you want mediation?" is not enough. If a solicitor has the wrong impression of mediation and says it is "Sitting in a room, listening to whale music", then what chance has someone got of making an informed choice about whether mediation is for them. Therefore a party has to be informed about how mediation works for them, what the benefits are and what the downside might be. They need to know that they can have a choice of mediator or not, and so on.

Finally after adhering to the key principles, mediation, in my opinion, should also be provided to participants for free to remove a barrier to those wishing to take part; after all people do not get charged for using the police, for being imprisoned or for having to have social worker intervention. Mediation is every bit as useful as these agencies and yet recently has been referred to as a 'luxury' service. As I have said, mediation can be used in many arenas and as long as the facilitators use the principles, the results are mainly positive. If there are failures then it is usually down to one of the principles being overlooked. Because mediation is about empowerment and puts the responsibility of the resolution back to the disputants, they are the ones responsible for the solution and for keeping that agreement going. To highlight this I am going to share with you a case study where all the principles were met, and another one which failed to meet a number of key principles.

One of the cases which was really powerful was working on a planning issue in Bolton on a case between local residents and a planning application for an Islamic community centre. The local residents had generally been against this application and had submitted many objections. We were contacted by a local housing group and asked to assist in the communication between the three sides: the planning department, the local residents and the leaders of the community centre. Communicating directly with each person on this case, we began to see a picture emerge – the local residents were worried that the community centre would turn out to be a mosque and their main worry was about parking in the streets which was already a problem after 5:30 in the afternoon. Not all residents wanted to attend; however those that did had a strong voice and had also discussed the issue with other residents. The community centre and members from planning were also keen to get involved. A meeting was facilitated and all sides had the opportunity to discuss their concerns. Once a number of the local residents had met the leaders of the community centre, they began to build up trust and put a face to a name. The local residents were invited to visit the site and were assured that non-Muslim groups would also be able to access the meeting rooms. A number of the local residents removed their complaints and general feeling about the centre improved. Some of the local residents attended the opening, with one local resident deciding he wanted to assist in the training of the junior football team. It also helped to ease racial tension which was growing in that area.

Of course running a mediation service has not always gone smoothly and sometimes cases can go horribly wrong. When complaints come in about the service or the staff members it is important to use the same philosophies for staff and volunteers too. Whenever a complaint or a commendation is received, the mediators on the case are always involved and updated. Whether it be a commendation or complaint, we contact the service users to identify specific points which they thought went well or should have been done differently. Obviously it is always trickier handling complaints rather than commendations. A case which sticks out for me was when two of our mediators were working on a very sensitive case with two men who had mental health issues, one of the parties was English and the other was from the Middle East. The mediators had come back happy that they had got an agreement. However, within a day we had a phone call from a very irate and emotional service user. On hearing how upset he was, I decided to answer this call in person. A colleague and I went out the next day and listened to what had happened. The issues were many. He had respiratory problems and the venue had a lot of stairs. Because of this when he arrived he was already feeling weakened and exhausted. The mediators had also been informed, in confidence, that he felt afraid of this man and moreover got panic attacks in confined spaces. Unfortunately, the meeting room was very small and throughout the mediation he stated that he was feeling uneasy. He felt that his comments had not been taken on board and that one of the mediators had taken the side of the other party, who was Middle Eastern. The complainant reported that the mediator, who herself came from that area, had tried to explain about the 'fiery nature' of Middle Eastern people. He had subsequently felt that the agreement was not a fair agreement and that he had signed it while feeling vulnerable. I let him know that we take every complaint seriously and said that we would talk to the mediators about this, get their perspective and get back to him with any feedback. We would also hold off sending out the agreement until we had talked with both mediators and the other party. I also informed him that we would be speaking with the housing association as they needed to be aware that there was a problem on this case. On meeting with the mediators we discussed every aspect of the case. There were feelings of defensiveness at first, but using the statement that the complainant had written, we looked through the letter and established how they were feeling about this and what their thoughts were. We also looked at what could have been done differently to avoid one party being left feeling like this. I asked them what extra support the service could have provided. Done in this way it was still a sensitive and difficult conversation to have but by the end of the meeting we had some ideas of what should have happened, and what we felt should be learned by everyone concerned. Together we decided what needed to happen to make it right. We also contacted the other party and asked him how he felt about the agreement. On hearing that the agreement was not going to go ahead he was initially angry and frustrated about wasting his time attending a meeting. I offered to come out and visit him but he refused. Cases like this are few but when something happens it is important to address it rather than bury it. It is also important to include the people who were involved, so they can get information and feel that they are being taken seriously. On feeding back to the housing association and the complainant, it was positive to hear that both felt more involved. The housing association also had a clearer way of dealing with the case and the complainant was relieved we had not just put his comments down to his mental health.

When conflict occurs there is always the opportunity that people become locked into defensive positions, either physical or metaphorical. By involving and informing people in any process this level of defensiveness is reduced. By getting the parties involved to decide on ways forward, mediation can offer positivity and a brighter outlook. Also, because each case responds to the individual needs of the parties, it really does seek to address inequality and provide a bespoke service to all. When I attend conferences or talk to people who come from a more punitive background who favour the 'tough love' approach, I am often challenged and questioned. Occasionally I am called a hippy or an idealist, which could quite possibly be true. My one firm belief is this: that all people no matter how young or old or whatever abilities and skills they possess do have opinions and feelings. When those opinions and feelings are ignored, that produces dissatisfaction and anger and can lead to impasse. By respecting individuals and realising everyone has a right to think and feel differently, mediation can help in a number of cases. Those where it is inappropriate, where the parties themselves have felt it not to be for them, we have a host of other interventions and legislation to fall back on. By not using a very simple and quick intervention, services could be losing money, time and resources fighting a battle that need not have taken place.

This contribution is part of the grammar of more co-productive policy making; it adds a part of the structures on which to hang conceptual frameworks. Mediation principles speak to ways in which the ideals of co-production can be translated into practice, grounded in workable strategies and made into everyday practice. Their emphasis is on the basis for structuring interactions to better guarantee constructive future-facing outcomes. This helps us to move away from a focus on structures per se, specific institutional structures and other more tightly bounded spaces as the sites for policy dialogue. As a process of dialogue with unknown outcomes and non-directive facilitation, mediation is a living example of one version of incomplete design.

The author poses some seemingly contradictory experiences and beliefs. Mediation is premised on the core belief in human beings' skills, for example in being able to emphasise and reflect. However, the contributor also documents and acknowledges people's very human frailties. Her contribution rescues the possibility of maintaining an asset-based approach in the face of aggression, parochialism and cultural conflict. She helps to do this by placing them in a broader empathetic context, for example understanding how people can react defensively if they feel backed into a corner – literally in the case of one of her clients. She also reminds us of the necessity to keep a future-orientated and problem-solving focus in circumstances where some of the parties have become 'locked into defensive positions', where the past has a stranglehold on their ability to see the larger goals or common good.

By acknowledging people's emotions, mediation explicitly reintroduces this aspect of human responses back into public dialogue as a potentially constructive force. Underlying this contribution are some big ideas: first that there may not be a single truth to be discovered about a conflict, merely contrasting perspectives. Second, that the perspectives of those involved must be acknowledged if the process is to be effective and productive: as Maura Rose says, it 'is about empowerment and puts the responsibility of the resolution back to the disputants; they are the ones responsible for the solution'. Third, ultimately what matters in the process is not the competing or conflicting views of the parties, but whether they can achieve mutually agreeable outcomes.

Constructing and managing mediation is, as the author points out, more than simply 'banging heads together'. It suggests that facilitation is a necessary and identifiable skill in its own right. Many of the sensitive, controversial and complex policy negotiations that happen in boundary spaces will require this advanced level of facilitation. Experiences of this mediation service, and others like it across the UK and elsewhere, suggest effective facilitation skills can be taught. New ways of doing policy making will require new skills for those leading policy dialogue. However, the fact that they can be taught does not guarantee that they will be learned. Indeed, this contribution highlights in several places some of the criticisms of mediation directed at this work, and the author, over the years. Some portray mediation as a 'soft' and marginal activity, contrasted with the 'hard' mainstream policy levers of legislation and enforcement. This stereotype of alternative ways to approach policy as idealistic, naïve or peripheral is challenged by this contributions.

FOUR

Debating co-productive policy design

The aim in this book is to frame a debate on how policy making may be better able to address some of the wicked and squishy problems facing societies. The intention has not simply been to offer an empirical description of how policy making works, though many of the contributions are illuminating in that regard. Rather, the aim is to initiate a conversation driven by theory and informed by practice, about how policy actors can imagine and realise a co-productive alternative to conventional policy design.

The book was conceived as a conversation between theory and practice. It started by generating theoretical tensions, highlighting the limitations of conventional policy design. It then set out some tentative framings of different elements of vision for co-productive policy design and the practices, or 'grammar', which may help to realise vision. Specific contexts for these broad theoretical ideas were provided by a series of diverse contributions. Through their grounded efforts to do policy design differently, these contributions offer insightful reflections from policy makers, practitioners, researchers and activists who are actively engaged in this debate.

This chapter reflects on the challenge, creativity and inspiration provided by the contributions to challenge, deepen and develop the theorising of the opening chapters. *Challenging*, because there remain many lively debates between ideas, stances and tactics advocated by the group which has produced the book. If each of the 12 sets of contributors (made up of 30 individuals) do not necessarily agree with each other, nor do they all entirely accept all aspects of the arguments set out in the opening chapters, or at least some of the nuances of those arguments. As part of the attempt to 'model' some of the very ideas we advocate, this chapter reflects on these debates. *Deepening*, because specific examples in specific contexts reinforce and illuminate the broader theoretical points. *Developing*, because the contributions prompt amendments, additions and changes in emphasis from the original heuristic. As befits the iterative, incomplete and inclusive ideas advocated, the book is structured so that this chapter critically reappraises the ideas set out at the start. This is a relatively unusual approach to the structure of a book. It is attempted so that the dialogue and iterations in the arguments are deliberately presented in an explicit way. Chapter Four therefore returns to the theory of the opening chapters, but with a fresh perspective generated by the contributions, and with debates not previously covered. A combination of theory and practice are used to explore these new topics, bringing in reflections from the vignettes together with additional ideas from the literature where needed to deepen or develop the ideas in the heuristics.

The contributions generate complex issues, which cannot be ignored if co-production is to become a serious contender. These include the feasibility and possible methods of change, the degree to which this is idealistic, how co-producers might protect themselves from being co-opted, how this takes account of deep value conflicts, and how to reconcile strong leadership with less hierarchical structures, and retain leadership while valuing a range of different forms of expertise, including experiential expertise.

Figure 6 summarises the conversations between theory and practice that are discussed in this chapter. The chapter recaps briefly on the need for change in conventional policy design, but also the potential of and constraints on change, before exploring in more depth the various illuminations offered by the contributions about the visions and grammars of pre-figurative co-productive models. This chapter discusses some of the tough questions and dilemmas raised by the conversation between the opening chapters and the contributions. How can change be created and what are some tools for creative disruption? What strategies can be used in the absence of positive-sum understandings of power? How can vision offer leadership if it is in a non-dominating setting? What happens when there is a clash of vision and values? Will citizens come forward, and in what forms? How is expertise respected without being diluted or pushed out? What might an 'incomplete' policy design look like?

The need for change in conventional policy processes, and its prospects

For many within conventional policy design, its appropriateness is self-evident: it is said by its defenders to produce policies that are strategic, cost-effective, efficient and accountable. A more co-productive alternative, from this perspective, is premised on a level of involvement and deliberation for which there is little appetite and which may produce decisions that are populist but not necessarily representative; that are also short-termist, with indeterminate costs and

Figure 6 Points of debate between conventional and co-productive policy design

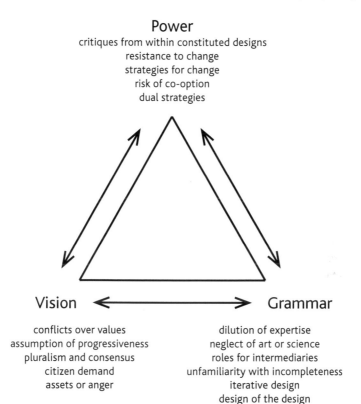

Power
critiques from within constituted designs
resistance to change
strategies for change
risk of co-option
dual strategies

Vision ⟷ Grammar

conflicts over values
assumption of progressiveness
pluralism and consensus
citizen demand
assets or anger

dilution of expertise
neglect of art or science
roles for intermediaries
unfamiliarity with incompleteness
iterative design
design of the design

a lack of evidence of their ability to enhance policy outcomes. The tradition of conventional policy making is perceived to have endured because it offers the best way of making policy that liberal western democracies have yet constructed.

In the opening chapters, a critique was offered of this apparently self-evident case. It is to be expected that there is more onus on challengers to the status quo to make their case than there is the incumbents to defend theirs. Conventional systems have many strengths, which were highlighted in Chapters Two and Three, such as their focus on instrumental rationality, and how best to achieve policy outcomes that matter for the lives of citizens. Recognising the need for structures of governance is another key strength. Yet what can be seen from the contributions are signs of recognition of the limits of conventional designs. Many of those inside the policy process are recognising that the conventional policy process may not be tenable or fit for purpose as new crises and challenges emerge. There are cracks and fissures within the system that allow for the possibility to open up new ways of shaping and influencing policy design.

Some of the initiatives presented are illustrations of a growing unease from actors within existing systems about how far the conventional model can be sustained. Simon Burall and Tim Hughes' work focuses on the UK 'Open Government' experience of a much bigger global initiative for more transparent, participatory and accountable government. Robert Rutherfoord and Lucy Spurling showcase an attempt at 'Open Policy Making', using the example of a UK government programme to decentralise decision making to citizens and transfer control over public resources. These contributions are premised on a fundamental critique of conventional models and promote the ideas that local knowledge and the involvement of new groups will produce more effective policy outcomes. The 'establishment' itself is advocating change. In relation to the heuristic, the contributions suggest that the divisions between the models are not as stark or absolute as suggested by Figure 4.

Several of the contributions have an explicit emphasis on the need for change. In their own ways, all of the contributions imply a cogent and compelling case for change; they expose the limits of what has gone before as well as showcasing or prefiguring what might otherwise be. Jess Steele poignantly reflects on how, to citizens coming forward with the intention of making positive change in their communities, traditional responses from conventional policy often feels like 'being "done to", over and over again'. Katy Wilkinson's darkly humorous portrayal of policy crisis in the 'Department for Biblical Disasters' shows the tragic mismatch between the messiness and complexity of the problems faced by a rigid and binary system. In this system, there are two modes: no crisis, or 'peacetime', and full-on crisis, or 'wartime'; as she says, 'there is no in between state'. Toby Blume also describes the rigidity of institutional structures and ways of seeing of conventional designs, where citizens play a peripheral role. Although coming from quite different perspectives and positions, Paul McCabe in York and Teresa Cordova and Moises Gonzales in New Mexico illustrate 'problematic development decisions' produced by conventional processes which fail to adequately reconcile sustainability with growth and economic development, or sufficiently broker between the needs of settled communities and future households. Maura Rose argues that rising racial tensions in one community in Bolton, England were exacerbated by attempts to suppress or ignore people's views, leading to dissatisfaction and anger. Toby Blume in Lambeth, London, Teresa Cordova and Moises Gonzales, and Dan Silver and Amina Lone in the North West of England in Salford, all speak powerfully about negative, pathologising, stigmatising and damaging deficit-based models of communities and neighbourhoods. Images of 'sink estates' or 'war zones' populated by criminal elements are belied by the reality of citizens' and communities' myriad creativities and problem-solving abilities seen throughout all 12 contributions. The contributors from the Morris Justice Project send a similar message in the context of the more malignant aspects of power in some constituted institutions. In the South Bronx, the negative consequences of some policies fell most heavily on already stigmatised communities, who displayed their resourcefulness in challenging policing policy.

However, despite the increasing credibility of arguments for co-productive policy designs, this does not mean that alternatives will 'occur spontaneously' (Ostrom, 1996, p. 1082). While there is a desire for more co-productive elements within conventional policy design, achieving this change continues to prove more elusive. Change is difficult to achieve. The specific and partial understanding of power for some within conventional policy designs – as set out in Chapter One – is that power is zero-sum, one body has power, or someone or somebody else has; it exists for the taking and is not shared or jointly created. If this is the case, the emphasis in the conventional policy process is then to minimise perceived risk to power holders. What is illustrated by the contributions is how this risk aversion can have a paralysing effect and reinforce the existing way of doing things. Katy Wilkinson shows how the perception of reputational risk or potential for flak for a central government department in working with different stakeholder groups means that the expertise and insight of scientists and citizens is often relegated to a marginal role of advice and consultation. It is used to bolster existing policy prejudices – described by some commentators as 'policy-based evidence making' – and to place policy making beyond politics. Katy Wilkinson's piece also gives a glimpse of how, with the same actors, there can be rapid change. In her contribution, it was an emergency that generated better policy designs by bringing in additional expertise, and developing systems for iterative problem solving. However, this period was all too brief, and change-resistant systems were also quick to reconstitute themselves. Simon Burall and Tim Hughes' example showed how civil society groups engaging in a government-convened attempt at collaborative policy making were undermined by 'red herring' questioning of the legitimacy of their representative claims. The politics of constituted power, therefore, are at their worst when they are about sustaining the current allocation of 'who gets what, when and how' and avoiding flak, scrutiny and protecting reputation and position.

Even with the best of co-productive intentions, governments can sometimes act as a 'civic *dis*abler' (Sirianni, 2009, emphasis added). The contributions make reference to hard-bitten struggles, hard-fought battles, setbacks, disappointments and let-downs. As Lowndes and Roberts (2013, p. 184) have noted, 'forgetting' established practice can be hard to do. As Toby Blume's account illustrated, it is easy to revert to the familiar; the usual way of doing things is so entrenched that it is difficult to advocate and introduce change. Those who are committed to change can find it challenging to develop the creativity and flexibility required to identify and reach even a commonly defined goal of co-productive policy design.

How can change be created?

Chapter One made a case for conscious, planned policy design which also incorporates iterative reflection. Chapter One proposed 'policy design for foxes', meaning not a grand, once-and-for-all policy prescription for a single solution but an approach built up of many smaller strands, which are thoroughly tested along the way. However, the contributions illustrate that more co-productive policy designs were being conducted in parts rather than wholes. A co-productive approach is not the model which currently exists in most places. Therefore, the first step is the creation of change in a resistant and risk-averse system. Reflection on the contributions helps to iterate these very ideas – strategies to generate policy *change* for foxes. While some contributors talked of 'strategic intent' to make interventions in the policy process, others were prompted by issues (police brutality), events (riots) or opportunities (occupation of a building, impetus of a government pilot). The contributions present three key messages that build on the ideas in the opening chapters: using moments of dislocation to create change; consciously generating creative disruptions in policy; and re-emphasising and acknowledging emotion in policy processes.

First, the contributions point to the potential to exploit, disrupt and reappropriate the temporalities and rhythms of conventional policy making. As Katy's insights into the handling of an animal health crisis in central government illustrates, crises, policy failure and external events can offer moments of dislocation which do not only reinforce or exacerbate existing policy narratives but can be taken advantage of to generate change. Those seeking an alternative way of making policy can use these moments of dislocation to press forward with change. In

Bradford, Michaela Howell and Margaret Wilkinson's example shows them attempting co-design which built on local 'appetite for change', at a time of a local public spending crisis, with the added momentum of being part of a national government decentralisation programme. In Simon Burall and Tim Hughes' example, the awareness within civil society groups of the potential flak for the government if the open government plan was not acknowledged by them as a real partnership and the need within government to make an 'eye-catching' policy statement on a particular date gave them power within the process. Understanding and being informed of policy's rhythms, knowing how to play the game, can inform and maximise the effectiveness of an intervention.

The second strategy is consciously generating creative disruptions, such as Toby Blume's use of the repetitive why (also known as 'five whys') technique. Proposed as a way of getting to a deeper understanding of root causes of problems, it offers a challenge to what exists – why do things have to be the way they are – and opens up the possibility of change. Jess Steele's methods are different, but also attempt to disrupt a '"magical reality" in which things could not be any different'. As one member of the Morris Justice Project puts it, 'it doesn't have to be like this'. Ostrom's acute observations, set out in Chapter Three, are that for co-production to be more efficient than production by one group or another, 'each has to have something that the other needs' (Ostrom, 1996, p. 1079). Recognition was given in the contributions to the importance of 'doing politics' in order to assert and establish that mutual need. More diverse stakeholders in the policy process need to 'do politics' to ensure the presence of varied forms of expertise and for a wider range of groups to 'get a seat at the table'. Contributors draw attention to different tactics and practices of 'doing politics'. For Jess Steele, 'doing politics' involves traditional forms of political participation coupled with direct action. Jess Steele, Raza Planning and the Morris Justice Project employ the tactics of community organising: building local knowledge through listening, developing diverse networks, realising the power of numbers, conducting power analysis, generating visibility and creatively mobilising. One illustration of this power is offered by the Morris Justice Project: 'When you ask us, you're not just asking one person, you are asking a group that has systematically asked a thousand of their neighbours.' The example of MapLocal in Birmingham, England, shows the potential for technology and social media to shift the parameters of 'doing politics', allowing communities to 'shout a little louder' in the policy process.

Decentralisation and devolution of powers to local areas and neighbourhoods was used as another example of the technique of creative disruption to overcome the problems of institutional stickiness (Pierson, 2002). In the case of Robert Rutherfoord and Lucy Spurling's contribution, new community rights were created by central government as a mechanism for citizens to have more 'hard' legal powers to disrupt conventional systems. Elsewhere, academics Phil Jones and colleagues describe some of this legislation as having taken a 'flamethrower' to the existing planning system. However, one of the civil servants' lessons from the government programme discussed is that decentralisation in this case needed to go further to 'align incentives' for genuine shifts in control over budgets for public funding.

A third strategy for creating and facilitating change that can be discerned in the contributions is re-emphasising and acknowledging emotion in policy processes, as also recognised in design thinking literature (Burns et al, 2006, p. 14; Boyer, Cook and Steinberg, 2011, p. 46), which exhorts designers 'don't forget to laugh' (Allio, 2014, p. 26). Design is 'human-centred' and uses 'professional empathy' (Allio, 2014, p. 8). Emotions featured as barriers to change, as seen in Toby Blume's contribution, where one response was to 'cling to the familiar'. Change is intensely emotionally charged: people feel uncomfortable, awkward, frustrated, as well as joyous and empowered. Acknowledging these, often denied, emotional dynamics is a crucial part of establishing meaningful alternatives. As the Morris Justice Project described it, a willingness to 'stretch beyond what's comfortable and learn from each other' is essential. Raza Planning talk about their emotional connections to place, and the 'laughter' that helped generate their vision and principles. Jess Steele talks of delight as well as despair. Michaela Howell and Margaret Wilkinson's example from Bradford, West Yorkshire, describes how creative exercises took participants out of their comfort zone, but that feeling uncomfortable was a powerful move in itself. Emotion also could be seen as an expression of one of Ostrom's conditions for successful co-production: input is incentivised appropriately. As she puts it, 'incentives help to encourage inputs from both officials and citizens' (Ostrom, 1996, p. 1082). Crucial incentives are provided by focusing on 'enduring' issues which have a direct impact on the lives of those participating. The contributions tapped into these sorts of concerns, planning and infrastructure developments, employment and skills, public order and criminal justice.

What strategies can be used in the absence of positive-sum understandings of power?

Chapter One discussed the paradoxes of power, including the dangers of co-option into constituted models. It argued against a strategy of perpetual resistance, and for the possibilities of the integration of more co-productive approaches within formal institutional policy settings. However, in a situation where a fully constitutive alternative has not been fully realised, then a risk remains of potentially 'abandoning a critical distance and capacity for alternative resistance strategies' (Coafee and Healey, 2003, p. 1997 cited in Taylor, 2007, p. 311). Phil Jones and colleagues remind us that the language of co-production may be used in contexts where it is still the reality that co-production is possible 'so long as communities are happy to co-produce the things that policy makers want'. As Simon Burall and Tim Hughes recognise, attempts to reconstitute the process take place in a primarily constituted approach, which means that the policy process can be 'a site of tensions between what civil society wants and what government is prepared to do'. What are the status quo challengers to do in the interim? If they are not to stand permanently outside a fully or even semi-constituted model, then how can they avoid the dangers of stepping into a still partly un-reconstituted policy arena where they lack power?

In the opening chapters, an understanding of power was presented which rejected a coercive model of power and argued in favour of more relational notions of power. Such an argument is all well and good, but what if citizens and others are dealing with situations dominated by more coercive forms of 'power over'? Some contributors do see power in a more nuanced way to include both forms. For example, Raza Planning and Jess Steele both talk about power as control over land and other physical assets and financial resources; but this is in addition to the power they see in relationships between citizens, the ability to mobilise collectively and the strength of numbers. Advocacy of constitutive models in the contributions is made in full awareness of the realities of the sharpest edges of hard power. Maura Rose says she is accused of being an 'idealistic hippy' and does not reject the label. Other contributors would not describe themselves as idealists but as realists. Labels aside, the contributors share a sense that the alternatives to change are crucial to get away from the current situation of poor quality policy decisions and suboptimal policy outcomes. Some contributors are inside the system working for change; others present a defiant face to power from outside. Partly, this is a function of the degree to which constituted institutions present themselves as impermeable, corrupted or open and willing to have honest dialogue. Strategies must vary depending on circumstance.

Reflecting on the contributions helps to resolve some of these issues and tensions. What can be learned from the contributions in response to the issues of co-option and hard power is the value of a 'dual strategy'. Jennifer Dodge (2010), in her work on environmental advocacy, talked about the importance of retaining an antagonistic 'outsider' position while also negotiating an 'insider' position: agitation with deliberation. Such a strategy recognises the risks of co-production. Specifically, domination or capture by particular groups; the exclusion and marginalisation of others; conflict, at times leading to paralysis and deadlock; lack of innovation, capacity and sophistication; and inhibited strategic thinking (Fung, 2001; Boyte, 2005). The 'dual strategy' approach is analogous with a long-standing debate within community organising and draws on Alinskyist organising tactics of power analysis (Alinsky, 1946, 1971), which can be used to great effect, as illustrated by Jess Steele, and Teresa Cordova and Moises Gonzales. Similarly, Fung and Wright (2001, p. 26) argue that 'democracy-enhancing collaboration is unlikely to be sustained in the absence of an effective countervailing power ... a combination of both insider and outsider strategies [is] likely to be most effective'. Marilyn Taylor (2007, p. 311) suggests that 'community empowerment is likely to require insiders and outsiders, those who choose to enter invited spaces and those who prefer to operate in their own "popular" spaces. Indeed, citizens need their own popular spaces to develop their own independent narratives and voices, whether or not they then decide to enter invited spaces.' A dual strategy fulfils one of Elinor Ostrom's conditions for effective co-production, set out in Chapter Three, that there must be flexibility for participants: 'options must be available to both parties' (Ostrom, 1996, p. 1082).

How can vision offer leadership if it is in a non-dominating setting?

As the contributions show, the imperatives and practices of conventional policy making do not go away just because of a hope or attempt to do things differently. Attempts at co-production – as Simon Burall and Tim Hughes observe – 'do not happen in a vacuum', but rather in a 'sea of other policy processes'. The contributions acutely articulate the frustration that citizens can feel engaging with this conventional process which often seems so abstracted and disconnected from their lives. Also the anger and infuriation felt when their knowledge, expertise, energy and sense of 'having right on their side' are co-opted, undermined and marginalised. It is clear from their accounts that the contributors are not naïve; they recognise the workings, reach and implications of constituted power. But the vision they hold and articulate challenges the sense of inevitability of how things are currently done.

In these contexts, the contributions show the value of having, in the case of Raza Planning, 'conscious and explicitly stated mission and principles', and with the Morris Justice Project, to 'believe in the justice possibilities'. Brett Stoudt and colleagues worked from a value base with 'theoretical frameworks rooted in solidarity'. Vision here is not just an expression of 'good intentions' but a stated intent to make an intervention, which can in turn inform value-driven practice and value-led policy. Values are a form of 'art', or leadership, as emphasised by Robert Rutherfoord and Lucy Spurling's contribution. Relational forms of power do not negate the need for muscular leadership, or, as some prefer, 'stewardship' (Allio, 2014, p. 12; Boyer, Cook and Steinberg, 2011). On the contrary, an explicit articulation of co-productive values can provide 'contours for action', informing, guiding and giving a purpose for action, and transforming values into action via strategic intent (Boyer, Cook and Steinberg, 2011, p.23). In Lambeth, York and Bradford, the visions for the city or neighbourhood were negotiated and mediated through strengthened roles for local civic leaders. Whereas in Jess Steele's and Raza Planning's contributions, individuals take leadership roles in collective action; civic leadership is provided by 'brothers and sisters with whom we laugh and break bread', a crucial way recognised elsewhere of filling vacuums in leadership (Allio, 2014, p. 14). As Teresa Cordova and Moises Gonzales articulate, 'the set of values and principles provide the guiding light for action as well as the basis to care'. Michaela Howell and Margaret Wilkinson concur, arguing that grammar only emerges from a vision. But, as Raza Planning and the Morris Justice Project assert, having this vision and leadership is 'not an excuse' or a substitution for drawing on relevant experiential and scientific expertise. Rather, expertise is marshalled and mobilised through the statement of explicit principles, in order to shape interventions in and challenges to the conventional policy process.

As Jess Steele suggests, being right is not enough. Robert Rutherfoord and Lucy Spurling offer a different formulation of this same point – that having 'persuasive business cases' was not enough to persuade institutions to give citizens more control over resources: that is, hard power. The contributions also repeatedly acknowledge that while different types of knowledge are necessary to develop a co-productive alternative, knowledge is not sufficient to be constitutive of a more democratic policy process on its own; as Jess Steele sharply observes, 'knowledge is not power'. Rather, they demonstrate that knowledge has to be effectively marshalled as part of broader organising efforts. One of the many inspirational aspects of the contributions is the ways that newly emerging grammars – or institutional structures and processes – have been created around new values and respect for knowledge.

What happens when there is a clash of vision and values?

If action and grammars are shaped, channelled and mobilised through values, then this raises some complex issues about what those values are, and how far values can ever be fully shared across different interests, groups and ideological preferences. For example, taking Katy Wilkinson's example, there is the National Farmers Union, representing the interests of farmers, which advocates badger culling to reduce transmission, believed to be by badgers, of an infectious disease in cattle (bovine tuberculosis). Positioned against this is Badger Trust, which represents its members and local badger groups, and whose core purpose is the conservation, welfare and protection of badgers. As is so sympathetically set out in Paul McCabe's contribution, grassroots mobilisation is not inherently progressive (Fischer, 2000; de Filippis, Fisher and Shragge, 2010). What does this mean for co-production, given that, on the whole, the visions articulated and implied in the contributions are progressive and informed by principles of social justice. Of the people involved in this book that have the space to publicly declare their positions, all want to construct a progressive policy alternative, aimed at creating greater and more equally distributed social benefits, in response to complex policy challenges.

But this is not a simplistic aspiration of consensus; there needs to be respect for difference. This argument can be applied within networks or people who work together. The members of the Morris Justice Project describe themselves as a 'research collective that experiences misunderstandings, frustration and disagreement – and that's okay', adding that going through conflict strengthens their analysis. But they also have a set of shared values and interests on their side. What happens when there are more severe clashes between coalitions based on deep disagreements? In electoral politics, debates about values and ideologies are mediated through political party politics and the pluralism of the ballot box. The opening chapters talked about how formal party politics can be sullied by politicking, but another piece of the co-produced jigsaw is to strengthen formal democratic spaces and encourage electoral and party participation. The approach advocated here is in favour of this: it is not a case against party politics, quite the contrary, but we want to extend the scope of democratic engagement beyond this arena. If by politics we are referring to values and vision, then we want the opposite of what Simon Burall and Tim Hughes describe as things which 'churn just below the surface [but] are rarely talked about'. In surfacing deep values there is likely to be lively contestation and debate. Other writers have made a case for the positive benefits of political conflict. The contributions show how conflict can help generate mobilisation and debate. But without some level of consensus, how can policy be agreed and implemented? Respect for difference has benefits, but by itself might lead to inaction due to lack of agreement. But agreement is not always desirable or possible. Neither route seems to provide a sufficient resolution. As Dryzek and Niemeyer (2006, p. 647) point out: 'It makes little sense to be for pluralism, against pluralism, for consensus, or against consensus.' What then is the answer?

One formulation by Dryzek and Niemeyer (2006, p. 647) is for: 'pluralism at the simple level combined with meta-consensus on values, beliefs, and preferences'. In a situation of disputed values, there should be a recognition of the legitimacy of those disputed values (Dryzek and Niemeyer, 2006, p. 638). This type of meta-consensus is 'especially urgent in situations featuring deep difference in identities and value commitments' (p. 647). Where 'powerful actors invoke questionable empirical claims in support of their material interests' (p. 647), then there is a need for meta-consensus about the credibility of disputed beliefs about the impacts of policies. And finally, where 'one or more actors is in a position to manipulate decision processes (through, for example, the range of options on the agenda or the order in which votes are taken)' (p. 648), then it is crucial to focus on getting meta-consensus about the nature of the disputed choices for specific policies. Their framework also parallels the conclusions that can be drawn from the contributions.

For meta-consensus on values, some contributions showed how 'win–win' outcomes were possible even in situations of strong conflicts of interest. In the Raza Planning example, win–wins included cheaper roads, enhanced landscape and protection for local businesses where the development of transport infrastructure was reconciled with respect for the community's natural and economic resources and assets. This consensus was based on the establishment of an overarching set of interests, within the context of their vision, to which different interests could align themselves. Paul McCabe also talks about the need for shared vision and common purpose in a similar way. For meta-consensus on beliefs, Maura Rose suggests how misplaced beliefs about the consequences of policy proposals, like the Muslim community centre, might be challenged, conversely using respect for the 'right to think and feel differently' to evolve greater agreement. And meta-consensus on preferences is seen in Robert Rutherfoord and Lucy Spurling and Michaela Howell and Margaret Wilkinson's descriptions of local pilot projects that required some level of consensus. In their pilot areas of decentralised decision making, agreement was needed specifically over what the local priorities were, and how to make them happen.

Will citizens come forward, and in what ways?

A long-standing and hard-to-resolve debate on any form of public participation is whether citizens have the motivation and desire to get involved in decision making, as well as the capacity and resources to do so. Some of the answers to these questions must come from robust empirical research, including data on levels and types of citizen participation (such as can be found in Dalton, 2009), as well as field trials to test ways to stimulate additional civic behaviour (John et al, 2013). Measuring levels of participation within conventional systems only tells part of the story. By its very nature, currently untapped potential – or latent demand – is hidden and therefore hard to assess until an alternative is presented to people. Community organising – a method used in Jess Steele's and Raza Planning's contributions – is specifically design to mobilise people who are not active, by tapping into their passions, frustrations, skills and sense of personal agency. In one of the pilot areas in the government's decentralisation pilot, the organisations were surprised by the demand that was revealed – or generated – through their efforts. Toby Blume tells of 3000 citizens commenting on Lambeth Council's plans for more cooperative ways of working. Katy Wilkinson mentions the high level of public interest in policy issues and also spontaneous mobilisation of opposition to specific policies.

Several contributions pose a puzzle of simultaneously low and high levels of participation. For example in York, where there were sparsely attended public meetings at the same time and on the same topics as had generated petitions from 8% of the city's population. In part, this puzzle is resolved by recognition of the distinction between 'invited' participation, where the parameters are set by the state, and 'popular' participation, which is organised and led by citizens (Cornwall, 2004).

The participative intent of the former is often not realised. In part this is due to the format (John, 2009) – though, as demonstrated in Dan Silver and Amina Lone's piece, their public meetings in Salford and Manchester on the riots were relatively well attended – but more significantly because of the dominance of constituted power.

What is also interesting is not whether citizens will come forward or not, but what forms this takes when they do. Paul McCabe illustrates how with difficult and contested policy issues, such as planning and housing development, inviting the views of citizens can feel to those inside a conventional policy design akin to opening the door to an angry mob. He acknowledges the possibility of a dark and primal fear of the other. This is not to deny that sometimes people are angry, resentful, upset or vicious. Dan Silver and Amina Lone describe the riots in Salford as being widely seen as a demonstration of anger against the police. Events like those of summer 2011 in the UK are complex and extreme cases, with differing interpretations, and there were damaging effects of these events for all of the actors involved. Facilitated dialogues like the Community Conversations act as a reminder not to see the angry mob as something 'other'. Community Conversations, including discussion about the causes of the riots, seemed nuanced, subtle and comprehensive, suggesting what could be possible through more co-productive approaches.

More broadly, there are many different things that could be going on when citizens' mobilisation appears as angry protest. It could be the case that some of the forms engagement takes are a product of constituted systems that hold citizens at arm's length from decisions, offer limited sets of options without opportunities to develop alternative ideas, just to accept or reject what has been offered. Perhaps citizens' assets do not appear at their finest when 'their agency [is] constantly and fatally submerged', to use an expression from Jess Steele, whose contribution makes the point: 'Of course, as always, those with power were able to play out their values in the real world while those without power became angry and disengaged.' Maura Rose sets out her 'firm belief' that when people's 'opinions and feelings are ignored, that produces dissatisfaction and anger and can lead to impasse'. Her examples show how empathy may unlock solutions where people have become 'locked into defensive positions, either physical or metaphorical', unable to see shared goals. Some of the pejorative reaction to citizen anger may also lie in the distaste for expressions of emotion in a dispassionate ultra-rationalist constituted world. Anger is not always recognised as potential positive mobilisation, and conventional approaches tend to prefer to suppress such manifestations of passion. Fear of people's anger might also be connected to other assumptions in conventional designs that people have fixed preferences rather than understand the prospects for amended preferences based on dialogue, reflection and deliberation. One alternative hypothesis suggested by the contributions, and which needs to be further explored and tested, is that alternative forms of more co-productive policy design open up citizens' assets for democratic problem solving. Collective mobilisation might not need to be synchronous, as suggested by the example of MapLocal, which allows for asynchronous participation of individuals in a wider conversation.

How are different forms of expertise respected without being diluted?

The contributions have demonstrated various grammars of co-productive policy design, including how not to be too quick to ascribe particular knowledge to particular roles or individuals. Instead they advocate looking more openly at the multiple assets which different individuals and constituencies can bring to policy processes. Opening up the notion of expertise can work to draw in the most marginalised groups into the policy process – for example, the traditional communities engaged in the work of Raza Planning and rioters in the Reading the Riots work. Ostrom (1996, p. 1082) points to the need for synergies, when 'inputs are diverse entities and complements, synergy can occur' (p. 1079). The contributions show that co-productive efforts demand a triangulation of different complementary forms of expertise. Thus not marginalising technical, legal or scientific expertise, or neglecting leadership, but valuing them together with local knowledge and experiential expertise.

In Chapter Two a tightly bounded model of policy making was rejected. The boundaries being rejected were those that confined specific skills and roles to particular groups. For example, in the contributions, civic leadership was being provided by others to complement democratically mandated leaders, drawing on different bases for legitimacy and accountability in its widest sense. Several contributors also suggested that even in a tightly bounded model, lines were in reality much more porous and blurred. However, synergy of expertise demands that art, craft and science are in balance, or at least represented in proportion to the demands of the specific context. Policy still benefits from imagination and leadership, combined with scientific evidence, plus direct experience. In a more co-productive approach, these forms of expertise are utilised and represented, rather than a formulaic notion of specific groups, and therefore some people or groups might bring a combination of an evidence base of tried and tested interventions, and some untried innovative suggestions, as well as reflections based on their own experiences. What this looks like in practice can be seen across the contributions, with people outside traditional academic institutions doing research, or professionals reconnecting with their own lived experience in the Bradford example by Michaela Howell and Margaret Wilkinson. Other contributions point to the value of skills such as facilitation and mediation, research and evidence gathering and organising and creative mobilisation, without ascribing these skills as being held solely by a particular group. The contributions also challenge a repeated misinterpretation of co-production: that drawing together these different forms of expertise implies their dilution. Co-production is importantly about respecting and learning from different forms of expertise, not abandoning differences or replacing the domination of one by another.

While co-production is mutually transformative – as the Morris Justice Project reflected, 'our assumptions of each other, policing, and research were challenged and complicated' - transformation does not mean that differences in values, interests and expertise are elided. For example, the contributions from Raza Planning and the Morris Justice Project show that the involvement and mobilisation of communities does not mean that the rigour of academic research is abandoned. As Teresa Córdova and Moises Gonzales reflect, the 'quality of the work really matters. Never at any point did anyone ever question the quality of our work. You want to make sure that what you are doing is tight.' Their 'analytical rigour' was not displaced by their values, 'quite the contrary'. The Morris Justice Project opened up statistical analysis through 'stats-n-action', a back-pocket report and sidewalk science. At the same time they demonstrated the power of combining research and experiential expertise to effect change. As one member commented, 'In order to speak back informed and with authority, we needed to "come from a place of knowing."' Michaela Howell and Margaret Wilkinson illustrate how first-hand storytelling of experience gave their data 'a human face'. As Paul McCabe reflects, bringing in citizens' expertise does not replace the need for other forms of expertise, such as city leaders. But rather, as Raza Planning showed, knowledge of planning processes and techniques can be used to facilitate the inclusion of a wider range of voices into decision-making policy choices. In Deptford, the Magpie project described by Jess Steele was a way to collectivise specialist knowledge.

Some work takes place in a circumstance where conventionally tightly bounded models continue to dominate. Other approaches are working in a more co-productive way with multiple forms of expertise. Both situations suggest that there are boundaries, with the implication that they need to be spanned. A number of the contributions cited the significance of intermediaries or 'boundary spanners' who were able to facilitate and mediate relationships between types of knowledge and expertise. Jess Steele describes how an 'escape[e]' from the local council helped citizens rescue a physical asset in Deptford. Raza Planners were able to act like 'deliberative practitioners' in their ability to listen empathically, build and sustain relationships and manage conflict. In their account of the Reading the Riots project, Amina Lone and Dan Silver illustrate the importance of having trust and credibility within different constituencies in order to initiate dialogue on a contested, sensitive and complex issue. Michaela Howell and Margaret Wilkinson show how trusted intermediaries can galvanise participants and support them to deal with the uncertainty of incompleteness. Maura Rose's view shows the importance, at points, of an independent figure, recognising that conflict is likely and demands not only mitigation but clear strategies for mediation.

What might 'incomplete' policy design look like?

In debates about change in public policy-orientated organisations, caution has been urged about avoiding an 'organisational fix' (Durose et al, 2013b) – that is, not trying to impose completeness on a process. Overly rigid policy designs were identified in the opening chapters as one of the negatives of conventional approaches. An argument was made for policy processes that are able to handle uncertainty and flexibility in response to circumstances and to change. These ideas have been referred to as 'incomplete' policy designs. While the precise outcomes may end up being specified as the process develops, what is specified from the outset is the 'design of the design', or what Goodin (1996 p. 28 cited in Lowndes and Roberts, 2013, p. 187) calls 'designing schemes for designing institutions'. Incompleteness balances value rationality with instrumental rationality to produce outcomes that also matter and meet shared values.

Part of the reason why policy should not be neatly fixed by professional policy makers then left unamended is that incompleteness involves openness to being 'palpably and directly affected' by the participation of citizens and to their involvement as co-designers of the policy process (Fung, 2001, p. 79; Garud, Jain and Tuertscher,

2008). As was seen in the government programme presented by Robert Rutherfoord and Lucy Spurling, engaging with communities had quickly and significantly changed local plans. As Maura Rose asserts, it may mean that the outcomes have a greater likelihood of being positive for all involved. Phil Jones and colleagues showcase how technologies can be used as tools for including citizens on technical issues, like spatial land use planning. MapLocal is literally and conceptually a new way of seeing. Michaela Howell and Margaret Wilkinson show an equally powerful set of 'low tech' tools, such as storytelling about people's journeys, mapping and prioritising circles and action charts.

Incompleteness in policy contexts is shown by the contributions to be a challenging notion to execute. Toby Blume's experiences in local government in London are instructive: 'Embarking on a journey whose eventual destination we cannot predict – without pre-empting where citizens will want to go – can be unnerving.' He describes how a lack of prescription in incomplete designs means that policy implementation requires interpretation. Thus, unfamiliar and new demands are placed on those involved, with risks of misinterpretation. However, the contributions also suggest ways to manage incompleteness. Policy options, choices and specifications of outcomes evolve through the process. However, these processes are deliberately designed and intended to produce concrete policy outcomes – there seems little point otherwise. In the Bradford example, the proponents of alternative methods had to convince other actors that there would be tangible results, despite being unable to list these in advance. As Michaela Howell and Margaret Wilkinson say, their mantras were to 'trust in the process', not for the sake of the process, but to deliver results, and to therefore 'focus on action' to achieve outcomes. Toby Blume encourages a focus on 'the art of the possible'. Raza Planning draws attention to the value of 'learning by doing', reflecting that, 'you learn by actually engaging in the process. The process of engagement is what teaches us how to engage. Which also means that sometimes you are going to make mistakes.' Robert Rutherfoord and Lucy Spurling illustrate how processes and relationship should not be 'directive', but instead 'develop in an iterative and co-productive way'. The programme they discuss was intended to 'test proposition[s]'. Incompleteness implies a recasting of traditional notions of policy 'failure' as part of an iterative process of learning and adaptation.

Another theme across the contributions was 'relationships, relationships, relationships'. Members of the Morris Justice Project call themselves a 'family of a different kind'. Relationships are referred to in the sense of, as Raza Planning term it, both 'being' and 'getting' 'in there' – so building tightly bonded relationships within a particular community but also bridging relationships able to generate more diverse coalitions. This emphasis on relationships is underpinned by a positive-sum conception of power – power is the property of relationships between people. It can be generated, shared and is not diminished by being distributed. These relationships can generate new possibilities, challenge the usual ways of doing things and create alternatives. One condition for successful co-production from Ostrom's work is that 'participants need to be able to build a credible commitment to one another so that if one side increases input, the other will continue at the same or higher levels' (Ostrom, 1996, p. 1082). This notion of a 'credible commitment' fits with the contributions' understanding of how relationships can help manage incomplete policy designs. They offer an alternative to mechanisms in conventional designs for holding people to account for their contributions and outputs. In traditional models, policy might specify a series of predefined outputs, against which delivery could be judged to have succeeded or failed. However, if the contours of a policy are shaped as it evolves, and iterations take account of lessons from earlier attempts, then relationships help deliver the process and outputs, and ensure actors are accountable to one another. Relationships are hard currency. Relationships and process are not a substitute for action and outcomes, but are the activity through which it is hoped that better outcomes will be achieved. For instance – as also shown in Michaela Howell and Margaret Wilkinson's contribution – in Jess Steele's example of replacing a large-scale 'solution-focused [...] master plan' with one which was community led and process and relationship focused. One corollary is the idea that facilitation skills, such as detailed in Maura Rose's contribution, cannot be dismissed as a 'luxury' or 'sitting in a room, listening to whale music'.

Conclusion

This chapter has sought to challenge, deepen and develop the theorising set out in the opening chapters of the book. It reinforces the need for change in the conventional policy designs, but what is clearly articulated is the growing questioning of the limitations, appropriateness and sustainability of the conventional policy process from inside and outside. Nevertheless, the scope for change is constrained by the difficulties of establishing new ways of doing, regardless of the level of commitment to the ideas. Even recognising the agency and efficacy of those up for the challenge, co-production remains a 'daunting' ambition. But the theorising and empirical insights in this book show us that we should remain hopeful about the prospect for change. The chapter has also set out what we have learnt about the vision and grammar of a co-productive alternative.

Moving towards co-productive policy design poses difficult questions and a series of dilemmas for participants. One crucial concern is when those moving towards more co-productive approaches are met with others who have a more zero-sum notion of power. Not meeting half way might risk less powerful participants being co-opted, and losing critical distance. Strategies for handling these dilemmas included a dual insider and outside strategy – working with those in a conventional power position, while retaining the option to resist co-option. Other strategies for generating change were to understand its rhythms, being opportunistic and seizing the moment; to knowingly disrupt rhythms and established practices and look for techniques of creative disruption, as well as acknowledge the human and emotional side of change.

Attempts to reconstitute the policy process do not exist within a vacuum and conventional policy designs can feel deeply entrenched and immutable to change. The contributors show how the strength of their vision gave them a sense that things could be different. Relational forms of power do not negate the need for muscular leadership or stewardship. Expressing values provided 'contours' and leadership that mobilise action; practice is explicitly value driven. But what happens when there is a clash of values? The contributions show the potential for 'win–win' strategies to be developed even in a context of fierce debates over values. Surfacing differences in values can be useful in generating respect for difference and in mobilising broader participation. What the contributions point to is meta-consensus, which does not mean ignoring value differences but rather working to identify points where consensus on values, preferences and beliefs may be possible.

The appetite of citizens to get involved is always questioned and apathy assumed. Apathy is belied by the simultaneous realities of low levels of formal invited participation and often unwanted relatively high levels of informal, popular but non-progressive participation which is not concerned with social justice or alternative solutions. The contributions point to the value of other strategies for popular participation which might generate higher levels of socially progressive and constructive participation, notably community organising. A crucial lesson from organising is that it is important to recognise, seek to understand and harness emotion, not fear it. Emotion is an important route to involvement. Through being involved in co-productive processes, the assets held by citizens are opened up. The more they engage, the better able they are to engage.

Recognising the valuable assets which citizens can bring to the table does not diminish the forms of expertise existing within conventional forms of policy. Instead, it acknowledges that these different forms of expertise can be complementary. The contributions show us that we should avoid ascribing particular forms of expertise to particular groups but also that challenging these conventional tightly bounded demarcations demands nuanced, careful mediation and facilitation.

Generating change comes from flexible strategies, which recognise the interdependency and significance of both the vision and grammar of co-productive policy design. It is important that the grammar of co-production remains 'underspecified' (Garud, Jain and Tuertscher, 2008) in order to be open to being 'palpably and directly affected' by the participation of citizens (Fung, 2001, p. 79). But dealing with the uncertainty of incompleteness can be difficult. What the theorising and empirical insights presented here suggest is that incompleteness can be managed through building relationships of trust and effective process which gives space for experimentation and failure. This avocation is not a cop-out from focusing on outcomes, but a way of achieving better outcomes.

CHAPTER FIVE

Governance for co-productive policy designs

This book advances an emergent critique that conventional, constituted approaches to policy making and analysis are limited in their potential to address 'wicked' and 'squishy' policy problems which we face as a society. These problems range from the challenges of a super-diverse society to environmental sustainability to the future of public services. Experiences of failure in conventional policy designs are unremarkable. To ordinary citizens, this policy failure often 'presents itself as a glaring discrepancy between the official rhetoric on an issue and the reality on the ground, as being de facto abandoned by public officials or as being excluded from the central institutions of society' (Wagenaar, 2007, p. 28). Failures are extreme cases, but there is also a growing sense, shared by some policy makers and other policy actors, that current models are simply insufficient to generate the level of creativity and innovation needed.

Yet it is vital to retain a commitment to the idea that the policy process has the potential to be more than a 'fuzzy gamble' (Dror, 1986). The arguments presented in this book go beyond critique, to draw on and appropriate the rich lineage of co-production as a lens for contesting and reimagining the concept of power, the visions and grammars that frame, inform and guide policy design. Modelling a commitment to incomplete design (Garud, Jain and Tuertscher, 2008), the book aims to offer a contribution to 'the practical work of experimentation' (Lowndes and Roberts, 2013, p. 189) and begin to theorise co-productive policy designs.

This book has worked with grounded, powerful reflections on the potentialities of co-producing policy from policy makers, researchers, practitioners and activists. These contributions are important, not for developing a 'how to guide' of who, what, where, when and how for co-producing policy, but rather because they embody the importance and value of policy experimentation. From these insights, it is asserted that there can be co-productive alternatives which are able to 'mobilise and use the knowledge, resources and energies of empowered citizens' (Agger, 2012, p. 29), that also reinvigorate rather than dilute Lasswell's

(1971, p. x) vision of the policy process as 'creating knowledge needed by the democratic polity'.

This book has demonstrated a growing appetite for change being advanced within and outside of conventional policy design. It has set out features of vision and grammar for a co-productive alternative. What underpins co-productive designs is not only recognition of how zero-sum power works, but the positive-sum alternative to it: how to generate power through articulating values and using those values to inform practice. Building positive-sum power is not about espousing false consensus. It comes from articulating the emotional effects of policy, surfacing differences and working through them to identify opportunities for meta-consensus. It comes from retaining the flexibility to work in a way which is appropriate to the circumstances. To have grammar that enables resistance and collaboration, according to what secures better policy outcomes. To be comfortable in this incomplete view of the policy process demands respect for different forms of expertise, nuanced facilitation and relationships of trust.

The current context makes a shift towards constitutive policy making daunting, but more important than ever. Recognising that co-production of policy making is 'inescapably a normative project' acknowledges an intention to remake and institutionalise values and power relationships (Lowndes and Roberts, 2013, p. 187). Co-production may be understood as radical and transformative, but it also builds on and reinvigorates a rich intellectual lineage and grounding in democratic practice. Co-production aims to reposition citizens as an 'active and part of a common solution to social problems' (Brannan, John and Stoker, 2006). This is all well and good, but advocates of co-productive approaches may need to do intellectual battle with policy zombies. They may need to defend themselves against charges that co-production is yet another policy unicorn; those arguing for co-production do not believe in unicorns. However, it is true that co-productive policy designs run the risk of falling into the category of 'inspiring' but 'marginal' (Boyte, 2005). The theorising and empirical insights presented here are prefigurative of a different way for doing policy. Importantly, they do not put forward one rigid prescriptive model in place of another. The book has presented the argument that activity at different scales is valuable and, as the Morris Justice Project exhorts us, to 'dream big; work local'. The aim here is not to present something for 'scaling up', instead, co-production provides a way of 'scaling out' and proliferating policy experimentation.

Chances of proliferation are arguably stronger as more exemplars are created. Conditions for successful co-production are said to be 'most likely to be met' (Ostrom, 1996, p. 1082) in a context of decentralised or polycentric governance, that is arrangements with 'many centres of decision-making, which are formally independent of each other' (Ostrom, Tiebout and Warren, 1961, p. 831) and which 'offer citizens opportunities to organise not one, but many, governing authorities' (Ostrom, 1996, p. 1082). These 'messy' self-governing arrangements are found to 'significantly outperform' larger, unified, more distant public government and allow for more effective sharing of resources (Ostrom, 1999, p. 526). Such arrangements have been developed to draw citizens into making key policy decisions – for example Archon Fung's (2001) work in Chicago.

In Fung's example, local government provides a framework, specifying broad outcomes. Local groups, which involve citizens, professionals and public organisations, are able to 'set and implement, through deliberative processes, the specific ends and means toward broad public aims' (Fung, 2001, p. 75). This approach offers better adapted rules and draws in local knowledge (Ostrom, 1996; Lowndes and Roberts, 2013), facilitating policy experimentation and innovation. Local government offers support, monitors performance outcomes, exerts sanctions and intervenes in the case of failure. This system of 'accountable autonomy', 'allows those closest to concrete public problems to innovate and utilise their utility' (Fung, 2001, p. 75), but also allows citizens to play different roles according to their interest, ranging from seeking formal authority through election, attending monthly meetings, to continuous and direct participation (Fung, 2001, p. 78). The notion of polycentrism tallies with Dryzek and Niemeyer's (2006, p. 647) take on democracy and their avocation of 'pluralism at the simple level combined with meta-consensus on values, beliefs, and preferences'. Polycentrism allows for generative possibilities and a way of negotiating power inequities through proliferation of a variety of different institutional forms. As Mary Parker Follett (1998, p. 39) once wrote, 'Unity, not uniformity, must be our aim. We attain unity only through variety. Differences must be integrated, not annihilated, not absorbed.'

Polycentrism allows people to come together at different scales, according to their interests and with different forms of interaction (Ostrom, 1989). These multiple, overlapping governing authorities allow for self-organisation and for public authority to be shared (Salamon, 2002): for the strategic and the local to come together in complement. Polycentrism mixes decentralised and general governance, where 'rules at a large system level can be written in a general form that can then be tailored to local circumstances' (Ostrom, 1996, p.

1082). Polycentrism 'reframes the debate between participatory and representative democracy by highlighting the importance of both' (Boyte, 2005, p. 523). Polycentrism may offer us a way of thinking about how the co-production of policy making can be 'scaled out'.

These reflections on polycentrism suggest governance arrangements which can facilitate co-productive policy design. This book opens the debate about the desirability and feasibility of change and puts forward the vision and grammar of an alternative. The book has been conceived as a conversation between theory and practice. We now want to continue that debate and conversation. We do so sharing Bob Jessop's sense of a 'self-reflexive irony', in which we 'recognise the likelihood of failure but always proceed as if success were possible, seeking creative solutions, while always acknowledging and engaging with the limits of any such solution' (Jessop cited in Taylor, 2007, p. 314).

Co-producing research

Working alongside 30 individual contributors, the authors are two researchers working in research-intensive higher education institutions in the UK. We are long-standing collaborators whose research interests convene around the politics, policies and practices of participation, particularly at the neighbourhood or local level. The scholarship of individuals such as C. Wright Mills, Harold Lasswell and J.K. Gibson-Graham inspires us in claiming a role for research in building public value and generating new democratic potentialities. We see ourselves as engaged scholars, who want to promote democratic and progressive values through our work, particularly through our collaboration beyond the academy with policy makers, practitioners, activists and ordinary citizens. Our work is informed and, we would argue, strengthened by recognising the value of different forms of expertise and by actively seeking to contribute and have appeal and resonance outside of academia.

We are conscious of – and indeed, have sympathy with – the accusation of a 'relevance gap' (British Academy, 2008) which is oft made regarding academic research. We recognise that the ways that research is weighted and valued within the academic community can serve to perpetuate a particular hierarchical ordering that disincentivises collaborative, transdisciplinary and applied work (Dowling, 2008). This ordering speaks to a wider debate in the social sciences and humanities about the purpose and value of research. Research that involves collaboration outside academia, that is problem centred and seeks to address real-life concerns is too often dismissed or devalued within the academy. Such work is perceived as simply fulfilling a technocratic demand for 'evidence' for policy making or as a naïve co-option or collusion with a wider neoliberal project. The work of Gibson-Graham presents a more hopeful position. Drawing from theories of performativity, Julie Graham and Kathleen Gibson assert the constitutive possibilities of research in shaping 'worlds that exist and in bringing new worlds into being' through collaboration inside and outside of the academy. We share their questioning of how as academic researchers we may 'become open to possibility rather than limits on the possible?' (Gibson-Graham, 2008, p. 614).

So, what have we learnt from the experiences of authoring this book? The book continues our critical reflection about the participatory nature of our own practice (Durose et al, 2011; Beebeejaun et al, 2013, 2014; Richardson, 2014). As scholars working in the field of participation, we are conscious that research about participation in the policy process has rarely, in itself, been participatory. This book offers us an important opportunity to reflect on the practice and governance of research. In a recent article, we explored the power of published or written text as one of the exclusionary devices of the academy (Beebeejaun et al, 2013). However, in earlier papers and books, we too have excluded our community and non-academic collaborators from the process of writing. We wanted, in our advocacy of co-production, to use these approaches in this current work. We wanted this book to exemplify some of the substantive ideas that it conveys, such as giving respect and value to different types of knowledge, including experiential expertise alongside theoretical insights, and acknowledging the iterative processes of idea formation, through a move away/move towards a more dialogic form of knowledge production.

Could we have gone further? Of course. We see this book as a step along in generating the vision and grammar of co-production in research. At times it seemed hard to avoid some crude and inaccurate implications that academics are not also practitioners or that practitioners do not theorise or write on their own platforms. Despite this, the idea of co-producing a written piece is not principle for the sake of worthy principle. Some of the same frustrations as with conventional policy processes drive co-production of research. The failure to integrate different forms of expertise is not only infuriating and upsetting to the excluded subjects of research (Gallaher, 1971) but wastes crucial human assets/capital to help us figure out how to be a better society, and to articulate ideas in a more rounded and grounded way.

To help present some radical and alternative ideas, we have curated contributions from policy makers, researchers inside and outside the academy, practitioners and activists. They are all actively engaged in bringing citizens into the policy process, across research, analysis, making, implementation and evaluation. We were able to convene this book and draw in a range of policy makers, practitioners, researchers and activists because of our longstanding and trusted networks. Most of our collaborators are people who we have met over the years whom we have felt inspired by. But we are conscious that there are power dynamics within these relationships. As academic researchers, we are often in a privileged position, able to leverage resources, give time and priority to these sorts of projects and have a platform through publishing. We were keen to use this privilege to give space to those outside the academy to share their stories, reflections and analysis.

Collaborating with policy makers, practitioners and activists outside of the academy does have fundamental implications for our research practice. It does not mean abandoning our role or expertise as researchers. Instead, co-production of research means respecting and valuing different forms of expertise in the research process. Co-production of research also allows the authority, resources and status of the academy to contribute as part of advocacy coalition for social and policy change. Something that our contributors showed is not only needed, but also possible. We hope that doing this work within the academy will contribute to questioning our disciplinary parameters and institutional incentives. More broadly, to help in democratising our institutions and promoting democratic and progressive values that in the current context seems more important than ever.

References

Agamben, G. (2005) *The state of exception*, Chicago: University of Chicago Press.

Agger, A. (2012) 'Towards tailor-made participation: how to involve different types of citizens in participatory governance', *Town Planning Review*, 83(1): 29–45.

Agranoff, R. (2007) *Managing within networks: adding value to public organizations*, Washington, DC: Georgetown University Press.

Alford, J. (2009) *Engaging public sector clients: from service delivery to co-production*, Basingstoke: Palgrave.

Allio, L. (2014) *Design thinking for public service excellence*, Singapore: UNDP Global Centre for Public Service Excellence.

Alinsky, S. D. (1946) *Reveille for radicals*, New York: Vintage Books.

Alinsky, S. D. (1971) *Rules for radicals*, New York: Vintage Books.

Allison, G. T. (1971) *Essence of decision*, New York: Little Brown.

Arendt, H. (1963) *On revolution*, New York: Viking.

Arnstein, S. (1969) 'A ladder of citizen participation', *Journal of the American Institute of Planners*, 33: 216–224.

Atkinson, D. (2012) *Nourishing social renewal*, Brewin: Studley.

Atkinson, R. (2003) 'Addressing urban social exclusion through community involvement in urban regeneration', in Imrie, R. and Raco, M. (eds) *Urban renaissance? New Labour, community and urban policy*, Bristol: Policy Press, 101–119.

Audit Commission (2003) *Making ends meet*, London: Audit Commission.

Bang, H. (2005) 'Among everyday makers and expert citizens', in Newman, J. (ed) *Remaking governance*, Bristol: Policy Press, 159–178.

Bardach, E. (2011) *A practical guide for policy analysis: the eightfold path to more effective problem solving*, 4th edition, Washington, DC: CQ Press.

Barker, A. (2010) *Co-production of local public services*, London: Local Authorities Research Council Initiative.

Bason, C. (ed) (2014), *Design for policy*, Farnham, Surrey: Gower Publishing.

Baumgartner, F. and Jones, B. (1993) *Agendas and instability in American politics*, Chicago: University of Chicago Press.

Beck, D. and Purcell, R. (2013) *International community organising: taking power, making change*, Bristol: Policy Press.

Beebeejaun, Y., Durose, C., Rees, J., Richardson, J. and Richardson, L. (2013) 'Public value or public harm? Towards co-production in research with communities', *Environment and Planning C*, early view

Beebeejaun, Y., Durose, C., Rees, J., Richardson, J. and Richardson, L. (2014) 'Beyond text: exploring ethos and method in co-producing research with communities', *Community Development Journal*, 49(1), 37–53.

Benjamin, W. (1921) *Critique of violence*, New York, NY: Schocken Books.

Bernalillo County (2011) *International Trail Scoping Report*, Bernalillo County Public Works, www.bernco.gov/uploads/FileLinks/df6a90ac60074c829ceb4889d9b62a70/International_Trail_Scoping_Report.pdf

Berry, N. (2012) 'Scaling up is not always best', *The Guardian*, 11 October, www.theguardian.com/public-leaders-network/2012/oct/11/locality-public-sector-scaling-design

Bobrow, D. B. and Dryzek, J. S. (1987) *Policy analysis by design*, Pittsburgh: University of Pittsburgh Press.

Bovaird, T. (2007) 'Beyond engagement and participation: user and community co-production of public services', *Public Administration Review* (September/October): 846–860.

Bovaird, T. and Loeffler, E. (2012) 'From engagement to co-production: the contribution of users and communities to outcomes and public value', *Voluntas*, 23(4): 1119–38.

Bovens, M. and t' Hart, P. (1996) *Understanding policy fiascoes*, New Brunswick, NJ: Transaction Publishers.

Bovens, M., t'Hart, P. and Peters, B. G. (2001) *Success and failure in public governance: a comparative analysis*, Cheltenham: Edward Elgar.

Boyer, B., Cook, J. W. and Steinberg, M. (2011) *Recipes for systemic change*, Helsinki, Finland: Sitra.

Boyte, H. C. (2005) Reframing democracy: governance, civic agency, and politics, *Public Administration Review*, 65(5): 518–528.

Bradwell, P. and Marr, S. (2008) *Making the most of collaboration: an international survey of public service co-design*, London: Demos/Price Waterhouse Coopers.

Brannan, T., John, P. and Stoker, G. (2006) 'Active citizenship and effective public services: how can we know what really works?', *Urban Studies*, 43: 993–1008.

Brewer, G. D. (1974) 'The policy sciences emerge: to nurture and structure a discipline', *Policy Sciences*, 5: 239–244.

British Academy (2008) *Punching our weight: the humanities and social sciences in public policymaking*, London: British Academy.

Brudney, J. L. and England, R. E. (1983) 'Towards a definition of the coproduction concept', *Public Administration Review*, 43(1): 59–65.

Burns, C., Cottam, H., Vanstone, C. and Winhall, J. (2006) *Transformational design*, London: Design Council.

Burton, J. (1986) ''The theory of conflict resolution'', *Current Research on Peace and Violence*, 9(3): 125–130.

Bussu, S. and Galanti, M. T. (2014) 'Facilitating co-production: from a literature review towards a working definition', a paper presented at the Political Studies Association Conference, Manchester, April.

Butler, D., Adonis, A. and Travers, T. (1994) *Failure in British government: the politics of the poll tax*, Oxford: Oxford University Press.

Cabinet Office (2001) *Professional policy making*, London: Cabinet Office.

Cahill, C. (2007) 'Doing research with young people: participatory research and the rituals of collective work', *Children's Geographies*, 5(3): 297–312.

Cabinet Office (2012) 'Co-Chair vision: UK priorities for the Open Government Partnership', www.gov.uk/government/publications/open-government-partnership-uk-co-chair-vision

Cahn, E. and Gray, C. (2012) 'Co-production from a normative perspective', in Pestoff, V., Brandsen, T. and Verschuere, B. (eds), *New public governance, the third sector and co-production*, Abingdon, Oxon: Routledge.

Caplan, N. (1979) 'The two-communities theory and knowledge utilization', *American Behavioral Scientist*, 22(3): 459–470.

Carley, M. and Baley, R. (2009) *Urban extensions, planning and participation – lessons from Derwenthorpe and other new communities*, York: Joseph Rowntree Foundation.

Cimasi, R. J. (2013) *Accountable care organisations: value metrics and capital formation*, Boco Raton, FL: CRC Press.

City of Albuquerque (2012) *International District Sector Development Plan*, Planning Department, www.cabq.gov/planning/residents/sector-development-plan-updates/international-district-sector-development-plan

City of Albuquerque (2014) *'Our Town' initiative in Albuquerque*, Cultural Services Department, www.cabq.gov/culturalservices/ourtownprogram

Clarke, J. (2005) 'New Labour's citizens: activated, empowered, responsibilised, abandoned?', *Critical Social Policy*, 25: 447–463.

Clegg, S. R. (1989) *Frameworks of power*, London: Sage.

Cohen, M. D., March, J. G. and Olsen, J. P. (1972) 'A garbage can model of organizational choice', *Administrative Science Quarterly*, 17(1): 1–25.

Collins, H. M. and Evans, R. J. (2002) 'The third wave of science studies: studies of expertise and experience', *Social Studies of Science*, 32(2): 235–296.

Conroy, M., Clarke, H. and Wilson, L. (2012) *Connected health and social care communities*, Swindon: AHRC.

Cooke, B. and Kothari, U. (2001) *Participation, the new tyranny?*, London: Zed Books.

Córdova, T. (2011) 'Community-based research and participatory change: a strategic, multi-method community impact assessment', *Journal of Community Practice*, 19(1): 29–47.

Cornwall, A. (2004) 'New democratic spaces? The politics and dynamics of institutionalised participation', *IDS Bulletin*, 35(2): 1–10.

Dalton, R. J. (2009) *The good citizen: how a younger generation is reshaping American politics*, revised edition, Washington, DC: Congressional Quarterly Press.

Davies, H. T. O., Nutley, S. M. and Smith, P. C. (2000) *What works: evidence-based policy and practice in public services*, Bristol: Policy Press.

De Filippis, J., Fisher, R. and Shragge, E. (2010) *Contesting community: the limits and potential of local organizing*, New Brunswick, NJ: Rutgers University Press.

Denis, J. and Lomas J. (2003) 'Convergent evolution: the academic and policy roots of collaborative research', *Journal of Health Services Research and Policy*, 8(2): 1–6.

Department for Communities and Local Government (DCLG) (2013) *Neighbourhood community budgets: research, learning, evaluation, and lessons*, London: Department for Communities and Local Government.

Design Council (2013) *Design for public good*, London: Design Council.

DesignGov (2013) *Design thinking compendium*, Canberra, ACT: Australian Government.

Dewey, J. (1934) *Art as experience*, New York: Paragon/Putnam's.

Dodge, J. (2010) 'Tensions in deliberative practice: a view from civil society', *Critical Policy Studies*, 4(4): 382–404.

Diers, J. (2004) *Neighbor power: building community the Seattle way*, Seattle: University of Washington Press.

Dowling, R. (2008) 'Geographies of identity: labouring in the neoliberal university', *Progress in Human Geography*, 32: 812–820.

Dror, Y. (1986) *Policymaking under adversity*, New Brunswick, NJ: Transaction Publishers.

Dryzek, J. S. and Niemeyer, S. (2006) 'Reconciling pluralism and consensus as political ideals', *American Journal of Political Science*, 50(3): 634–649.

Duncan, S. (2005) 'Towards evidence-inspired policy making', *Social Sciences*, 61: 10–11.

Dunleavy, P. (1995) 'Policy disasters: explaining the UK's record', *Public Policy and Administration*, 10(2): 52–70.

Durose, C., Greasley, S. and Richardson, L. (eds) (2009) *Changing local governance, changing citizens*, Bristol: Policy Press.

Durose, C., Justice, J. and Skelcher C. (2013) *Beyond the state: mobilising and co-producing with communities – insights for policy and practice*, Birmingham: University of Birmingham.

Durose, C., Justice, J. and Skelcher, C. (2015) 'Governing at arm's length: eroding or enhancing democracy?', *Policy & Politics*, 43(1), 137–53.

Durose, C., Beebeejaun, Y., Rees, J., Richardson, J. and Richardson, L. (2011) *Towards co-production in research with communities*, Swindon: AHRC.

Durose, C., Mangan, C., Needham, C. and Rees, J. (2013a) *Transforming local public services through co- production*, Birmingham: AHRC Connected Communities/Department for Communities and Local Government/University of Birmingham.

Durose, C., Richardson, L., Dickinson, H. and Williams, I. (2013b) 'Dos and don'ts for involving citizens in the design and delivery of health and social care', *Journal of Integrated Care*, 21(6): 326–335.

Esaiasson, P. and Narud, H. M. (eds) (2013) 'Between-election democracy: an introductory note', in *Between-election democracy: the representative relationship after election day*, Colchester: ECPR Press.

Etzioni, A. (1988) *The moral dimension: towards a new economics*, New York: Free Press.

Etzioni, A. (1993) *The spirit of community: rights, responsibilities and the communitarian agenda*, New York: Crown.

Evans, B. with Vujicic, M. (2005) 'Political wolves and economic sheep: the sustainability of public health insurance in Canada', in Maynard, A. (ed), *The public–private mix for health*, Abingdon, Oxon: Radcliffe Publishing, 117-140.

Ewert, B. and Evers, A. (2012) 'Co-production: contested meanings and challenges for user organisations', in Pestoff, V., Brandsen, T. and Verschuere, B. (eds), *New public governance, the third sector and co-production*, Abingdon, Oxon: Routledge.

Festinger, L. (1957) *A theory of cognitive dissonance*, Stanford, CA: Stanford University Press.

Fischer, F. (1995) *Evaluating public policy*, Chicago: Nelson-Hall.

Fischer, F. (2000) *Citizens, experts, and the environment: the politics of local knowledge*, Durham, NC: Duke University Press.

Fishkin, J. S. (1997) *The voice of the people*, Durham, NC: Duke University Press.

Fishkin, J. S. and Luskin, R. C. (2000) 'The quest for deliberative democracy', in Saward, M. (ed), *Democratic innovation: deliberation, representation and association*, London: Routledge.

Fogg, R. W. (1985) 'Dealing with conflict: a repertoire of creative, peaceful approaches', *The Journal of Conflict Resolution*, 29(2) 330–58.

Foucault, M. (1979) 'Governmentality', *Ideology and Consciousness*, 6: 5–21.

Follett, M. P. (1924) *Creative experience*, New York: Longman Green and Co.

Follett, M. P. (1998) *The New State: Group organization the solution of popular government*, Philadelphia, PA: Pennsylvania State University Press.

Forester, J. (1999) *The deliberative practitioner: encouraging participatory planning processes*, Cambridge/London: MIT Press.

Freire, P. (1996) *Pedagogy of the oppressed*, London: Continuum.

Fung, A. (2001) 'Accountable autonomy: toward empowered deliberation in Chicago schools and policing', *Politics and Society*, 29(1): 73–103.

Fung, A. and Wright, E. O. (2001) 'Deepening democracy: Innovations in empowered participatory governance', *Politics & Society*, 29(1): 5–41.

Gallaher, A. (1971) 'Plainville: the twice-studied town', in Vidich, A., Bensman, J. and Stein, M. (eds), *Reflections on community studies*, New York: Harper and Row, 285–303.

Garud, R., Jain, S. and Tuertscher, P. (2008) 'Incomplete by design and designing for incompleteness', *Organization Studies*, 29: 351–371.

Gaventa, J. (2005) *Claiming citizenship: rights, participation and accountability*, London: Zed Books.

Geva-May, I. with Wildavksy, A. (1997) *An operational approach to policy analysis: the craft*, Boston: Kluwer Academic Publishers.

Geva-May, I. and Pal, L. (1999) 'Good fences make good neighbors: policy evaluation and policy analysis', *Evaluation: The International Journal of Theory, Research and Practice*, 5(3): 259–277.

Gibson-Graham, J. K. (2008) 'Diverse economies: performative practices for "other worlds"', *Progress in Human Geography*, 32(5): 613–632.

Gilmore, R. W. (2007) *Golden gulag*. Berkeley, CA: University of California Press.

Goodchild, M. (2007) 'Citizens as sensors: the world of volunteered geography', *GeoJournal*, 69(4): 211–221.

Grant, W. (1997) 'BSE and the politics of food', in P. Dunleavy, A. Gamble, I. Holliday and G. Peele (eds), *Developments in British Politics 5*, Basingstoke: Macmillan, pp. 342–53.

Green, D. P. and Gerber, A. S. (2003) 'The underprovision of experiments in political science', *ANNALS of the American Academy of Political and Social Science*, 589: 94–112.

Greene, J. A. (1999) 'Zero tolerance: a case study of police policies and practices in New York City', *Crime and Delinquency*, 45(2): 171–187.

Hallsworth, M., with Parker, S. and Rutter, J. (2011) *Policy making in the real world, evidence and analysis*, London: Institute for Government.

Hansard Society. (2013) *Audit of political engagement 10: the 2013 Report*, London: Hansard Society.

Harcourt, B. E. (2001) *Illusion of order: the false promise of broken windows policing*, Cambridge, MA: Harvard University Press.

Hardt, M. and Negri, A. (2002) *Empire*, New Haven, CT: Harvard University Press.

Hatchard, J. L., Fooks, G. J., Evans-Reeves, K. A., Ulucanlar, S. and Gilmore, A. B. (2014) 'A critical evaluation of the volume, relevance and quality of evidence submitted by the tobacco industry to oppose standardised packaging of tobacco products', *British Medical Journal Open*, 4(2): 1–9.

Heskett, J. (2001) 'Past, present and future in design for industry', *Design Issues*, 17(1), 18–26.

Heskett, J. (2005) *Design: a very short introduction*, Oxford: OUP

HM Government (2010) *Decentralisation and the Localism Bill: an essential guide*, London: Her Majesty's Government.

HM Government (2011) *Community budgets prospectus,* London: Her Majesty's Government.

HM Government (2012) *Civil Service Reform Plan,* London: HSMO.

HM Treasury (1998) *Statistics: a matter of trust*, Cmd 3882, London: TSO.

HM Treasury (2003) *The Green Book: appraisal and evaluation in central government*, London: TSO.

Hogwood, B. W. and Gunn, L. A. (1984) *Policy analysis for the real world*, Oxford: Oxford University Press.

Horne. M. and Shirley, T. (2009) *Co-production in public services: a new partnership with citizens*, London: Prime Minister's Strategy Unit.

House of Commons Science and Technology Committee (2006) *Scientific advice, risk and evidence-based policy making*, London: HMSO.

Hughes, R. (1998) 'Considering the vignette technique and its application to a study of drug injecting and HIV risk and safer behaviour', *Sociology of Health and Illness*, 20(3): 381–400.

Jessop, B. (2003) Governance and metagovernance: on reflexivity, requisite variety and requisite irony, Department of Sociology, Lancaster University, www.lancaster.ac.uk/fass/resources/sociology-online-papers/papers/jessop-governance-and-metagovernance.pdf

John, P. (2009) 'Can citizen governance redress the representative bias of political participation?', *Public Administration Review*, 69(3): 494–503.

John, P. (2012) *Analyzing public policy*, 2nd edition, Abingdon, Oxon: Routledge.

John, P. (2015) 'The three ages of public policy: Theories of policy change and variation reconsidered', Paper prepared for the panel, 'The political science of public policy', held at the American Political Science Association meeting, San Francisco, 3-6 September 2015.

John, P., Cotterill, S., Moseley, A., Richardson, L., Smith, G., Stoker, G. and Wales, C. (2013) *Nudge, nudge, think, think: experimenting with ways to change civic behaviour*, London: Bloomsbury Academic.

Jones-Brown, D., Stoudt, B., Johnston, B., and Moran, K. (2013) *Stop, question and frisk policing practices in New York City: a primer*, 2nd edition, New York: John Jay College Center on Race, Crime and Justice.

Kelling, G. L. and Wilson, J. Q. (1982) '*Broken windows: the police and neighborhood safety'*, *The Atlantic Monthly*: March: 29–38, www.theatlantic.com/magazine/archive/1982/03/broken-windows/304465/

King, A. and Crewe, I. (2013) *The blunders of our governments*, London: Oneworld.

Kingdon, J. W. (1995) *Agendas, alternatives and public policies*, 2nd edition, New York: Longman.

Kretzmann, J. P. and McKnight, J. L. (1993) *Building communities from the inside out: a path toward finding and mobilising a community's assets*, Evanston, IL: Institute for Policy Research.

Kurniawan, M. and de Vries, W. T. (2015) 'The contradictory effects in efficiency and citizens' participation when employing Geo-ICT Apps within local government', *Local Government Studies*, 41(1): 119–36.

Lambeth Council (2011) *Sharing power: a new settlement between citizens and the state*, London: London Borough of Lambeth.

Lambeth Council (2013) *Lambeth Community Plan*, http://moderngov.lambeth.gov.uk/documents/s55297/06b%2020130403%20Community%20Plan%20FINAL.pdf

Lasswell, H. D. (1936) *Politics: who gets what, when, how*, London: Whittlesey House, McGraw-Hill.

Lasswell, H., 1971 *A pre-view of policy sciences*, New York: American Elsevier.

Lasswell, H. D. and Kaplan, A. (1950) *Power and society: a framework for political inquiry*, New Haven, CT: Yale University Press.

Leadbeater, C. and Cottam, H. (2007) 'The user generated state: public services 2.0', in Diamond, P. (ed.) *Public matters: the renewal of the public realm*, London, Politicos

Li, Y. and Marsh, D. (2008) 'New forms of political participation: searching for expert citizens and everyday makers', *British Journal of Political Science*, 38: 247–272.

Light, A., et al (2013) *Effectiveness in action*, Connected Communities 2012 Summit follow-up funding and co-design and co-development award.

Lindahl, H. (2007) 'Constituent power and reflexive identity: towards an ontology of collective selfhood', in M. Loughlin and N. Walker (eds), *The paradox of constitutionalism*, Oxford: Oxford University Press, 9–24.

Lindblom, C. E. (1959) 'The science of "muddling through"', *Public Administration Review*, 19(2): 79–88.

London Borough of Lambeth (2011) 'The Co-Operative Council sharing power: a new settlement between citizens and the state', London: London Borough of Lambeth, http://moderngov.lambeth.gov.uk/mgConvert2PDF.aspx?ID=26390

London Borough of Lambeth (2013a) 'Co-Operative Council Transformation Programme – commissioning cluster workstream. Proposals to establish new co-operative commissioning structure: business case', London: London Borough of Lambeth.

London Borough of Lambeth (2013b) *Lambeth Council's Community Plan 2013–16*, London: London Borough of Lambeth.

Lowndes, V. and Roberts, M. (2013) *Why institutions matter: the new institutionalism in political science*, Basingstoke: Palgrave MacMillan.

Lowndes, V. (2005) 'Something old, something new, something borrowed ... How institutions change (and stay the same) in local governance', *Policy Studies*, 26(3/4): 291–309.

Lukes, S. (2005) *Power: a radical view*, Basingstoke: Palgrave MacMillan.

MacDonald, H. (2013) 'Courts v. cops: The legal war on the war on crime', *City Journal*, www.city-journal.org/2013/23_1_war-on-crime.html

March J. G. and Olsen, J. P. (1989), *Rediscovering institutions: the organizational basis of politics,* London: Collier Macmillan.

Maude, F. (2013) 'Francis Maude's letter to UK OGP civil society network', www.gov.uk/government/publications/francis-maudes-letter-to-uk-ogp-civil-society-network/francis-maudes-letter-to-uk-ogp-civil-society-network

May, P. J. (1991) 'Reconsidering policy design: policies and publics', *Journal of Public Policy*, 11(2): 187–206.

Maynard-Moody, S. and Musheno, M. (2003) *Cops, teachers and counsellors: stories from the front line of public service*, Ann Arbor, MI: University of Michigan Press.

Miles, M. B. and Huberman, A. M. (1994) *Qualitative data analysis*, 2nd edition, Thousand Oaks, CA: Sage.

Mills, J. and Robson, S. (2010) 'Does community organising empower or oppress?', *CDX magazine*, winter: 12–14.

Mintzberg, H. (2005) *Managers not MBAs: a hard look at the soft practice of management and management development*, San Francisco, CA: Berrett-Koehler.

Mouffe, C. (2000) *The democratic paradox*, New York: Verso.

Mouffe, C. (2013) *Agonistics: thinking the world politically*, New York: Verso.

Mulgan, G. (2005) 'Government, knowledge and the business of policy-making: the potential and limits of evidence-based policy', *Evidence and Policy*, 1(2): 215–226.

Myrdal, G. (1972) 'How scientific are the social sciences', *Journal of Social Issues*, 28(4): 151–170.

Needham, C. (2011) *Personalising public services: understanding the personalisation narrative*, Bristol, Policy Press.

Needham, C. and Carr, S. (2009) *Co-production: an emerging evidence base for adult social care transformation*, London: Social Care Institute for Excellence.

Needham, C. and Mangan, C. (2014) *The 21st century public servant*, Birmingham: University of Birmingham.

Newman, J. (2012) *Working the spaces of power: activism, neoliberalism and gendered labour*, Bloomsbury: London.

Nicolini, D. 2013. *Practice theory, work, and organization: an introduction*, Oxford: Oxford University Press.

Olsen, J. P. (1997) 'Institutional design in democratic contexts', *Journal of Political Philosophy*, 5(3): 203–229.

O'Donovan, B. and Rubbra, T. (2012) *Public services, civil society and diseconomies of scale*, London: Vanguard Consulting/Locality.

Orr, K. M. and Bennett, M. (2009) 'Reflexivity in the co-production of academic-practitioner research', *Qualitative Research in Organisations and Management*, 4: 85–102.

Orr, K. M. and Bennett, M. (2010) 'Editorial', *Public Money & Management*, 30(4): 199–203.

Ostrom, E. (1990) *Governing the commons: the evolution of institutions for collective action*, Cambridge: Cambridge University Press.

Ostrom, E. (1993) 'A communitarian approach to local governance', *National Civic Review*, 82(3): 227–233.

Ostrom, E. (1996) 'Crossing the great divide: co-production, synergy and development', *World Development*, 24(6): 1073–1087.

Ostrom, E. (1999) 'Coping with tragedies of the commons', *Annual Review of Political Science*, 2: 493–535.

Ostrom, V. (1989) *The intellectual crisis in American public administration*, 2nd edition, Tuscaloosa, AL: University of Alabama Press.

Ostrom, V., Tiebout, C. M .and Warren, R. (1961) 'The organisation of government in metropolitan areas: a theoretical inquiry', *American Political Science Review*, 55(4): 831–842.

Parsons, W. (2002) 'From muddling through to muddling up – evidence based policy making and the modernisation of British government', *Public Policy and Administration*, 17(3): 43–60.

Pateman, C. (1970) *Participation and democratic theory*, Cambridge: Cambridge University Press.

Pearce, J. (2011) *Power in community: a research and social action scoping review*, Swindon: AHRC.

Pelletier, D., Kraak, V., McCullum, C., Uusitalo, U. and Rich, R. (1999) 'The shaping of collective values through deliberative democracy: an empirical study from New York's North Country', *Policy Sciences*, 32(2): 103–131.

Pestoff, V. (2012) 'Co-production and third sector social services in Europe – some crucial conceptual issues', in V. Pestoff, T. Brandsen, and B. Verschuere (eds), *New public governance, the third sector and co-production*, London: Routledge.

Pestoff, V., Brandsen, T. and Verschuere, B. (eds) (2012) *New public governance, the third sector and co-production*, Abingdon, Oxon: Routledge.

Pierson, P. (2002) 'The limits of design: explaining institutional origins and change', *Governance*, 13(4): 475–499.

Pohl, C., et al (2010) 'Researchers' roles in knowledge co-production: experience from sustainability research in Kenya, Switzerland, Bolivia and Nepal', *Science and Public Policy*, 37(4): 267–281.

Polya, G. (1945) *How to solve it*, Princeton, NJ: Princeton University Press.

Porter, L. (2010) *Unlearning the colonial cultures of planning*, Farnham, Surrey: Ashgate.

Preskill, H. and Beer, T. (2012) *Evaluating social innovation*, Center for Evaluation Innovation, www.fsg.org/tabid/191/ArticleId/708/Default.aspx?srpush=true

Pressman, J. L. and Wildavsky, A. (1979) *Implementation: how great expectations in Washington are dashed in Oakland: Or, why It's amazing that federal programs work at all, this being a saga of the economic development administration as told by two sympathetic observers who seek to build morals on a foundation of ruined hopes*, Berkeley: University of California Press.

Putnam, R. D. (1995) 'Bowling alone: America's declining social capital', *Journal of Democracy*, 6(1): 65–78.

Rams, D. (1995) *Weniger, aber besser* [Less, but better], Hamburg, Germany: Jo Klatt Design and Design Verlag.

Rawls, J. (1999) *A theory of justice*, Cambridge, MA: Harvard University Press.

Resource Center for Raza Planning (RCRP) (2013) *The Rio Arriba Indo-Hispano homeland: a living culture corridors plan*, Indo-Hispano Field School, School of Architecture and Planning: University of New Mexico.

Richardson, L. (2013) 'Putting the research boot on the policy-makers' foot: can participatory approaches change the relationship between policy-makers and evaluation?', *Social Policy and Administration*, 47(4): 483–500.

Richardson, L. (2014) 'Engaging the public in policy research: are community researchers the answer?', *Politics and Governance*, 2(1): 31–43.

Richardson, L. and Durose, C. (2013) *Who is accountable in localism? Findings from theory and practice*, Birmingham: AHRC Connected Communities/Department for Communities and Local Government/ University of Birmingham.

Richardson, L. and Le Grand, J. (2002) 'Outsider and insider expertise: the response of residents of deprived neighbourhood to an academic definition of social exclusion', *Social Policy and Administration*, 36: 496–515.

Rittel, H. W. J. (1966) 'Instrumental knowledge in politics', in Krauch, H. (ed) *Beiträge zum Verhältnis von Wissenschaften und Politk*, Heidelberg: Studiengruppe Für Systemforschung, 183–209.

Rittel, H. W. J. (1988) 'The reasoning of designers', Arbeitspapier zum International Congress on Planning and Design Theory in Boston, August 1987, Stuttgart: Universitaet Stuttgart, Schriftenreihe des Instituts fuer Grundlagen der Planung.

Rittel, H. W. J. and Webber, M. M. (1973) 'Dilemmas in a general theory of planning', *Policy Sciences*, 4: 155–169.

Robinson, J. and Tansey, J. (2006) 'Co-production, emergent properties and strong interactive social research: the Georgia Basin Futures Project', *Science and Public Policy*, 33(2): 151–160.

Rose, N. (1999) *Powers of freedom reframing political thought*, Cambridge: Cambridge University Press.

Rothstein, H. and Downer, J. (2012) 'Renewing Defra: exploring the emergence of risk-based policymaking in UK central government', *Public Administration*, 90(3): 781–799.

Russell, B. (1954) *Human society in ethics and politics*, London: Allen and Unwin.

Sabatier, P. A. and Jenkins-Smith, H. C. (eds) (1993) *Policy change and learning: an advocacy coalition approach*, Boulder, CO: Westview Press.

Salamon, L. (ed) (2002) *The tools of government: a guide to the new governance*, Oxford: OUP.

Schneider, A. and Ingram, H. (1997). *Policy design for democracy*, Lawrence: University of Kansas Press.

Schön, D. (1983) *The reflective practitioner: how professionals think in action*, New York: Basic Books.

Sen, A. K. (2003) *Stir it up: lessons in community organising and advocacy*, San Francisco: Jossey-Bass.

Sharp, E. (1980) 'Toward a new understanding of urban services and citizen participation: the co-production concept', *Midwest Review of Public Administration*, 14: 105–118.

Sieyès, A. E. J. (1789) *What is the third estate?*

Simon, A., Cordova, T., Cooke, J., Aguilera-Harwood, P. and Miera, B. (2004) *A dialogue for sustainability: people, place and water*, Annual proceedings, Council of Educators in Landscape Architecture (CELA), Charleston.

Simon, H. A. ([1969] 1996) *The sciences of the artificial*, 3rd edition, Cambridge, MA: MIT Press.

Simon, H. A. (1991) *Models of my life*, Cambridge, MA: MIT Press.

Sirianni, C. (2009) *Investing in democracy*, Washington, DC: Brookings Institution Press.

Skelcher, C., Mathur, N. and Smith, M. (2005) 'The public governance of collaborative spaces: Discourse, design and democracy', *Public Administration*, 83(3): 573–596.

Smith, G. (2005) *Power beyond the ballot: 57 democratic innovations from around the world*, London: The Power Inquiry.

Social Action and Research Foundation (SARF) (2012) *A tale of two cities*, Manchester: SARF.

Stoker, G. (2013) *Why policy-makers ignore evidence*, Public Policy@ Southampton, http://publicpolicy.southampton.ac.uk/why-policymakers-ignore-evidence/

Stoker, G. and John, P. (2009) 'Design experiments: engaging policy makers in the search for evidence about what works', *Political Studies*, 57(2): 356–373.

Stone, D. (1997) *Policy paradox: the art of political decision-making*, New York: W. W. Norton.

Stoudt, B. G., Fine, M. and Fox, M. (2012) '"NYC eats its young": growing up policed in the age of aggressive policing policies', *New York Law School Law Review*, 56: 1331–1372.

Stoudt, B. G. and Torre, M. E. (2014) 'The Morris Justice Project', in Brindle, P. (ed), *Sage cases in methodology*, London: Sage.

Strauch, R. E. (1975) '"Squishy problems" and quantitative methods', *Policy Sciences*, 6: 174–184.

Susskind, L. and Elliott, M. (1983) *Paternalism, conflict, and coproduction: learning from citizen action and citizen participation in Western Europe*, New York: Plenum Press.

Swyngedouw, E. (2005) 'Governance innovation and the citizen: the Janus-face of governance-beyond-the-state', *Urban Studies*, 42(11): 1991–2006.

Taylor, M. (2007) 'Community participation in the real world: opportunities and pitfalls in new governance spaces', *Urban Studies*, 44(2): 297–317.

Thompson, J.D. (1962) 'Organizations and output transactions', *American Journal of Sociology*, 309–24.

Torre, M. E. and Ayala, J. (2009) 'Envisioning participatory action research entremundos', *Feminism and Psychology*, 19(3): 387–393.

Torre, M. E. and Fine, M. (2005) 'Bar none: extending affirmative action to higher education in prison', *Journal of Social Issues*, 61(3): 569–594.

Unger, R. (2004) *False necessity: anti-necessitarian social theory in the service of radical democracy*, revised edition, London: Verso.

US National Design Policy Initiative (2009) *Report of the U.S. National Design Policy Summit*, US National Design Policy Initiative.

Verschuere, B., Brandsen, T. and Pestoff, V. (2012) 'Co-production: the state of the art in research and the future agenda', *Voluntas*, 23(3): 1083–1101.

Wagenaar, H. and Cook, S. N. (2003) 'Understanding policy practices: action, dialectic and deliberation in policy analysis', in Hajer, M. and Wagenaar, H. (eds), *Deliberative policy analysis: understanding governance in the network society*, Cambridge: Cambridge University Press, 139–171.

Wagenaar, H. (2007) 'Governance, complexity, and democratic participation: How citizens and public officials harness the complexities of neighborhood decline', *American Review of Public Administration*, 37(1): 17–50.

Wainwright, M. (2012) 'Salford meeting calls for gentler policing, youth opportunities and more thoughtful coverage by the media', *Guardian*, 8 March, www.theguardian.com/uk/the-northerner/2012/mar/08/reading-the-riots-community-conversations-salford

Walt, G. (1994) 'How far does research influence policy?', *European Journal of Public Health*, 4: 233–235.

Ward, K. (2006) 'Geography and public policy: towards public geographies', *Progress in Human Geography* 30(4), 495–503

Weil, M. (1986) 'Women, community and organising', in Van den Bergh, N. and Cooper, L. B. (eds), *Feminist visions for social work*, Silver Springs, MD: National Association of Social Workers, 187–210.

Weiss, C. (1993) 'When politics and evaluation research meet', *American Journal of Evaluation*, 14(1): 93–106.

Whitaker, G. P. (1980) 'Co-production: citizen participation in service delivery', *Public Administration Review*, 40(3): 240–46.

Wildavsky, A. (1979) *Speaking truth to power: the art and craft of policy analysis*, New Brunswick, NJ: Transaction Press.

Williams, P. (2002) 'The competent boundary spanner', *Public Administration*, 80(1): 103–112.

Williams, P. (2012) *Collaboration in public policy and practice: perspectives on boundary spanners*, Bristol: Policy Press.

Wright Mills, C. (1959) *The sociological imagination*, Oxford: Oxford University Press.

Yanow, D. (2004) 'Translating local knowledge at organizational peripheries', *British Journal of Management*, 15(S1): 9–25.

Yin, R. (2009) *Case study research: design and methods*, 4th edition, Thousand Oaks, CA: Sage.

Young, I. (1990) *Justice and the politics of difference*, Princeton, NJ: Princeton University Press.

A combined subject and conceptual

Index

with acknowledgements to originators

A

Authors of this book:
committed to:
  answer 'so what' question 3
  battling policy shibboleths 3
  co-production of research 204
  modelling dialogic form 6, 204
  incomplete, iterative approach 5, 177
  possibility of democratic co-production
    3
conscious of 'relevance gap' in research
    203
proceeding as if success is possible 202
    Jessop
rationale for their belief in change 17
reflect upon governance of research 204
scholars collaborating beyond
    the academy 203

B

Bolton Mediation Service 168
**boundary/ies including boundary-
spaces,**
boundary spanners, *Williams,*
  'policy entrepreneurs', *Kingdon*
  between academics and policy-makers
    27
    Caplan
  boundaries – low permeability 27
  boundary spanners:
    'jacks of all trades' 45
    Williams
    'soft skills' of 45, 113
    translators of values
    Burton
  feature of rigid delineation of roles 27
    Agranoff
  policy entrepreneurs 28, 123
  replacing party political spaces 45
Bradford Trident:
  community-owned and run 158
'bricolage' supports iteration 48
    Lowndes and Roberts

C

change:
  co-productive alternatives not
    spontaneous 49
  danger of powerlessness 19, 185
  desire for co-production 181
  emotion an appropriate incentive 184
    Ostrom E
  extremely emotionally charged 184
  limits of present policy 180
  possibilities of, pre-figured in
    co-productive models 178
  strategy of 'perpetual resistance':
    argued for 19
    seen as counter-productive 185
citizens:
  active role in co-production implied 33
    Ostrom E
  alternatives – hidden latent demand 190
  apathy belied by popular participation
    197
  capacities questioned 190
  civic leadership – role of individuals
    in 187
    Allio
  co-designers of policy process 194
    Fung
  community organising 115-124, 186,
    197
  concerned to enhance capacities 44
  deficit-based model stigmatises 27
  empathy unlocks defensive positions
    191
  empirical research shows capacities 190
    Dalton
  grassroots mobilisation 188
    Fischer de Filippis et al
  mechanisms to hold power to account
    18
  opposition to specific policies 190
  solving problems 122
    Alinsky
  spaces: 'invited' and 'popular' 186
  stimulation of civic behaviour 190
    John et al